SECRET PROMISE

JOAN LIVIERI

Copyright © 2025 Joan Livieri
All rights reserved
First Edition

NEWMAN SPRINGS PUBLISHING
320 Broad Street
Red Bank, NJ 07701

First originally published by Newman Springs Publishing 2025

ISBN 979-8-89061-897-9 (Paperback)
ISBN 979-8-89061-898-6 (Digital)

Printed in the United States of America

For Mallory Joy, your belief that *Secret Promise* must be shared. This is for you.

1

August 1973, Touring Italy

Having left her tour group, Laura Kincaid ambled along Rome's side streets absorbing as much of its culture as possible at her own pace. This vacation being all she hoped for—hearing melodious Italian voices coming from sidewalk cafes added one more memory to take home to Vermont. Heading toward the famous Spanish Steps, she jumped back as a moped whizzed around the corner. The driver grinning—she had another Rome moment to add to her memory box.

Enraptured, Laura suddenly felt her breath cut off as she was shoved against a wall with sharp points of stone piercing her back. Two youths—one is yanking at her purse's shoulder strap and the other pulling on her arm to get her to let go and ripping her blouse—popping its buttons. Laura tightened her grip determined to keep her purse. "No, no," she cried, "please…"

Someone shouted "Alt"—Stop! They bolted without their pickings, not looking back.

Laura's savior, an irate young woman, hurried to her, said, "Those gypsies, they bring shame to my country."

Shaken, her legs barely keeping her upright, Laura managed, "Thank you. Gratzi."

"You are Americano, si?"

Laura nodded while pulling at her blouse and trying to still her trembling.

"I speak English. Come," patting Laura's arm, "I cannot leave you here."

"Oh no, thank you but I must go to my hotel."

"You must let me help you. It is not good for you to travel about in your torn blouse. I live at the next corner. Come," she softly insisted, "we will have wine and I will mend your blouse."

Laura did need to gather herself. This woman's gentleness turned Laura's mind into accepting her assistance. "If it is not too much trouble," Laura held out her hand, her knuckles sore from the boys pulling on her purse strap, "I'm Laura Kincaid."

Taking Laura's hand, she said, "I am Trista Serrano," Trista used her mother's name—the Deluca family name being well know for its affluence in business. "I'm glad to meet you but not like this."

"You saved me." Laura held back tears hiding under her lashes, and nervously explained, "I was scared yet determined to keep my purse."

"You were very coraggioso—brave."

Climbing a narrow darken stairway and entering Trista's second-floor apartment gave Laura a view of Italian life separate from her hotel rooms. Sun lines cross through tilted wooden blinds exuding a quiet comfort and inviting one to want to relax on the brown leather sofa. An upholstered chair, its cushion smashed from use blended with the colorful rug spread over rust-colored tiles made the room perfect in Laura's eyes. A low marble top table displayed a few magazines, a candy dish, and a bottle of wine on a separate tray with glasses. Laura was drawn to a huge painting of a flowered garden—bright blooms surrounding a fountain set inside a stoned wall.

Laura was in awe, and Trista smiled. "I love flowers, and it is a gift from my brother."

"It's magnificent—so real that you want to smell the flowers."

"I enjoy it every time I look at it."

Trista flipped a switch turning on a ceiling fan that began to whir softly. She opened a narrow glass-paned door leading onto a small balcony of potted plants. The afternoon air entered mixing with the fan's stirring.

"First a glass of wine and then I sew."

"Oh no, you've been very kind, I can repair my blouse."

Trista's dark eyes along with her flawless complexion and petite figure made Laura's sixty-seven inches feel graceless. Laura envied her rescuer's velvety black hair wishing her plain brown was as lustrous.

"No, no, the nuns have taught me well. Let me show off my tiny stitches."

Laura felt embarrassed to remove her blouse and sit in her camisole and jeans when Trista offered her a silk mini robe. Donning the elegant garment, Laura sighed, "This is gorgeous."

Intent with her stitching, Trista's brow puckered. "Those Gypsies are a menace. I'm sorry it has spoiled your visit."

"Our guide warned us to hold tightly to our purses, and I did. More important is how may I repay you?"

Trista stopped sewing, "Please, this is nothing." She began to move the needle again and said, "Tell me about you…America. When I was five I was in New York. I don't remember it; just that they said I was there. I have been to London and schooled in Geneva. My padre doesn't like for me to travel. If not for my brother I would not have this little apartment for myself." She raised an eyebrow, adding, "But sometimes I sneak away…I love Paris."

"You know I never thought first of Paris it has always been Rome for me—your history and food. Paris to me is glamour while Rome has it all—a warmth that comes from people's smiles, their voices—I revere its history. This visit is more than I expected with no disappointments."

Trista eyed Laura and smiled. "I don't see a ring so you are not wed."

Laura shook her head. Perhaps it was the wine and Trista's warmth as well as the cozy ambiance, she divulged, "I'm fulfilling my dream to visit Italy. Too, I'm away from a guy hounding me to be more than a friend."

"Hounding? That word I do not know."

A devilish look came into Laura's eyes. "It means he is chasing me. You know how a dog chases after something it means to catch?"

Trista laughed. "Si, now I understand, and you do not like him?"

"He's nice as a friend but there's no special feeling." Taking a sip of wine, added, "If you know what I mean. I've always hoped to feel something special."

"Ah, si, now that I understand. You want the spark."

The vibrancy in Trista's reply was not lost on Laura. "Spark? So you have it—that special feeling with someone?"

Trista nodded while tying off the last button. "I match a couple of buttons; there is not so much a difference with the others."

"Thanks." Laura stood to put on her blouse. "So tell me," she gently prodded, "what is it like to have that special spark?"

Holding her glass of wine, ready to sip but stopped and Trista's voice softened; she said with intensity, "It is wonderful. When he touches you or if you touch him it's an unknown sudden reaction—something ignites but you can't identify it. It jolts you and you feel it and it stays with you. There's a sudden zing that hits you that must be existing deep within you waiting for that moment. It will multiply and erupt—you can't stop it. It stays with you in mind and body. The spark is magic." She sighed, "Wait for it, Laura, and don't settle for less. Though I must warn you there is a wounding aspect if the spark is one sided—not reciprocated, you know? Then you must let go and wait until you find the mate that responds in kind. Otherwise, I believe life would be unbearable and heartbreaking. Fortunately, Antonio and I have found our spark together. When I told him my feelings he couldn't believe that his were the same." Her voice warmed, "It's the most exciting sensation in the world. I have it with my Antonia." Glowing, she went on, "I have not mentioned this to anyone, but I am sure Antonio and I will soon wed."

Laura stepped over to hug Trista. "I'm so happy for you. Antonio is a very lucky man, although I bet he already knows it."

Trista beamed. "Si and if he does not know then I will be sure to tell him." She refilled their glasses. "Let us drink that you will also find your special connection."

The mood was pleasant as the two women sat in silence for a few moments.

"So tell me, Laura Kincaid, more about you."

"There's not much to tell. My parents died when I was fifteen. I live with my grandmother and her sister these last eight years. They are in their eighties and I try looking after them but I confess I think it's the other way around. They are so good and sweet. I love them. We live in Stowe, Vermont. It's mostly known as ski country. I work at a posh resort, Cloud Nine, as reservations clerk plus fill-in duties when needed. Naturally the busiest time is winter—hopefully with lots of snow."

"Do you ski, Laura?"

"Not well. I rather enjoy sitting in front of a fire watching its flames. Do you ski?"

"No." Trista's voice waivered, "I never was permitted to learn." Then her voice brightened, "But my brother loves to ski and goes away whenever he can—he's very very good."

"Maybe some day you can suggest that he bring you and Antonio to Stowe. They can ski and you and I can visit."

Trista knew that was impossible. "Maybe, who knows."

Laura stood. "I must go, Trista. The group I'm with will be worried. We're departing in the morning for home. I can't thank you enough. I wish I could do something for you. I think that if I were here longer we would be close friends."

"Let us exchange addresses. I'd like to keep in touch with my new American friend."

"I was going to suggest the same. I'm delighted to have met you, Trista Serrano."

"It has been my pleasure, Laura Kincaid. You are a very nice person."

They hugged. Laura said, "Be happy with Antonio. I'll search for that spark."

"Don't give up. It'll be worth it, you'll see." Trista called for a taxi.

"Goodbye, Trista."

"Arrivederci, my new friend."

One last smile as Laura waved.

* * * * *

Trista knew she was early. Antonio said she was to come at eight o'clock, but her joyous news was too good to wait another thirty minutes. Bubbling, Trista was not only going to have Antonio's baby but they would soon wed. Her life couldn't be any better. Too, she made a new American friend. There is much happiness to share with Antonio.

"Oops," she cried as Trista's strap on her sandal gave way so she kicked them both off and ran up the stairs to Antonio's rooms. She was searching for her key when she noticed the door ajar. Her warm glow blossomed and increased as she discovered Antonio was already home.

She pushed in the door, her bare feet making her entrance unnoticed. About to drop her sandals and purse she heard Antonio's acerbic tone lash out. "I told you I will have the Deluca bid—possibly tonight. I have his sister in my pocket," he snickered, "and in my bed."

A gruff voice threatened, "Dominic will kill you if he finds you using his sister to steal his calculations. Remember, we must have the information direct from his papers."

"You worry for nothing." Trista heard Antonio exude certainty. "Just so I get the money for this job, it'll all be worth it."

Trista froze, despair struck like an iron weight as she strained to keep her knees from buckling while her heart pounded and bile filled her throat. She heard chairs shoved and movement—it took less than a second for her to race out the door. She had to get away. Her purse and sandals slamming wildly against her body—running in bare feet, tears crashing against her eyelids with desperation pounding inside of her.

How she made it back to her apartment never entered her mind all she knew is that she had no alternative but to disappear before Antonio came looking for her. She couldn't disgrace her family by becoming a mother without marriage. Yet she couldn't let them worry about her so she must be astute and secretive. She needed to think how best to vanish and leave no clues. How? Pacing, she crossed her arms, gripping them. Tears gushed forcing her to shove her knuckled fist at her mouth to push back her sobs. How? How can I do it?

SECRET PROMISE

There is no one I can trust. Oh Dom, why didn't I listen to you? It was then she spied her sewing box. The buttons! She fell back on the sofa taking a deep breath and feeling a slight sense of relief—she had a way to save her family and her baby…the Americano.

A short while later, with her emotions guarded, Trista was knocking on the apartment manager's door. "Signore Bellini," she shoved a wad of money into his hand, "please look after my garden. I'm off to Firenza for a celebration holiday. I don't know how long I'll be gone. Gratzi."

2

August, Stowe, Vermont

Cloud Nine's reservation cards were stacked on Laura's desk. She stretched, covered a slight yawn—almost finished.

Mr. Irwin walked into her office carrying his mug of coffee. "Laura, I checked with Mrs. Meriwether"—he sipped from his mug—"and she isn't sure what her family plans will be. Still, hold her usual Thanksgiving reservation and remind me to check with her around the end of October."

Laura jotted the memo in her log. Holding up two cards, she said, "I have last year's reservations ready for this coming season—these two are questionable."

Leaning his shoulder against the door jam, her boss said, "I hope it's not that college fraternity."

She laughed. "No. One is a Mr. and Mrs. Alec Moore, a London address, and the other is a Dominic Deluca. It says Rome with no address."

Mr. Irwin narrowed his eyes, thinking, and then said, "The Moores were honeymooners. They didn't take to skiing at all. I doubt they'll return. Leave the Deluca file open. Don't send our usual announcement as Mr. Deluca doesn't require a notice or invitation. Should he contact us—always accept his request as Clouds's personal service is automatically available to him—no confirmation required."

Laura grinned. "He's from Italy, so he must be okay."

"Ah yes, you said you fell in love with Rome."

"I'll never forget Rome. It captivated me." Laura clipped a note on his card. "Mr. Deluca's card shows he stayed four days. Do I hold a suite for him?"

"He will stay in either of the two suites not open for tourists. We've found that it's prudent that the suites remain vacant for our special unexpected guests. Cloud Nine always accommodates those opting to select our small inn for their holiday."

"I take it that Mr. Deluca is a very important man."

"He is, and a very private one. He is wealthy and could stay at any resort or be welcomed in any private home, yet I believe he comes to Stowe and Cloud to enjoy skiing. It is my understanding that in America he intentionally keeps a low profile. He is very family-oriented, caring for his parents, and adores his younger sister."

"He's not married?"

"Not that I'm aware, but he could be."

Sliding the Deluca card into her open file, she said, "I'll be sure we keep the usual suites available."

"Very good." He turned to go, "Thanks, Laura, for coming in like this. With this racket going on with restorations it can be maddening."

"I don't mind."

Mr. Irwin left, and Laura put Meriwether and Deluca reservation cards in the hold file.

*****

January 7, Stowe

Laura entered Cloud's rear entrance. "It's cold, cold, cold!" Kicking off her snow boots she pushed them over with others on the mat.

Pete, Cloud's handyman, grinned. "Yeah—it keeps Stowe in snow and us happy."

"I'm glad you're here, Laura," Mr. Irwin's voice carried into the room, "Stop in my office as soon as you can."

Nodding for Laura to take a seat, said, "I'm pleased with our holiday bookings, but I'm also glad the holidays are over." He reached for his coffee mug.

"It has been hectic but everyone was in a celebrating mood and it became contagious. You outdid yourself, Mr. Irwin, with generous food, drinks, and gifts. Cloud Nine's New Year's Eve party proved successful. I don't think there were many skiers on the slopes until late afternoon. But they all wore smiles."

Mr. Irwin picked up a sheet of paper, "We still have some good weeks of skiing left and we must keep on our toes." His eyes assessing, said, "I know I have put a lot of extra work into you, and I value your diligence." He smiled. "I'm going to increase your salary by 10 percent."

She beamed, "Thank you."

"No thanks necessary. Actually, Laura, I'd like for you to work with us year-round. There will be summer visitors and then autumn with our maples—Cloud Nine should take advantage and remain open. Spring will be our off-season, time for improvements, also taking time off, then will be acceptable."

Pleased to be working full time, Laura said, "Mr. Irwin, I'll do my best. I look forward to new challenges."

Confident with his decision, he said, "Good." He passed the sheet of paper toward her.

Perusing the message, her tone said it all, "Is he for real?"

"Now, Laura, he's only asking we guard his privacy. That we can do."

"Asking? He's demanding it. We are to keep anyone from invading his space." Laura grinned. "I suppose we can erect an electric fence around him and I can stand guard, or follow him about giving anyone the evil eye if they dare approach him."

Mr. Irwin appreciated her sense of humor, yet he said, "I know you'll remember that Cloud, without question, caters to its guests."

"Of course, though I wonder if he wants the slopes to be available only to him and I'm to keep his ski's waxed."

Mr. Irwin couldn't help but grin. "Mr. Deluca must be satisfied with our services or he wouldn't be returning. We will do all for his comfort. I don't doubt that he's here to rest as well as to ski. Though wealthy he is a working man and travels the world."

"I'll give him personal Cloud Nine treatment. He'll have no complaints."

"That's why I rely on you, Laura. We want Mr. Deluca to continue to consider Cloud his personal retreat."

Laura scanned the paper. "He's to arrive on the fifteenth. No word how long he'll stay."

"However long it is, I'm putting Mr. Dominic Deluca in your personal care. I trust you will see he receives our top-most services."

Laura left Mr. Irwin's office. Mr. Deluca, you old grouch, I'll take good care of you…just you wait and see.

*****

January 17, Cloud Nine

Mr. Irwin walked into Laura's office.

Tapping the Deluca reservation card on her desk, she said, "Mr. Deluca's reservation said the fifteenth. I've kept his suite polished, the fireplace filled with burning logs for days and the man hasn't the courtesy to notify us of his delay."

"Mr. Deluca is signing in now."

"What?" Laura rushed past her boss. "For heaven's sake, why didn't you tell me?"

Mr. Irwin, grinning, said to the empty room, "I just did."

Laura arrived at Reception and jerked to a halt. There was not an old man at the desk, but a tall frame filling the area. A black cashmere overcoat blanketed his wide shoulders with a maroon plaid cashmere scarf hanging longer on one side. His opened coat revealed a black turtleneck sweater and black jeans—one pant leg was hooked up on a black leather boot. He wore no hat—his long raven hair rested on the coat's collar with a few windblown strands resting on his forehead. She heard his voice—velvet-edged with the Italian sound, asking if his suite is ready.

"Good day, Mr. Deluca. We have been looking forward to your arrival." Laura's smile was met with stormy dark eyes.

"I'm sure," his tone cold. "Now if you will direct me to my suite."

The warmth in Laura's eyes vanished. Taking a second good look at Cloud Nine's esteemed guest, she reached to take his small bag when his hand flashed to stop her. His touch on top of her fingers infused a shock that she quickly pulled her hand back only to catch the inside of his hanging scarf and pulling it down further. Startled, she inhaled as her eyes captured his stare. She felt like a deer caught in headlights. Her green eyes turned luminous though she didn't know. Astounded, it felt as though someone hit her with a giant snowball—a soft gasp escaped. She forced air into her lungs and then as if someone pricked her fingers she pulled her hand from under his scarf. Doing her best to steady the unexpected jolt, said, "Sorry, I...I was going to carry it for you."

Dominic concealed his bewilderment at the unexplainable sudden zing that raced through him. Stepping away and pulling at his scarf, said, "If you will show me the way, I will settle in."

"Yes, yes of course." Eying his stacked luggage, she said, "I'll have your bags brought up." She stepped aside on the bottom step to allow him to go first.

"After you," he said, without smiling.

Laura posted a smile of nonchalance. He followed her. Her hips moved side to side with each step and no matter how she tried to stop their motion—it was impossible. His dominance being something she'd never dealt with and then the unexpected jolt from him that she didn't understand flying through her minutes ago was bewildering.

Laura twisted the brass key in its lock. She pushed the door open and stood aside.

His tone remained cold as icicles hanging on eaves. "After you, Signorina."

Laura walked in flipping the wall switch lighting several lamps giving the room an inviting setting—noting that everything was in good order. The fireplace emitted warmth with a couple of logs glowing red. The suite was large, but with Mr. Deluca, its size seemed to diminish. Looking up at the handsome man made her stomach knot. Power emanated from him—she was still shaken from his touch, yet she was determined to give him Cloud's finest service. "How may I help you, Mr. Deluca?"

Dominic looked around the suite while removing his coat dropping it on a chair and then pulling at his scarf leaving it atop his coat. Laura's eyes froze on his long muscular form. "This will do."

Laura's green eyes flashed, disguising her anxiety over the power this man exuded, she felt it and said, "We aim to please, sir."

For a moment he studied her intently. "Then you know I expect no interruptions. See that I will not be disturbed."

"We are aware of your desire for privacy and you shall have it. My name is Laura Kincaid, if you need any special service call the desk. I will personally see that you are accommodated."

If she had blinked she was sure she would have missed his near smile. But then the superiority in his voice belied what she thought she saw. "Tonight I will dine here. I see the wine cupboard is stocked." He picked up a bottle, eyed the label, put it down, and said nothing. "Send up whatever you think will appease hunger."

Laura almost saluted. "Yes, sir! Fish, poultry, or beef?"

"Surprise me, Signorina Kincaid." His voice was dominant. "I presume the lifts open at dawn?"

"Yes, from dawn to dusk if there is no fog or white-out."

"Excellent." Dominic picked up an apple from the scrumptious fruit bowl, flipped it in his hand, and then set it down. Laura couldn't help but notice his long fingers catching the apple while her memory jogged back to his incredible touch. "What time is the first-morning meal served? And when during the day is your dining room less busy? And the same for the evening—the less crowded the better. I have no desire for idle chatter."

"I've listed the restaurant hours on the desk tablet. Breakfast is served at five—rarely does anyone take advantage of early hours enabling you to enjoy your meal in solitude. A noon meal is anyone's guess—depends on skiers' delight—some order lunch in their room. The dining room serves fewer people at five to six-thirty. Evening dining—guests usually dine around seven. The last dinner meal served is at eight-thirty. Then many of our guests linger and do not leave immediately."

Dominic remained standing and didn't move, taking in her clarity and business acumen, yet not the least condescending.

Laura pulled her shoulders back not realizing her breasts stood out more. Her eyes met his. "Will there be anything more, Mr. Deluca?"

"If there is, I would have spoken."

Laura recognized his haughty tone. Well. Sir, I've had enough of your arrogant manner. She replied with a tinge of sarcasm, "Of course, I should have known. Please accept my apology. I'll see to your dinner."

Dominic watched as she quietly pulled the door closed. Pulling off his sweater, he uttered, "The lovely Signorina has a busy tongue."

* * * * *

Laura was in the dining room and standing off to one side, sipping coffee at 5:00 a.m. She meant to be on her toes until Mr. Deluca fell into his routine—determined to prove to Mr. Irwin that she was proficient at keeping Cloud's A-guest content and with no complications.

Dominic walked into the empty dining room glancing around and saw Laura. He did not acknowledge her, but he could feel his gut twist a bit. She looked beautiful with her slacks hugging her hips and a fitted green sweater outlining her generous breasts. Her brown hair was tied back and shining in the window's morning light. He noticed that she quickly set down her cup and moved toward him.

Laura didn't hold back a wide smile. "Good morning, Mr. Deluca."

He said nothing, barely nodding to acknowledge her greeting while taking in the warmth radiating from her rosy lips and her gleaming green eyes. Unaccustomed to this unexpected reaction from a woman, he couldn't stop his pulse from skipping extra beats.

Not to be deterred by his silence, Laura continued, "If you'll come this way I have a table ready. The view from last night's snowfall is beautiful—its pristine condition has yet to be trampled. Oops"—she bit her lip—"I forgot, you don't appreciate idle chatter." Was that a wink, or did she just blink, Dominic wasn't sure. She moved with the swing of her hips, again aware that he was behind her. She pulled out the chair, stood aside, and raised a hand for the waitress.

"Molly will serve you. I wish you a good day." She left and didn't look back.

Dominic admired her tenacity. Whether she was mocking him wasn't important as rarely did anyone stand up to him—especially the opposite sex. He smothered a smile and thought of his sister, Tris. She would argue the sky was green just to get him to respond to her chatter. Keeping in mind his need for undisturbed quiet he turned to the menu and the urge to test all that white powder.

Laura glanced back when she was sure Dominic couldn't see her—being in unfamiliar territory a wee bit of excitement zipped through her. She felt a rush of unfamiliar. *What is wrong with me? That man is arrogant and just a shade from being rude and I can't take my eyes off him. I wish I could touch his hand and see if I just dreamed it or if he really has the power to rattle me. I can't ask for certain he'll consider me daft.* Clenching her hands, she hurried to her office.

3

Three days later

Mr. Irwin smiled. "You're doing a great job with Mr. Deluca. He's pleased with his accommodations."

"You mean he actually has a good word for us? I'm surprised as he rarely says ten words."

"It is our privilege that he's chosen Cloud Nine to ski, Laura. We're a small inn and our amenities are unlike the offerings of our competitors so we see that our guests visit is unequalled with personal attention."

"It's just that I've never met anyone like him—not a sign of warmth yet very polite."

"It is not our license to question."

"I do understand, however…"

"Good." He interrupted, "Then you will be ready to drive Mr. Deluca to Montpelier in the morning."

Laura gasped. "What?"

"Mr. Deluca requested that you drive him to the capitol. He has an appointment."

Laura's pulse raced. The thought of being confined in the car with the man that twists her insides into slush every time she's near him—knowing his dark eyes miss nothing and just being near him gives her a buzz down to her toes. "But, Mr. Irwin…"

Mr. Irwin continued, "You'll use the Lincoln. I'm having it checked and fueled."

Laura liked her job, shading her anxiety, I can do this. "Very well."

He smiled. "There was never a doubt in my mind."

Laura left a message at the desk to notify her when Mr. Deluca returned from the slopes. Working at her desk, her head down, her hair having fallen forward, intent on checking February's reservations was how Dominic saw her when he stopped at her door. Her blanket of velvet golden brown hair hid her deep green eyes. He stared—the urge to let his fingers tangle in its wavy softness...Dio mio. "You wished to see me?"

Jerking her head up, brushing back her hair, said, "Oh, Mr. Deluca, you startled me." She rose, "Yes, I asked the desk to call me. I'm sorry they sent you here."

Dominic's voice resonated, "It is not a difficulty. What is it you need from me?"

Laura blushed. She could feel her face turning pink. She grinned. "We aim to please—what time do you wish to leave tomorrow for Montpelier?"

Dominic couldn't remember when he last saw a female blush and that included his sister. It annoyed him that he found it charming. His deep timbered voice, replied, "I must deliver some papers at the capitol. It will be a round trip. I will need you to wait."

"Yes, sir!"

Dominic bit the inside of his jaw not to smile. "We'll leave at nine."

"I'll be here. Anything more I can do?"

He took in the depth of her warm green eyes. He dated many beautiful women, some more glamorous than others, who no doubt spent the day in a salon, but this young lady with her natural poise and no vanity was refreshing. She took pride in her duties and he respected that. He was drawn to her and hadn't forgotten their stimulating touch, but common sense had him keep it masked while he kicked his arrogance up a notch. He could take the car and drive himself but when he observed Laura Kincaid—hearing her laugh—he wanted to enjoy some of that laughter. It was time to crack the shell he'd built around himself. And unbeknownst to this young lady's beautiful smile and sassy humor he thought her rather endearing. Mostly, Signorina Kincaid was not clawing to impress him—just doing her job and doing it very well.

Giving Laura one last look, he said, "Nothing else. Gratzi."

She smiled, hearing his mellow Italian. "You're welcome." The handsome man from Italy unsettled her.

Dominic nodded and left.

His aura hung in the air around her adding to the tingling in the pit of her stomach. She couldn't wait for tomorrow morning.

The roads were clear as Laura aimed the Lincoln north. She could feel Dominic look over at her and then turn his face forward. She made a point to keep her eyes on the road.

"Tell me, Signorina, would you care to stop for a cup of coffee? Or a cappuccino?"

Glancing over at him, her hands gripping the steering wheel, what is it with this man that my equilibrium goes out of kilter? He's indifferent to me. I'm his hired servant. "That would be nice." Then a flash of humor crossed her face. "We aim to please."

Dominic choked back his laugh. He liked her tease. "Then your aim is good please to refresh ourselves with a warm drink."

Laura smiled, again setting off Dominic's pulse to beat a shade faster.

Having enjoyed a cappuccino while discussing snowy weather, everything was fine until Laura reached for the check. Dominic's features; visually infuriated, stood, towering over her as he bent his head and whispered into her ear, "Never, Signorina, do that when you are with me, never!"

They were back on the road. She grasped the steering wheel, "Mr. Deluca, I apologize. You see, you are our guest. Cloud Nine wishes to aid you in every way possible. I meant no harm." She smiled. "Cloud is paying our way today, not me."

"Then let us understand, Miss Kincaid." His arrogance again was in full swing. "Mr. Irwin is offering the use of the automobile. For your time today, I will pay."

Furious, Laura said, "Oh no! This is part of my work." She mimicked, "Let us understand, sir, there will be no further discussion on compensating me for my time."

Dominic turned to look at Laura. He actually smiled, and it softened his dark eyes. His mouth was wide, and his teeth were white and straight.

Without thinking, she said, "You have a beautiful smile; you should use it more often."

He made no attempt to hide the fact that he was watching her or that her feisty rejoinder pleased him. "Grazie."

Tingling surged from Laura's fingertips, up her arms, and over to her heart. Suddenly the car's heater was no longer needed; her body temperature exuded more than enough heat. She couldn't have spoken at that moment and sounded rational. She bit the inside of her cheek.

Dominic knew where the pulse was beating under her ear and gripped the arm rest to keep from reaching over and touching that spot.

Adding miles they whizzed along. Finally, Laura decided she should say something—break the pressure built between them. "I toured your country last August. Italy is magnificent."

Dominic turned, eying her. "Si. But your country is also."

"Yes, it is, but visiting Italy fulfilled my dream. My tour went to many places."

Glad for the change, their uneasiness lessened. "So tell me, Signorina, what did you discover most interesting? Please do not tell me it is the Coliseum."

She didn't hesitate. "Michelangelo's *David*."

"Ahh, si, his talent cannot be matched. You like Firenze?"

She turned quickly to smile her eyes reflecting delight. "Florence…oh yes, but Rome took my heart." She watched the road sign and turned. "But I had an experience with gypsy boys—they tried to take my purse but I hung on and, fortunately, was helped by a young lady." Laura stopped talking, concentrating on the directions to the state capitol.

"That is very bad. I'm sorry."

"It turned out well, I made a friend. She...oh, here we are. I'll drop you off right here and find parking. I'll wait for you in visitor's reception."

Dominic hated to leave her but he had to deliver the calculation he promised. It was a personal favor for a friend of a friend. "I won't be long. Be careful, Signorina." He gave her a conspiratorial wink.

The gentle sound of his voice affected her more than she wanted him to know. She had to sheath her inner feelings. "Not to worry, Mr. Deluca, I'll be fine."

* * * * *

Heading back to Stowe, the atmosphere was pleasant and hassle-free. Laura learned there was a gentle side to Dominic Deluca that for some reason he concealed. Fighting to control her swirling emotions, she stayed quiet.

Again, a while later, she broke their silence. "Do you like traveling, Mr. Deluca?"

"Not really. I do so because of my business, but I prefer to stay near home."

She wanted to ask if he had a busy social life but knew she would be overstepping boundaries that had nothing to do with her job.

Dominic turned to sit at an angle. His arm reached across the back seats. The tips of his fingers were barely touching the tip of Laura's hair resting on her shoulder. He said, "I care for my mother and father, also my sister. They make each day I live happy. Traveling is a necessity, and taking personal quiet time is too."

"You're lucky to have a family. I have my grandmother and aunt. They are dear to me."

"Your mother and father?"

"They died years ago."

He moved his hand away from Laura's tresses before he caved and fingered its silkiness.

The Lincoln ate up the miles. The quiet in the car was soothing. It appeared that neither of them needed further conversation. When

SECRET PROMISE

Laura turned onto Highway 100, Dominic noticed an ice skating sign. "Do you skate, Signorina?"

"Skate?" Taken aback at his unexpected question, she added, "You mean ice skating?"

He couldn't hold back his chuckle.

Laura brought her hand up to stifle her giggles.

"Si," he said, teasing, yet his eyes were compelling, "you know—those shoes with steel blades attached to their bottoms."

Laura was a good skater. In awe at his sudden kidding, she just answered, "Yes."

Amusement flickered in the eyes that met hers. "A sign back there advertised skating and if you wish, we could go back."

Laura eased on the accelerator, though her heart was racing. "I'd like that, if you have the time." She was already looking to turn around.

"Let's hope they have skates to rent or we can find somewhere to buy some."

There was something especially charming about this man who purposely acted arrogant. Laura, excited about the change in plan, grinned. "One way or the other we'll manage. I'll be happy to give you a hand should you slip…we aim to please."

His laughter was undiluted, "We shall see."

One hour later with rented skates but with new blue wool stockings, taking her hand, and even through their gloves felt the zing, they glided onto the frozen pond. There were only four other skaters in the afternoon, giving Dominic free reign to swing Laura around. Soon they were skating in unison, grinning, smiling, and laughing. The warmth that exuded between them—they never felt the cold temperature.

With one arm around her waist, he kept her close so their hips touched as they skated round and round. When they looked at each other, a strange sensation pulled them closer together. They both felt it not knowing that they were each experiencing that same allure.

If I keep looking at him, I'm going to make a fool of myself, wanting him to never let me go. How stupid I am. Laura pulled away, spun, and skated backward, and she started laughing.

He felt his body react. *She is so carefree. Her hair has fallen, yet she seems not to notice, and her rosy lips around that wide smile, I don't remember ever wanting to kiss a woman as I do this one.* Dominic grinned, enjoying this wonderful moment as Laura turned, waved, and began skating faster with ease.

"Catch me if you can," she called, gliding across the ice.

By now, it was getting late, and they were the only ones left, and he didn't think twice about giving chase—only he cheated. He cut across the ice, and now he was skating backward in front of her.

"Come." He held out his arms. "Let us take one more skate together."

She went into his arms and they made their own music. He wanted to kiss her rosy mouth but refrained later, and she wanted him to kiss her wondering what it would be like, but he'd never even think to kiss me. Again holding her close, neither spoke, both wanting to treasure the moment. They were going to have to leave, but just as well, more skaters arrived to enjoy the ice.

Dominic knew they were nearing the inn. "Signorina Laura, I would like, very much, if you would join me for dinner this evening. Will you say yes?"

Laura's pulse quickened, she was certain he could tell. Taking a deep breath, not wanting to appear eager, said, "Yes, Mr. Deluca, I'd like to have dinner with you."

"Excellent." He smothered his delight, "You must give me directions to your home."

"But you don't drive."

"Of course, I can drive. In fact, I'll use this very car to call for you."

Tilting her head, her eyes widen, "Then why did you have me drive you to Montpelier?"

His husky whisper, "Caro, mia, I wanted to enjoy your company."

Tingling, Laura flashed him a big smile, "Really?"

Dominic laughed at her genuine response. "Si, realmente."

Guiding the Lincoln to Cloud's entrance—Dominic reached over and touched her hand. Zing, his fingers vibrated. He felt the

SECRET PROMISE

jolt. He lowered his voice to a whisper, "Don't forget to give me your address. And I'd like it if you'd refrain from calling me Mr. Deluca. I'm Dominic."

Laura wanted to melt right there. She knew she was blushing. "I...I can drive over. I'll reserve a quiet table in the dining room."

He shook his head. "Non, I would like to take you to dinner but not here."

Laura's smile told him he was going to enjoy the evening.

* * * * *

Wearing her best black sheath, the soft wave in her tawny hair glowing in the lamplight, and using a touch of blush she felt beautiful. Exhilarated, goose bumps danced on her arms thinking about her evening with Mr. Deluca...*Dominic. Magical. Please let him kiss me*. How it would be she couldn't imagine, but, oh, how she wanted it to happen.

"You did say seven-thirty, didn't you?"

Laura looked at her watch—eight o'clock. She peeked through the curtain for car lights but saw nothing. "He must have gotten lost, Gran."

"All he'll have to do is ask where Kincaid's live. He'll find you."

By nine o'clock Laura debated about calling him and decided not to. No one knew she was going to have dinner with Dominic.

"Laura dear, perhaps you should call." She heard the concern in Gran's voice.

Doing her best to hide her hurt, Laura said, "I'll think about it. Why don't you and Aunt Kate go to bed? I'm sorry to have kept you up so late."

"Not to worry. Come, Kate. We'll see you in the morning, dear."

Alone, a waterfall began falling with force off her cheeks.

At ten o'clock Laura checked the door and turned off the lamps. In her bedroom, she unzipped her dress and fell face down on her pillow to muffle her sobs.

* * * * *

Dominic couldn't wait to get gorgeous Laura Kincaid in his arms. He was going to kiss those rosy lips that had driven him crazy all day.

He was putting on his coat when there was a knock on the door and it opened. His cold voice was disapproving, "What are you doing here, Gina?"

"Dom…darling, at last, I've found you." She threw her arms around his neck. To move her away, he gripped her waist. She was kissing his cheeks—he turned his head to keep her from kissing him on the lips.

Pete stood in the hall watching.

Curses fell from Dominic's mouth while he removed Gina from him. He pushed the door shut in Pete's face. "I'll ask again, what are you doing here?"

The look he gave her—Gina knew he was masking his rage. Her black curls piled on the top of her head fell on the collar of her leopard coat. "Dom, I've been calling everywhere to find you, when I remembered you saying you like skiing in Stowe, America. I called everywhere until I found where you were registered. You don't have to be so hateful, it's lucky I had sense enough to fly here for you."

Not trusting her wily ways, knowing she never accepted that they were no longer a couple, his temper was about to rupture, "Will you make your point; I'm late for my appointment."

Sizzling with resentment, she sashayed over to him, her eyes searching for even a tad of tenderness. Finding none, she knew her news would pierce his heart, just as he did to hers. "Your sister is missing."

"Trista?" His voice chilled her, "You're lying."

"No, Dom, I'm not. Call home and talk with your mother. She is beside herself. Trista has disappeared and they are worried sick. You've got to come home, now!"

Dominic was on the phone. "Si, Mama…si, it is me." He listened, his mind filled with fearful images of his sweet sister. "Don't worry. Si, I'm on my way."

Pete knocked on the door. Gina pulled it open. "See that Mr. Deluca's things are shipped." Turning to Dominic, "My plane is ready. Luckily I have an ace pilot."

Dominic was beside himself. He wasn't listening to Gina. All he could think of was his mother crying and his father shouting for him to come home. *What can Tris be thinking? If she marries that snake, Antonio, I will strangle her after I kill him.*

Moving with haste, Dominic didn't look back but strode down the stairs with Gina and out the door.

* * * * *

Laura walked into Cloud's rear entrance and kicked off her boots. She called out a "Good Morning" and went straight to her office.

Struggling to keep her humiliation hidden, she decided not to approach Mr. Deluca. Better that he not know his no-show mattered. She'd keep busy and let the day move on.

Two hours later she couldn't stop the pounding in her head, a giant-size headache reaching down into the base of her neck—she wanted to die.

Mr. Irwin stepped into her office. "Did the trip to Montpelier go well yesterday?"

"Yes, as far as I know. Did Mr. Deluca have a complaint?"

"No, no, I just had Pete take down the mileage for our records and thought to check with you."

"There weren't any problems. You might ask Mr. Deluca."

"He's not here."

"Well, when he comes in from skiing."

"No, Laura, I mean he's gone."

She could actually feel the color drain from her face and was certain Mr. Irwin could hear her hammering heart.

"Laura?" She heard his voice, but it seemed far away. "Laura, are you feeling all right? Is there something I can get for you?"

To her dismay, her voice broke, "I…I'm sorry, I…"

He interrupted her, worried. "Look, you had a full day yesterday. I want you to go home for the rest of the day." He smiled "That's an order."

Laura nodded. The water building under her lids, burning—need to get a grip on her emotions, said, "Thanks, Mr. Irwin, I think I'll do that." She pushed the papers on her desk into the top drawer.

Laura was pulling on her boots when Pete walked in. "Hi...the Lincoln purred for you yesterday, didn't it?"

"Yes."

Pete leaned in to whisper. "I know we're not supposed to talk about Cloud's guests, but you know that Italian guy in Suite B?" He didn't wait for her response. In fact, Laura couldn't have been able to speak. "You should've seen the woman kissing him. Wow! He was holding her, and then he shut the door in my face." She could tell Pete was in awe. "She's a real beauty and uppity, you know the kind."

Laura had to know. "I guess that's when Mr. Deluca checked out."

"He didn't go near the desk but just walked out and got into her Mercedes."

"Perhaps he had an emergency."

Pete snickered. "She is some emergency if you ask me."

It was as if a steel arrow pierced Laura's heart. "It's best that we keep this to ourselves, Pete, and not repeat it. Privacy is Cloud Nine's edict."

"You always do the right thing for the Cloud and the people that come here. You can depend on me." He spied her with her boots on. "You going out?"

"Mr. Irwin is giving me the day off."

"You sure earned it having to put up with that guy."

Laura couldn't wait to leave. Slipping and sliding toward her car she held back her tears. Heading for home her thoughts were on Dominic Deluca. I've got to stop this idiotic dream I imagined with him. Cold tears leaked from the corners of her eyes as her crushed heart and humiliation swelled. She knew she was out of Dominic

Deluca's privileged class and should have known better. She uttered, "Stupid…stupid me. I've learned my lesson."

* * * * *

March 6, six weeks later, Stowe

"So dear, what are your plans, dear?"

Laura stirred her black coffee even though it didn't require stirring, "Hummm?" Laura still carried hidden hurt from Dominic's jilt—especially never hearing from him. Cloud received payment but no other word. She wanted to cry.

"Laura…yoo-hoo…come back to me."

Laura snapped out of her doldrums. "Sorry, Gran."

"Dear, you haven't been the same since…well you know."

"Gran…"

"Now don't interrupt," she gave her granddaughter a scold, "I recognized how excited you were about going out with him. He must be a nice man if you consider accepting, but he's not the only man who's never kept his word. I'm not making excuses, but maybe something happened and he had to leave." Gran grasped Laura's hand. "Let me finish before Kate comes in from her walk from the mailbox. Perhaps you put too much emphasis on the date and to him you were only going to be there to pass his lonely hours." She felt Laura flinch. "I know it must hurt, but still you can't let this continue to upset you. You're off for the month—I hope you do something special. I want to see your warm smiles again."

Laura kissed her Gran's wrinkled cheek. "I know I've been maudlin. I'm sorry, and I do know better."

"That's my girl. So what are you going to do with your time off?"

"I'm going to hang around and annoy you and Aunt Kate while watching the buds break open on the lilacs—spring's around the corner."

4

March 6, Burlington, Vermont

The nurse walked in carrying a pink blanket cuddled in her arms. "Here you are, Ms. Kincaid, your beautiful baby daughter."

Ms. Kincaid held out her arms from her position in the wheelchair. She carefully held her baby close to her heart.

The nurse smiled.

Holding her precious baby tears fell down her cheeks. "You're mine, Cella," she whispered. The nurse's aide came to push the wheelchair. "Thank you all," the new mother said as she was rolled toward the elevator.

One nurse walked along with mother and baby. "Are you sure, Ms. Kincaid, that you'll be all right?"

Anxious to depart and continue with her plan, Trista looked at the thoughtful nurse and smiled, and not wanting to raise suspicions, she said, "Thank you for asking. I'm fine. Cella's father is away and when he returns we're going to show off our baby to his parents."

The nurse nodded. "I wish you and Cella happiness; he's a very lucky man. All your papers and formulas are in your bag. Good luck."

Ms. Kincaid let out a small breath when the elevator door closed and the nurse's aide, indifferent to her, steered her toward the exit and the waiting taxi.

*****

March 12, Stowe

Gran, Aunt Kate, and Laura were in the kitchen that smelled heavenly from freshly baked cookies.

Taking a bite of an oatmeal cookie, Laura extolled, "Delicious."

The front doorbell rang. Rarely did anyone use the bell. Neighbors came to the back porch.

"I'll go," said Laura. Opening the door her eyes widened and her mouth fell open but no words came.

Holding a fluffy pink bundle, Trista smiled. "Hello, Laura Kincaid"—her Italian American words echoed—"I hope you remember me."

"Trista! Remember you? Of course, I do. I'm just so surprised. Come in."

Gran and Aunt Kate were standing in the hall.

Laura, hugging Trista, realized she was holding a baby. "Oh my gosh, Gran…Aunt Kate, this is Trista Serrano. Remember…the woman that saved me in Rome when two gypsy boys tried to steal my purse?"

Gran smiled. "It's nice to meet you."

Aunt Kate said, "Our Laura told us what you did. You were very brave."

Trista took in the three women. She said, "I have thought of Laura many times, never forgetting the nice person she is." Suddenly the bundle in her arm whimpered.

Gran spoke, "Come and sit and let us have a peek at your baby."

Trista entered an inviting sunny room—crowded with furniture, yet neat and homey. Books and magazines were stacked here and there. The small tables and floor were shiny from regular attention. A rocker with its worn indented pillow was near the fireplace. Lace curtains allowed sunshine to slip through. Its warm atmosphere helped ease Trista's resolution.

"Laura, would you like to hold Cella?"

"I'd love to."

"I'd like her to meet you."

Laura, taking little Cella, couldn't help but break into a grin. "My, Cella, you're as light as a feather." Using one finger, she traced it over Cella's tiny hand. "How old is she?"

"Ten days."

Gran eyed the young mother with misgivings. Trista's eyes bore dark circles.

Laura knew something was drastically wrong, but not wanting to add to Trista's discomfort, kindly suggested, "It's wonderful to see you. Please, say you'll stay and visit with us."

"Thank you. I'd like to very much."

"You may have Laura's room," Gran said. "It has a large dresser—I'll empty a drawer making it safe for your baby." She patted Trista's arm. "After you put your baby in her little bed, come and have a cup of tea with us. Too, you must be tired so why not rest for a while."

"Si. Thank you."

Gran and Kate went to the kitchen.

Laura stayed with Trista while she cared for Cella. "What happened to Antonio?"

Trista answered, her voice filled with hostility, "He is a swine. I never told him I was pregnant. I will explain later. Is that all right?"

"Of course. I'm sorry, Trista. I remember how much in love you were."

"He is no good. My brother was right but I didn't listen."

Laura didn't want to upset Trista; she didn't look well with her pale complexion. Traveling with a newborn when she should have been in bed—Laura surmised something dreadful occurred. Watching Trista settle her tiny baby in the drawer, Laura gently touched Trista's arm, "Let's go to the kitchen—it's where we spend a lot of time."

Trista's dark eyes watered, the tears hanging on its lashes. "You are my only hope."

Masking her confusion, Laura said, "What is it? I'll help if I can."

"I hope you remember those words."

A flicker of apprehension coursed through Laura—she'd have to wait until Trista was ready to explain.

Trista sat sipping coffee, and taking small bites from an oatmeal cookie. She didn't say much, doing her best not to let her nerves rattle the cup. She couldn't get up the courage to speak.

Gran noted the new mother's ashen complexion. "Perhaps you should rest, my dear. We can visit later."

"No please," her despair obvious as she rested her head in the palm of her hand for a few seconds. She needed these people to agree, especially Laura. "I have done something I am not proud. I ran away. It was necessary for me to come to America to see Laura."

Laura bit her bottom lip more confused than ever.

Trista's accent, suddenly more intense, said, "I need Laura's help. I am not married. My baby's father lied. I found he used me to steal information from my brother's work. He never loved me. There could be no marriage and because of my pregnancy I couldn't shame my family." Tears rolled down her face—clearing her throat, continued. "I could not do that to them." Her voice became a whisper, "I just could not." She pushed at her tears with the back of her hand.

Laura slid a paper napkin to her, still not understanding how she could help.

Trista's voice surged with anguish, "I went over and over in my mind trying to think of someone I could trust that had no connection with my family." She looked at Laura, "And I remembered the nice American…Laura Kincaid." Not realizing she was squeezing her fingers together until they whitened, went on, "I had Laura's address so I planed to Canada and then settled in Burlington where Cella was born—March second." Trista's eyes filled with tears, she dabbed at them with the wrinkled napkin. "The reason I have this big difficulty is should Cella's father find I have his child, his only interest would be money. My family is wealthy. He'd bargain or else expose my shame and I cannot let that happen to my family."

"That's blackmail…that's awful." Laura sat with her mouth open.

"Si, I know."

Laura said, "But your brother…"

Trista's eyes warmed. "He is wonderful and I know he would help me, but I would beg him not to tell my parents and it would put him to lie. No, I could not do that to him. Besides, he is busy and travels often."

Taking in Trista's torment, Laura asked, "How can I help?"

Trista's demeanor eased. "If you will, I need you to look after Cella when I return home."

"You mean Rome? Trista, surely you don't mean to go and leave your baby?"

"Si. I've shocked you, but it must be done."

Gran detected missing parts in the young mother's explanation. "My dear, there is more troubling you. We will talk after you've rested."

Trista bit the inside of her jaw. "I am sorry to bring my burden to your granddaughter, but as I said I have no where else to turn." Repressing her guilt took courage as living a lie was never a source she lived and yet knowing she was telling half truths, had to go on. "I wish to explain now, please," taking a noticeable breath, "when I was little I had headaches. My family took me to doctors everywhere and at the time no one had the right answer. Slowly my headaches lessened so much that my life was happy. Now I leap forward—I have to return to Rome for treatments. I have cancer in my lymphatic system. It was in remission, but no more. This disease attacks my lymph nodes that are important to my body's immune system. It will grow worse if I do not have the treatments. When I discovered I was pregnant, naturally I told no one and made up my mind to wait until after my baby was born to start the treatments. I cannot wait any longer."

Tears dropped off Laura's lashes. "Of course I'll look after Cella. If I can give you peace of mind, there is no question." Laura looked at her grandmother who had remained silent but Gran gave a slight nod. Anxiety eased all around. Aunt Kate perked up. "It'll be wonderful having a baby with us. How long will you have to leave her?"

Trista wanted to keep as close to the truth as possible. "I don't know exactly but knowing Cella is well cared for will help."

Laura reaching over to touch her friend, said confidently. "You can count on me."

"Grazie. I have one favor to ask, Mrs. Kincaid," looking at Gran, "if you please?"

"Yes?"

"I am not without resources. My family is what you say in America…rich. I also have my own money. Tomorrow, if Laura agrees I would like to go shopping and get things for Cella's care. I don't think it would be wise to take a tiny baby shopping, so I…"

Aunt Kate interrupted clapping her hands, "We'd love to look after her and you two girls can go out and have a nice day together."

"Wonderful," Laura approved. "But now you must rest. I'll check on Cella with you."

Trista's throat clogged—she could only nod.

The next day, shopping, Laura said, "You've bought Cella so many things."

"Why not? She deserves to have the best."

"You've certainly seen to that. She will lack for nothing." Not liking the growing dark circles around Trista's eyes, Laura suggested they have lunch.

"Wait, I would like to buy a gift for your grandmother and Aunt Kate. It will be a gift from Cella. Then we will eat."

Now Trista sat sipping tea—her hand shook.

"I'm worried about you, Tris…what can I do?"

She smiled. "You know, only my brother calls me Tris. I wish he could be here."

Laura pleaded, "Call him."

"No, no"—her anxiety was obvious—"it is as I said I couldn't ask him to lie." Biting the corner of her lip, she said, "Let's sit in the car. What I must tell you is very private."

The two women settled in Trista's rental. Laura, her wrist resting over the steering wheel looked at Trista, waiting. She had powered down the windows part way—the cool air wafted over them.

"Is it too cool for you?"

Trista shook her head, silent, trying to control her tremors. Taking a deep breath, said, "I need your promise that what I tell you will be our secret and not be repeated to another soul." She reached for Laura's hand. "Promise me," color drained from her face, "you must promise, please…"

Anxious for her friend, yet dismayed, Laura hastily responded, "I promise."

Trista relaxed her grip on Laura's hand. "Let me tell everything and then we talk."

"All right."

"When I found I was pregnant I knew I had to do whatever I could to protect my family. I also had to protect my unborn child from Antonio." She reached into her purse and handed her passport to Laura. "Open it."

Laura gasped—loud. "What is this? It is my name with your picture." For a long moment, Laura stared at Trista. "How? Why? I don't understand."

"I told you I had to protect those I love. With money, anything can be done. I needed to leave Italy. No one suspected a thing with your name. If I used my own I could be found."

"This still doesn't make sense."

Trista's voice faltered. "I made plans involving you—the perfect answer to my troubles. I'd first fly to Canada"—she half smiled—"I looked at an Atlas for Vermont as I would be using your identity—that is where you live and so then I settled in Burlington and waited for Cella to be born. I had a good doctor." She took another breath. "He knew I was unmarried and didn't ask questions. I lived quietly. Cella finally decided to enter my world. Here I am." Her voice wobbled, and tears fell. Reaching over to touch Laura, "I couldn't think of any other way."

"My god, Tris, what have you done?"

"Don't you see?" she cried, "I had to. Cella must have a chance to live with no shame and to be loved. I know you have a big heart. I'm counting on you. There is no one else."

Distraught, Laura's squeezing the steering wheel—her knuckles whitened. "But you can give her that in time. Why?"

"No, I can't. I'm dying. I'll have chemo, but there is little hope. My time is short. How could I leave my baby without a mother's love?" Tears coursed down her cheeks. "I became Laura Kincaid when I purchased my airline ticket…Trista Serrano disappeared."

Laura's heart was hammering. "You're telling me that you took my identification totally? For how long?"

"It was around September or maybe the last of August. Everything started moving fast as soon as I contracted for the passport. From there, I was careful not to be seen. Only until I boarded the plane did I feel I could relax."

Laura buried her upset. "This rental is in my name, right?"

"Yes."

"My god, Tris, do you realize if something happened and they contacted Gran, especially if I wasn't around to prove it's a mistake." Laura would have liked to shake her new friend, but not with her so ill, instead she vented, "Tris, I truly want to scream."

"Forgive me, I am a selfish person. If there was another way I would not have taken your name." She reached for Laura's hand discovering it cold. She bowed her head, distressed, knowing she had more to tell. "Laura, no one but you and me must know what I have done. No one!"

"But the man that made the passport knows."

For the first time, Trista smiled. "The old man is the most trusted printer in all of Italy. If he agrees to help you, no one will ever know."

"How did you find him?"

"It is not to be told. It is done and impossible to trace."

Accepting that she promised to keep Trista's secret, Laura said, "Little did I know that sunny day in Rome that two gypsy boys would open Pandora's Box."

"This secret you must carry is a burden, I know. However, anytime you need help, I'm leaving a letter with you for my brother. It'll be up to you to let him know."

"Oh, Tris."

Red eyes with darker circles met Laura's green eyes as Trista pulled a brown sealed envelope from her purse and handed it to Laura. "Inside is Cella's birth certificate and her hospital papers. Also, the letter for you to give my brother if you need him."

Stymied, Laura asked, "Didn't anyone question you about your stay in the hospital?"

"I didn't give them a chance. They did know that I was unmarried. They were polite and did what they were supposed to do. When I was discharged, my account was paid—the doctor too. There were no problems. They wheeled me to a waiting taxi—I rested a few days and, as I'd planned, found you."

"About the birth certificate…did you name Antonio?"

"Dio, never! I put my brother's name as the father."

Panic raced through Laura. "Your brother? You named him the father?"

"I did it so you will have the option of letting my brother take responsibility for Cella. I am going to die, that is a fact. My family will grieve and my brother is going to have to carry the weight my death will cause. Now you can see why I couldn't put Cella's birth in the middle of that. After some time passes, perhaps a year or two, you can contact him. I've written everything in detail so there won't be any difficulty for you. When I see him I'll tell him, leaving you free of explanations. His name, address, and telephone number are in this envelope. Use your judgment as to how you want to handle it. Her birth certificate names you as Cella's mother—this gives you the right as Cella's mother to do as you wish. Trust me on this, Laura; I know my brother will cause you no grief."

"That's good to hear." Laura held the thick brown envelope but didn't attempt to open it. "I promised to help you and I'll keep my word."

"It is our secret promise to each other. I ask that you not tell your family. It is not good of me to ask but the less people know of Cella's birth, the better."

"I agree. I won't mention this to Gran as it won't affect her. But she will wonder why you haven't returned. I wonder what people will say when they see me with a baby."

"Tell them that you are adopting her. Why not? Her birth certificate says Cella Rose Kincaid. Cella belongs to you until you call my brother."

"Tris, isn't there anything doctors can do for you?"

"There is nothing."

"My heart hurts for you. I'm so sorry."

"That you care is most important."

"Do you want me to call or write you?"

Trista grabbed Laura's wrist, nervously digging in her nails. "No! Never! When I leave you are not to make any connection with me." She was shaking. "This is our secret."

"Please, Tris, do not worry. I'll do as you ask. I promise."

"When I leave I will be gone forever from you and Cella. It must be that I never existed." She knuckled her tears. "As soon as I land in Italy I'll go at once to the ladies' bathroom—destroy the visa and passport. That will end our connection. No one can trace my movements."

Not wanting to upset her friend's fragile state, Laura thought to go to a lighter subject. "Remember when we talked about finding the right man and having that spark? I thought I found him, but it was only one-sided. He didn't respond."

The foreboding eased. Trista said, "Then you are lucky. But when it materializes make sure the fires truly burn between you both. Be wiser than me. The heart often leads before the brain kicks in."

"Isn't that the truth?" Laura shifted her body on the car's narrow seat.

"Just one more important matter. Where is your bank?"

"Not far. Do you need money? I have some."

"No, no, we are going to open a safe bank box for you. You can put Cella's papers in it, and I have money for you both. Everything about Cella will go in the box."

"Tris, I don't want any payment for caring for Cella."

"It is for her care and yours if you need it. I must do this."

Laura and Trista walked out of the bank—Laura slipped the silver key to Cella's life into her purse. "That is a lot of money, Tris. I'll not use it unless there's an emergency."

Trista shrugged. "It is only seventy thousand American dollars. When you need more, my brother will see to it."

Laura laughed. "Your brother sounds like a saint." Teasing, she asked, "Is he married?"

Trista's smile reached her eyes. "Maybe I should have brought him with me after all. I think that you would like him. He is a private man and can do anything and does it well. My one regret is that I didn't listen to him."

March 17 was a sunny day as Trista, all packed, picked up Cella, rocking her gently and kissing each of her tiny fingers. "Piccolo mia tesoro, my little treasure," she whispered, choking back sobs. She gave her baby to Gran.

Laura drove Trista back to Canada to catch her flight to Rome and returned the rental. She would return to Stowe by bus. The two women gently squeezed their hands together and then tightly embraced. Trista's voice choked. "I know, Laura Kincaid, that you will keep my secret, and I know with all my heart you will be a good mother. Gratzi."

The tears Laura tried to hold back ran down her cheeks matching Trista's.

"I promise, Tris. Goodbye."

"Ciao, Cella's mama." Tris turned, walked away, and didn't look back.

5

March 18, Rome

Dominic's haunted eyes stared at the small man standing in front of his desk. "You're telling me that after all this time you haven't found any trace of my sister's whereabouts?" He rubbed the back of his neck in frustration. "What has happened to her? Dio, I can't tell my parents that there is nothing." He pounded on his desk. "I know my sister wouldn't have disappeared unless she was forced. There has to be something we've missed, Flavio, but what?" Stress lines formed on his brow. "At first I thought it would be for ransom, but nothing—I don't believe she was taken. It has to be major for her, but what kind of trouble would cause her to leave and have no contact with her family?"

Flavio covered every connection to Trista Deluca. Nothing, not a clue. What Flavio didn't dare mention to his friend was that in his investigations, many times the girl runs because of pregnancy. Without proof, he'd be a fool to even suggest it—especially about Dominic's cherished sister. He leaned on Dom's desk. "I grabbed Antonio and shook him until his teeth rattled. Antonio doesn't know where she is. He said Trista was supposed to come to his place but she never showed. He went to her apartment and Bellini told him exactly as he told us that Trista was off to Firenze and he was to look after her plants. This time, I believe Antonio because I'm told he was looking for her everywhere and had no luck and couldn't even find anyone who saw her. He was mad at her for not showing up." Flavio rubbed his gray whiskers. "I know I mentioned this, Dom, but it looks like she planned to go away. Do you think she could possibly have changed her identification?"

Dominic rose from his chair and went to stare out the window, his posture rigid. "I don't know. Perhaps…but not the sister I know. Still, have you checked with Giovannetti?"

"Him? Oh yes. He professes that he is just a small local printer. Nothing more."

Dominic's face mirrored strain. "No one's seen her since last summer. What can she be thinking? I thought I knew Tris so well."

"Don't give up, Dom. We'll find her. I'll keep looking."

"Thanks, Flav. I know if anyone can find her it will be you. Do you need money?"

"You've paid me too much, and I give you nothing."

"Yes you have, Flav, you've assured me that Tris is not injured or in any hospital." He smiled. "And she hasn't been arrested for robbing a bank."

Flavio felt his client's anguish. "I'll find her, Dom." He picked up his hat and left.

Dominic rubbed his eyes, his fingers wet.

Trista walked out of the ladies' bathroom at Leonardo da Vinci International. She was tired, her pallor made her illness apparent. It is done. I have burned my fraudulent passport, visa, and ticket receipts. Laura Kincaid is no longer in Italy. She felt weak and was perspiring from the little effort it took to finish her maneuverings to keep her secret safe. She found a seat and slumped into it channeling her mind to bury her heartache. She wanted to call Laura to tell her that all the evidence was destroyed, but she wouldn't, she'd stick to her plan.

A short whiskered man stepped in front of her. "Perdono, you are Trista Deluca, are you not?"

Stunned, Trista stared at him but said nothing.

"Forgive me, Signorina, I am a friend of your brother. He is worried and asked me to find you."

Her voice low and tormented, she said, "My brother? How is he? I'm sorry…I'm so sorry." Trista swiped at her tears with the back of her hand. "I must call him."

Flavio's tone gentled. "He is fine. Call him and then I'll take you to him."

The ringing telephone annoyed Dominic. He was in his study finishing up work he'd never let lag before. Finally, grumbling, he picked up the receiver. "Deluca." He knew someone was on the line. "Ciao…hello, Deluca here." Then he heard her soft voice. "Dom?" His stomach contracted as his chest tightened and he held his breath, afraid to breathe—that he might lose their connection. "Tris?"

Trista's sobs carried through the phone. "Dom, oh, Dom, I'm so sorry."

"Where are you, Tris? Are you all right? I'll come and get you."

Flavio took the phone. "I've got your sister with me, Dom. We'll be with you as soon as we can get out of here…we're at Fiurnicino." Flavio heard not a sound. "Dom, are you still there?"

"Dio, Flav," his heart pounding while his breath caught in his throat. "Is she all right?"

"She's not injured, yet be prepared as she's very pale and I think she should be in bed. I think seeing you is what she needs right now."

"Hurry, please." Dom hung up. Tears smudged his paperwork. He cared not. Tris has come home.

* * * * *

March 20, Deluca Villa in Ronciglione

Trista lay in bed—ashen with dark circles shadowing her eyes. Dom sat beside the bed, grasping his sister's small hand—gently rubbing his thumb over it.

"Where's Mama…Papa?" Her voice croaked telling of her weakness.

Dom felt as if a fist punched his gut; said, "Papa is at the lake… you know how he likes to sit on the bench and watch the water. Mama is resting."

"It's all my fault." She turned her head, and though the pillow soft, the movement hurt. "But I…I had to, Dom."

"Tell me, Tris. Why did you have to go away? I'm here for you… you're my baby sister. We've always been honest with each other."

Trista pulled the sheet up to blot her tears. "I know—you're my best brother."

Dominic forced a chuckle. "You always say that knowing I'm your only brother. Yet you don't trust me. Why?"

"I do trust you, Dom. I just need to think." She took another short breath. "I promise I'll tell you."

Mama Deluca slowly walked in to join them.

Dominic stood. "Mama, you should be resting. Come, we'll let Trista sleep."

Mrs. Deluca bent over and kissed her daughter's forehead and then patted each of her cheeks all the while wanting to shout at God for not helping her baby. Leaning on her son's arm, she said, "My little bambina, I come back…you sleep and I pray."

"Yes, Mama."

* * * * *

"Buon giorno, Tris," Dominic entered, "I brought us breakfast."

She knew he did that so she'd eat. "I'm not hungry."

"Well, I am, and if you don't eat, then I can't. Not fair."

"Some melon then." She nibbled on a sliver of melon. Struggling for breath, she said, "You and I know I'm dying." She raised her fingers to stop him from speaking. Breathing more labored. "I hurt and I'm ready. I'm sorry to do this to my family."

"Hush"—his throat constricted—"no apologizing." Tears hung on his lids. "Little sister, I'd give my life if it would save yours."

"I know. Thank you for being here with me. I worry about you. Who's going to find you a wife?" She took a couple of short breaths. "I know of someone but she is far away."

Dominic let Trista talk, especially if it gave her ease. "When the time is right, I'll marry."

"You've never said…do you have someone special?"

"Why all these questions?"

SECRET PROMISE

"Promise me, Dom, that you won't marry Gina." Taking small breaths, she said, "She is not for you. Papa said Gina brought you home in her airplane. Where were you?"

"Never mind where Gina found me. She told me about you disappearing and everyone worrying."

"Dom"—he reached for his hand—"promise me you'll never marry Gina."

He noticed his sister's pinched expression. "I haven't any intention of marrying Gina, but who knows what the future holds?"

Taking a piece of melon, she said, "So you're not going to admit you have a sweetheart squirreled away?"

"I haven't...no squirrels and no nuts." He laughed and Trista smiled.

His sister's smile warmed his heart—hoping to keep her smiling he'd tell her a sweet memory. "Okay, I'll tell you something but there's not much to it. On one of my trips, I met a young woman. She's different because she's...I guess you could say she's plain in a charming way. Not plain...plain as in natural, no put-ons. She's a lady in every sense. I planned to take her out, but..." he didn't want to say that Tris's disappearance took precedence over that date, so he side-stepped his reason for not going. "Well you know how I am about business, it comes first."

"Maybe she would have been the one."

"I'll never know. It was on one of my travels, she's a working young lady. We can't predict how our lives will end." Then realizing what he'd said, chewing on the side of his jaw, apologized, "That was a rotten thing to say."

"Not to worry." She took extra breaths. "It's true, no one knows. As for me, look at it this way, all those headaches that went into remission gave me extra happy years."

"Are you certain, Tris? I worried about you with Antonio. I'm glad you came to your senses. Just like Gina is not for me, Antonio wasn't for you. You deserve better."

Trista knew without a doubt this was not the time to tell about Cella. "And so do you."

His heart was heavy, and he wondered how he was going to make it with his sister no longer a part of his life. They were close as brother and sister and that's why it bothered him that she wasn't willing to share her secret.

* * * * *

End of April

The doctor readied to leave. He'd known the Deluca family for decades. He had no words. There was nothing he could do. He wanted to suggest a priest, but from the pain in his friend's eyes, he couldn't. Instead, he nodded to Signore and Signora Deluca and quietly stepped out. How could he tell them their daughter was going to enter heaven soon? The priest would visit.

Dominic was called to return to the family villa.

A helicopter landed on the grass, and Dominic spied his father on the bench by the lake. He wanted to go to Tris, but his father needed him too.

Sitting beside his father, he gently encouraged, "Papa, you've got to be brave for us."

The old man aged more each day. He hadn't bothered to shave—more wrinkles were visible on his handsome face. "I don't have the strength, Figlio—son. Children are supposed to bury their madre and padre." Wiping his eyes, he said, "I'm glad you're here. Mama…"—he laid his hand on Dominic's shoulder—"what can I do for her and our poor bambina."

Dominic squeezed his father's arm—his own strength weakening with grief.

When Dominic entered the house he found his mother sitting with Trista. "I'm here, Mama." He embraced her. "I'll stay with Trista, why don't you go to Papa?"

Dominic pulled back the heavy drapes and opened the window—fresh air and sunshine invaded the room helping to ease a fraction of darkness ahead of them.

"Tris?" he whispered, his heart aching.

"I'm here." She didn't move. He sat, taking hold of her hand while caressing her arm. "Tris," his voice broke, "I'm here, sweetheart, wake up and let me see your beautiful eyes." She didn't move but lay on one pillow with a light coverlet over her. "Come on, Tris, wake up. I need you to hear me say I love you." He pressed her hand to his cheek.

"Dom?" Her voice was barely audible.

Tears rolled unashamedly, he nudged his shoulder to his face to blot them. "I'm here."

It was hard for her to concentrate. Her voice, so low that Dom had to lean close to hear. "I had to, Dom…no other way."

"What did you have to do, caro?"

"I'm a mother, Dom. I…I have a daughter."

Dominic was thunderstruck; never in all this time did he suspect that was her difficulty. Oh my sweet girl, why didn't you tell me?

"Dom," she gasped, "water."

He held her head as she sipped. Reaching for a towel he patted her chin and neck. "I got you wet." He sat closer taking her hand in his. There was no way he would let her know how her news shocked him. "So I'm an uncle. I'm proud of you, Tris. You must tell me where my niece is so I can be a proper uncle."

"She's safe. He can't find her."

He? Antonio? Not wanting to upset her, he gently probed to get as much information as he could. "You certainly fooled me. I couldn't find you. You left Italy?"

"Si."

Dom's first thought was to have Flavio find what airline she had flown, but remembered how thoroughly they had investigated. There had been no Deluca or Serrano on any flights. Gently urging, "Where did you go? Where is your daughter? Tell me, please. Let me do this for you, Tris."

"I knew you'd help. My baby…is loved."

"Who has my niece?" He was getting anxious. Tris being so frail it was difficult to press her.

"Promise…secret. Promise you won't tell Mama…Papa." She searched for another breath. "I don't want them to know." She became agitated. "Promise? You've got to," her breathing interrupting her plea. "You can't tell anyone about Cella."

"Cella? That's her name?"

Trista smiled, her darkened eyes seemed to gleam brighter. "I named…her. She's beautiful."

"I bet she looks like you." Dom wouldn't dare ask if Antonio is the baby's father. Instead, he said, "You didn't tell Antonio?"

She began to shake. "No. Never. Promise that you'll never tell." She tried to grip his fingers but had no strength. "Please promise me." She was trembling, and it scared him—he could do nothing other than promise he'd keep her secret forever.

Tiring, Trista's voice was fading.

"Tris, how can I find Cella?"

Her voice barely intelligible, murmured, "She'll get…touch…you." Weariness enveloped her as she tried to concentrate, "Safe box…address."

"Where, Tris? Who?" Anxiety rushing through him, "Please, try…"

Trista began to drift with Dom holding her hand—she smiled, sighed, and took her last breath.

He bent his head, crying. "Little sister, I failed to protect you." He whispered, "I won't fail you this time, Tris, I'll find my niece." He leaned over and kissed her goodbye.

Dominic with anguished eyes looked at his sleeping sister. You'd have made a wonderful mother, Tris, and I'm going to make a damn fine uncle. He silently closed the door to find his parents.

6

October, Stowe

The maple leaves were glorious in their usual extravagant bright colors. Laura's life matched nature's beauty—along with being the luckiest person in the world. She thought her work day would never end as she couldn't wait to go home.

Cella was calling her mama and that was music to her ears. Even though Gran's warning that there would be heartbreak ahead, Laura brushed it off. Cella Rose belonged to her, and she had the hidden silver key to prove it.

Almost skipping into the house, Laura called, "Hi, everybody, I'm home."

The house was exceptionally quiet—no radio playing in the background, silence. Her mind and body acting in unison she hurried into the living room and saw Gran laying on the couch with her body half on and half off. Falling on her knees, she cried, "Gran, are you all right? What happened?" Touching her gran's forehead and finding it cold, Laura gasped. Her fingers looked for a pulse, but she was too nervous to find it. She needed to find Cella and Aunt Kate, but she didn't want to leave her Gran. Shaking, she dialed 911 while calling out for Aunt Kate.

"Aunt Kate…" Laura hurried to her aunt's room and found her holding Cella—both asleep. Hearing the ambulance siren, she rushed to open the door.

Gripping her fingers, not realizing that her knuckles whitened, with tears falling, she told the medics how she found her grandmother. "Please…"

One medic said, "We're sorry. We can't tell you anything. We'll have to take her to the hospital. You understand we're not qualified to say…" He left the word hanging.

Laura nodded. She kissed her grandmother. "I'll come to the hospital."

The medic offered, "Why don't you call first? If you give us her doctor's name, it will help."

Laura swiped at her tears. "Yes. Thank you."

* * * * *

Aunt Kate's daughter attended Gran's funeral. Then she came to talk with Laura and explained that she was taking her mother back to Wisconsin to live with her. "Mom shows signs of dementia. I want her with me."

Laura, her heart aching over Gran's dying, said, "Of course. Aunt Kate is dear to me. I'll miss her."

Everyone had been so very nice. Mrs. Dupree offered to look after Cella until Laura could find someone permanent.

Holding Cella, kissing her pudgy cheeks, Laura couldn't help but give her baby a gentle squeeze, saying, "I'm lucky I have you. Mama is going to take care of you."

* * * * *

Laura, at her desk, with the telephone squeezed between her ear and shoulder saw Pete stick his head around the corner at her door and waved for him to come in.

He held his hat flipping it from one hand to the other. He hesitated, seemingly inhibited, and suddenly blurted, "Well, you see, Laura, my wife's sister is visiting with us from Pennsylvania. My wife wants her to stay until spring. Our house is small and it's going to be a long winter and I was wondering if you'd be interested in renting one of your rooms?"

Laura bit the inside of her lip. She didn't want to rent to anyone. "I don't think so, Pete. I'm sorry."

Pete's face dropped. "I understand, I just hoped…"

Looking at the man who was always there for her—plowing the snow from her drive, offering to make small repairs when needed… How can I refuse without at least talking with her…for Pete's sake, she smothered a laugh at her pun. "Pete, on second thought, why don't you have your sister-in-law stop over on Saturday? We can meet and see if it could work. You did say until spring?"

Pete's smile covered his weathered face. "Just 'til spring. Thanks, Laura." Grinning, he said, "Now all I have to do is convince my wife and Gretel."

* * * * *

Cella was napping and Laura had finished waxing the kitchen floor. Its uneven floorboards creaked in places, but she smiled knowing that her grandmother used to say those sounds matched her bones.

"Dear Gran," she uttered, "you left me your house and savings. How dear of you to think of me. If it's possible for you to hear me, I thank you so very much and Cella does too."

"Hello, is anybody home?"

I forgot…Pete's sister-in-law. "Come in, Pete."

"I brought Gretel over to meet you. My wife is shopping so this is working great."

Gretel stood beside Pete. Her brown wool coat with its velvet collar matched the coat's color. Laura noticed that Gretel wore shoes like Gran—black with laces. Her dark hair had traces of gray.

Laura held out her hand. "Hello. I'm Laura."

She appeared embarrassed. "I'm Gretel Kubek."

"I'll let you two ladies get acquainted." Pete backed out of the kitchen. "I'll be back."

Laura could have crowned Pete. "Mrs. Kubek, if you'd like to take off your coat you may hang it there on the coat tree and we'll have coffee."

"Please call me Gretel, and I'm sorry about intruding. I didn't know how to turn Pete down. He's so nice to me." She moved her shoulders. "I've decided to go back home."

Just then Cella's cry could be heard. "Excuse me, Gretel, I'll get my daughter."

Gretel looked around the old-fashioned kitchen—yellow walls with flowered curtains made the room cheerful.

"Here we are." Laura had a warm voice, smiling. "Cella, say hello to Mrs. Gretel."

Cella reached out and touched Gretel's offered hand.

"She's beautiful. May I hold her?"

Taking Cella on her lap, the baby quickly reached for the button on Gretel's dress. Gretel chortled, "You're a quick one, aren't you? Well, you can't have my button but you may hold it."

A few minutes later, Laura placed Cella in her highchair with a cookie.

Gretel sipped her coffee. "I hope Pete comes soon, I'm sorry to be a bother."

"Gretel"—Laura chewed her bottom lip, deciding and knowing Pete. "I wonder if you would do me a favor?"

Surprised, she answered, "Certainly, if I can."

"Pete suggested that you might be interested in having a room here so you can visit with your sister." Laura eyed Cella banging her cookie on the tray and then continued, "The lady that cares for Cella while I'm working is helping me temporarily. Would you be interested in taking care of Cella while I'm working? I can pay a little plus room and board and you can still be near your sister."

Gretel's beaming smile said it all. "Yes, I'd like to, if you're sure—I'll take good care of your beautiful daughter. You'll have no worries. Thank you."

A knock on the door and Pete moseyed in, not sure if he should smile.

"Peter, you'll never guess what Miz Kincaid is going to do. Why land's sake, I never expected this to be such a wonderful day."

Pete's gray eyebrows shot up. His sister-in-law's mood told all.

"I'm going to take care of this sweet little baby. I'm thrilled."

Pete's grin went from ear to ear. "I'll say, Gret, that little one is a charmer."

"We do have to make one change, Gretel. I'd like that you call me Laura."

Her cheeks pinked. "I can do that. Thank you…Laura."

* * * * *

November, Stowe

Laura studied the reservation cards for the coming Thanksgiving weekend. She carefully read each name to the very last. Settling back, disappointed—she wouldn't admit to anyone that she was hoping for a Deluca reservation.

Why do I punish myself over this man? He didn't have the decency to call to explain or apologize. Laura never got over the hurt of being stood-up. It was humiliating and still rankled. Dominic Deluca is an arrogant Italian who demands privacy and cares nothing about people's feelings. A bit of humor augured in and she laughed at her wanting him to come to ski so she could tell him what she thought of him. And it wouldn't be flattering. She swallowed the lump in her throat contemplating that in all likelihood he'd not given Stowe a thought. Then thinking of Cella carrying Italian blood in her tiny veins and her beautiful dark eyes were a lot like Dominic's. She couldn't help but smile. It must run in Italian families.

Never once did Laura rue the day she agreed to keep Tris's secret. Nothing in this world would make her open that safety deposit box. *It's my decision to contact her brother. I will not. Cella is mine.* Laura made up her mind—that brown envelope would remain unopened.

Many times Laura thought of Trista, wondering if the chemo helped or did Trista die as she predicted. Laura would continue to honor her word and make no contact.

Mr. Irwin interrupted Laura's reverie. "We're booked for the holidays—right through the New Year. I'll need you to work over this rush, especially if snow keeps falling."

Laura couldn't afford to pass on earning extra bucks, but she looked forward to Cella's first Christmas. She'd work around it. "Christmas Eve will start late with almost everyone taking a last run down the slopes—I can return around seven to be on hand for as long as necessary. Will that be okay?"

"I knew I could count on you, Laura. I'll be home all evening if you need me."

Laura held back her chuckle. *Mr. Irwin is spending the holidays with his family.* She said, "I don't perceive any problems, but I'll call should something unusual occur."

Mr. Irwin nodded and left.

7

January, Rome

"Flav, I can't believe there are no clues." Dom's maroon cashmere sweater and black jeans hugged his lean torso. Dark shadows appeared painted under his eyes. "I've got this dark cloud over my head. It's hard to accept Trista stumbled off somewhere and no one knows a thing."

"I'm sorry. There's nothing out there. Your sister mastered what a spy would envy. How she accomplished it, I don't think we'll ever know."

"But she said that someone would contact me. Who? You're sure you've checked on everyone no matter how insignificant or peculiar it might seem?"

"Dom, I've had men working on this full-time. I can't go on. Your sister left a dead-end." His tone gentled. "You can't allow this to rule your life."

"Easy for you to say," Dom groused.

"You're also my friend. Take some time—get away. Travel, ski, sail…take a few weeks. A holiday will be good for you. Get out of Rome or better yet, get out of Italy."

Dom held out his hand to Flavio, his grip solid. "You've always been a good friend, Flav, one I've counted on. You did bring Tris home to me. I thank you for finding her. Maybe I'll take your advice."

"I'll keep my eyes and ears open. I won't forget. Take care."

"I can't ask for more than that. Molte grazie."

Flavio left wishing he'd been able to have good news. He shook his head, muttering, "How'd you do it, Girl? How?" The elevator doors slid open. Flavio entered—the door swished closed.

* * * * *

February, Rome to New York City

Dominic's plan—go to Stowe for a couple of weeks—thinking Flav was right he should get out of Italy and his sister's haunting mystery. Besides he wondered if Laura Kincaid was still employed at Cloud Nine. He owed her an apology. Dominic hadn't forgotten that he left without leaving a word for her.

Stepping out of a restaurant Isabella saw Dominic passing by in a hurry. "Dom?" she called. "It is you!" A smile beamed as she went on to say, "How are you?"

Seeing Isabella Mancini, Dominic grinned. He looked to see if Lorenzo was with her. Taking Isabella's gloved hand he kissed each cheek. "This is a surprise. You look as beautiful as always."

"Go on, Mr. Flatter, you haven't changed." She gave him a hug. "It's been a long time—not married are you?"

"No, no, and don't get any ideas, Issy. And I'm fine, thank you for asking."

"Where were you off to in deep thought?"

He laughed. "I'm, thinking of taking a ski holiday in America."

Isabella's eyes matched her bright smile, "Wonderful! I'm returning to New York, come with me. Ren will like seeing his old friend."

"I need a change…but not another city."

Isabella's tone changed, "I know, Dom. I'm so sorry about Trista." She pinched his cheek. "And don't call me Issy."

Dominic laughed again. It felt good. "I take it you're living in New York."

"Yes, three quarters of the time." She reached to touch his arm, "I don't expect you to remember but its Ren's birthday and I'm planning a surprise bash. I could use your help."

"How so?"

She looked at her longtime friend determined to take him to New York with her. "I won't take no for an answer…while I'm organizing Ren's party you can keep him occupied. I really want to surprise him. You must stay with us while you're in New York."

Dominic liked the idea, it would be good to see Lorenzo and then he could go to Stowe. "How can I refuse you, Issy? I'm all yours, but just remember because you've leg shackled Ren, don't try to put that kind of blessing on me."

Isabella winked. "I won't…not for a while, anyway. We'll fly out tomorrow. Promise you won't change your mind."

"I promise."

* * * * *

Dominic and Isabella sat in the warm limo. Heavy snowflakes had New York traffic moving at a snail's pace.

"So when is this big birthday party going to happen?"

"Excited, are you?" she teased.

"I can't wait. I hope we're going to see a luscious female jump out of Ren's cake."

"You wish! But, no, darling, just a regular cake. I've already reserved a room at the Waldorf. You have to keep my husband busy for the next three days, notice I said days—not nights."

They both laughed.

* * * * *

Lorenzo walked into the living room glaring at Dominic. "I can't understand why I have to attend this dinner with you. And insisting I suit up as a penguin. I hate being tuxed-up."

Dominic put down his drink. "Stop bellyaching. If Issy didn't go out with her friends, you could stay home with her. However, seeing as I have to attend this dinner is reason to not leave you enjoying a quiet, alone evening."

Lorenzo chuckled. "You know if I wasn't so glad to see you I'd tell you to take your dinner and…" grinning, "but I'll have mercy and be a good paesano. How long is it going to last? And another thing," he scowled, "if I get raw chicken, I swear you're going to be wearing it."

Dominic got Lorenzo to his birthday party. Totally astounded, never suspecting—he embraced his wife, his eyes telling how much he adored her.

Realizing that he was missing something special, Dominic moved off to locate a drink. He thought of Laura Kincaid and their car trip and how much he wanted to kiss her full rosy mouth. Involuntarily his brow furrowed wondering if she married.

"Don't tell me, Dominic, you scrunch your forehead when you see me coming?" Gina leaned into him with a smile. "Aren't you happy to see me?"

Dominic had to smile—Gina was so obvious, she didn't seem to realize it or she just didn't care. It was when he smiled at her question, and she returned with her sexiest smile that a photographer snapped their picture. Dominic didn't particularly care—pictures were being taken all evening. Isabella wanted to make a memory book for Lorenzo because it would be his last birthday party.

"We don't do forty's," she teased.

A couple days later Dominic told his friends he was leaving to get in some skiing. Though they hated to see him go, they understood.

Dominic called his parents to check on them. He was all they had and he worried about them now more than ever.

Stuffing his belongings in his suitcase, his heart pounding as his father said his mother's blood pressure was too high. Her depression continued and would Dominic come home.

Explaining to Ren, he left in a rush, hailing a taxi, he must return to Italy. There would be no skiing.

8

February, Stowe

It was bitterly cold. The lifts were half empty. Only the brave or the crazy's were taking to the slopes.

Laura walked into Mr. Irwin's office; dropping off the guest list. She saw the New York Sunday paper in disarray across his desk. She naturally went to straighten it. That's when her stomach somersaulted and she couldn't exhale. She stared at a picture of Dominic Deluca and a beautiful woman—standing so close their bodies touching. Trembling she read the caption Loving couple enjoying birthday bash. The paper rattled as she folded it neatly leaving in on the desk yet wanting to throw it across the room while she screamed.

Mr. Irwin returned. "Oh good," he said, "I've been looking for you." Laura's silence went unnoticed. "Laura, you know how important the Merewether's are to Cloud Nine?"

Taking a deep breath, Laura said, "Of course. Mrs. Merewether is one of our most prestigious guests. I understand she has been involved with the Cloud for years—long before I came to work here."

"Exactly. So when she requires a particular act of goodwill from us—we do all in our power to come to her assistance."

Laura knew she was going to be nominated for some task to make the very wealthy Mrs. Merewether happy. "What does she require?"

Mr. Irwin spoke with iron resolve. "She asked that you escort her eight year old grandson to the airport. He is to fly to Paris. His parents are there and the child wants to be with them. Mrs. Merewether will do all in her power to see the child happy."

Laura struggled to maintain her composure. "How in the world am I supposed to take her grandson to the airport? Paris?" Her voice obviously unsteady, said, "Those flights leave out of New York. You aren't serious, Mr. Irwin?"

"Now Laura," Mr. Irwin said with calm, a smile appeared, "It will only take a day. You will travel in Mrs. Merewether's limousine. The limousine will come down from Maine with her grandson and pick you up and taking you to JFK where her chauffeur will take you directly to the Air France terminal. You are to see young Paul safely transferred to Air France security. The limousine will bring you back to Stowe." He relaxed with certain confidence knowing he could rely on her. "I'd do it, Laura, but Mrs. Merewether especially asked for you."

Laura shook her head. "I've talked with her often, but I didn't realize I made an impression."

"Evidently you have." Mr. Irwin smiled. "I knew promoting you to personally handle the Cloud's guests was a wise decision. I've had nothing but complements."

For a moment it took Laura's mind off the picture. She chuckled, "So now you tell me."

Mr. Irwin shrugged his shoulders, "Sometimes it's smart to keep employees in the gray area. It keeps them on their toes, but I apologize, Laura, you don't need direction."

"Like now?"

"Yes."

"When am I expected to go?"

"In two days. Her grandson is anxious. The chauffeur will give you the child's ticket and credentials. Think of it as a day off. Also, Mrs. Merewether implied that she would handsomely compensate you for your time."

"Is that acceptable with you?"

"Why not? You're acting on behalf of the Cloud—consider it a gratuity. Your weekly wage will not be affected."

"Thank you, Mr. Irwin. I'll telephone Mrs. Merewether."

* * * * *

New York City

The taxi slowly moved along the airport lane to reach Italia Airlines. Dominic sat back looking out the window. Suddenly, he yelled at the driver to stop. He shoved a wad of bills in the man's hand, grabbed his suitcase, and ran.

His heart hammering—he knew it was her. He couldn't be mistaken. She was holding a small boy's hand and talking. It was Laura Kincaid; there wasn't a doubt in his mind. Her curled hair was still so natural and her form was straight as she seemed to glide across the walk. Where did she come from? Dom wondered where the devil she was going. Who was the little boy? Dom was bumping into people looking over their heads and around them, but he missed her.

Laura was whisked forward and taken to the lounge for Air France elite passengers. She had no difficulty in getting Paul settled for his flight. Laura handed Paul Merewether's passport and credentials to the man in charge. "Please, will you give me a receipt for my friend?" Laura grinned. "I want to be sure you take extra good care of him. He's a sweetheart."

The small boy said, "Merci, Mademoiselle."

Laura telephoned Mrs. Merewether to confirm they arrived and all was well.

Laura hurried to return to the limousine as the chauffeur cautioned that airport security frowned on them blocking the passageway. Moving with unusual haste Laura was stunned and almost screamed when she was literally yanked and pulled into a man's arms.

"I knew it was you, Signorina." Dominic's smile could have lighted a runway in the dark of night.

Laura's mouth gaped, but her body tingled from her head to her toes. Awed, she stared into the handsome face she never forgot. "Dominic," she spoke in a broken whisper, "Deluca."

"Si. I am so happy to see you. Come, we will find a place and talk."

Laura's spirits plummeted. "I can't." She pulled away. He saw her eyes shine he was sure with tears. "I've got to go." She took a step away.

Dominic wasn't going to let her get away without knowing, "The boy?"

Laura's smile beamed only for him. "A friend that needed my escort."

Determine to keep her until he tasted her rosy mouth remembering how he wished to hold her. Before she could protest, he pulled her into his arms and matched his mouth to hers. Slowly he moved his tongue over her lips until she let him invade and taste her sweetness.

He murmured while continuing to caress her lips, "I don't want to let you go."

Frantic, Laura wanted to stay melting in his arms, but the chauffeur was waiting. She had to go. She was blushing as she took in the tall, handsome man that she was unable to erase from her thoughts. She let out an audible sigh when Dominic kissed her finger and pressed it to his mouth. Not wanting to cause the chauffeur an extra problem waiting for her, she remembered the New York photo.

"I've got to go." She began to forge ahead through the mobs of people.

Dominic wanted to go after her, to stop her but knew she was determined and he had to get over to the Italia terminal. He'd go to Stowe with her but his parents needed him.

He called out to her, "I'll call you."

Rushing, Laura glanced back as she waved. She heard him, hoping he'd keep his word and then she moved along with others hurrying to their destination.

Laura rode home in plush comfort, but all that mattered was having seen Dominic. And he kissed her right there. Thinking of his kiss wrapped around her like a warm blanket. The spark zinging and tingling. She'd never been kissed like that before. No wonder he was popular with the ladies. Laura thought about not wanting to make this trip and now she felt she owed Mrs. Merewether for putting her right where Dominic could capture her in his arms and kiss her. Laura reeling on waves of exhilaration was on cloud nine and then she chuckled…it being very apropos. He said he would call, and Laura was sure this time he meant it.

The chauffeur left her at Cloud Nine after Laura assured him she needed no further assistance.

It was late when she left a note that all was well and she'd be an hour late in the morning. It was a long day and she was anxious to get home.

Laura smiled and said good night to the night receptionist.

"You're here late, huh?"

"I am but now I'm going home and cuddling my daughter." Smiling, she went out to face her cold limousine, which started her laughing. The cold air causing her breath to smoke made her look forward to spring.

The receptionist answered the ringing telephone. He heard, "I'd like to speak with Signorina Laura Kincaid."

He replied, "You just missed her. She left to go home to her daughter."

Dominic choked. His stomach tightened before it dropped into a well of doom.

"Hello?" the receptionist called out, "Are you there?"

"Si. Did you say daughter? Laura Kincaid's daughter?"

"Yes, that's right."

Silence.

Frowning, the receptionist waited. "Hello…Hello?" He was unaware that at the other end of the line, the news hit the caller full force. "Hello?" he tried again. Silence, then heard a click—the connection was broken.

"Huh?" The night receptionist uttered, "It couldn't have been important." There being no message he didn't bother to record the call. He yawned, leaning back in his chair picked up the mystery he was reading.

Dominic dropped the phone in its cradle. His eyes pool with angst. He remembered that she said she had to go. He bit hard into his jaw. She's married, and yet she kissed me back. Dominic picked up a magazine, whacking it hard against his thigh—I thought she was different, but no she plays games like all the others and then slammed the magazine down hard on the table as some of its pages fluttered open.

* * * * *

Dominic studied the brandy swirling through the crystal glass; its contents eased the twisted knot in his chest but not in his thoughts. He sat in his apartment with one lamp lighted, the dark surrounding him seemed appropriate—it matched his mood. His mouth stayed tight and grim.

It was impossible to get Laura Kincaid out of his thoughts. He'd believed she was different, totally unaware of her allure. It had been her loveliness that came from within her that he couldn't forget. He fisted his hand wanting to hit something—she sure knew how to play innocent. His lips curled in disgust at himself. It rankled because he had let himself feel a surge of elation especially when he embraced her. Intoxication had taken over as he kissed her rosy mouth. She seemed so pure. For some reason, her kiss left a mark on him, remembering how he pressured those soft lips my nipping her full bottom lip so she'd open for him.

No one could have stopped him from tasting her so he could show her how enamored he was with her. Now it galled him. She accepted his embrace pretending to connect with him. Cold fury settled within him thinking of the electrifying spark and only with her. His melancholy served to shake him—it was like being dropped in the Atlantic without a preserver and wanting to drown.

A derisive smirk reached the corner of his mouth before he took a long drink, the brandy heating his body, as it also matched his bad temper. Dominic set the half-empty glass on the end table and leaned his head back on his favorite easy chair, closing his eyes while wrapping his heart in ice. And then he slept.

Demand for Dominic's expertise was backlogged. He'd get busy fulfilling contracts. He was a man of integrity, and his word was his honor. He'd put many requests on hold because of Tris trying to find information regarding her baby and then getting sidetracked over Laura Kincaid. He checked his calendar and sat down to get busy.

Flavio would have called if he discovered any news about Trista, so Dominic put his sister's secret on hold. As for Laura Kincaid, she no longer being of any consequence he took the memo with Cloud Nine's telephone number, wrinkled it, and with his long fingers pitched it into the wastebasket.

9

Jubilant, Laura wasn't bothered by freezing temperatures; today the cold couldn't penetrate the warmth reaching from the top of her head to the tips of her toes. Humming, she kicked off her boots and hung up her coat reliving Dominic's kiss and his promise to telephone.

Mr. Irwin greeted her. "I presume the Merewether trip enabled you to relish the comfort of her limousine?"

"Yes, quite an experience and very enjoyable."

"I perused your message and naturally you represented the Cloud as expected. Thank you, Laura."

Laura wasn't about to share seeing Dominic let alone his kiss that continued to send arcs of bliss through her. She savored that precious moment—reliving it over and over. Her smile extra bright, said, "Everything went better than I could have hoped. I'll call Mrs. Merewether to check that Paul is safely with his parents."

"Good…good, Laura, a capital idea." He turned and was gone.

Laura got busy but still every time the telephone rang, she silently said a little prayer, please God. But it was not to be. So at the end of the day, she cleared her desk and headed home. Her mood still upbeat, yet a tad disappointed. She was sure Dominic Deluca would have phoned, maybe tomorrow.

* * * * *

"Cella, you are growing so fast." Laura kissed one cheek and then the other. "Cella baby, you are going to be one year old." Laura laughed as Cella tried to return her kisses. Laura looked over at Gretel.

"Time has whizzed by, and I know you're anxious to go home. Thank you for your help caring for Cella. My little girl loves you."

"I hope so, Laura. She is precious, and I adore her. I'm going to miss you both. Spring slipped in on us before we knew it. You have been so kind, and with my sister nearby, I've had a wonderful visit."

*****

Laura lay in bed with the pillow over her face to smother her sobs—heartbroken waiting for Dominic's phone call—excited and believing he would call, in fact, still hoping yet knowing he wasn't going to ring her after all. Yet she had been so positive Dominic meant it when he called out to her. His words echoed in his mind again and again—*I'll call you, but he didn't.* The more she tried to ignore the truth and accept she's pursuing a dream, the more she'd think up excuses for him—*he's very busy…he's not feeling well…his parents or his sister needs him or maybe he forgot her number.* But Laura knew that wouldn't wash. Cloud Nine is not an unlisted number nor was hers.

Rising, Laura slipped on her scuffs and pulled back the curtain. A crescent moon way up—so far away, yet she wondered if Dominic would be looking at it. She rubbed her arms in the chilly night. I've got to stop this. I'm no match for the elegant women he desires. Laura mentally reviewed the picture of the gorgeous woman on Dominic's arm. Yet, goose bumps developed as she convinced her mind that there was joy when Dominic reached her—especially kissing her it had to mean something to him too—just thinking about his velvet warm kiss filled her with desire. Laura felt the dynamism of his arms as he held her close—she felt his solid strength. Tears flooded her cheeks landing on her nightgown. She kept telling herself that continuing to wait for his call that wasn't going to come was torment and she had to get on with her life. These last three weeks of hoping and waiting had to end. Let him keep his uncaring heart, enough is enough.

Tears hanging on her lashes she climbed back into bed. Biting her bottom lip realizing that their spark kept her vulnerable—she must lock it in her memory box—end it as silly dreams. Dominic Deluca's magic hurt yet she couldn't discard it entirely so she'd allow him only a corner of her heart and say goodbye. Too, I've got Cella Rose and he probably wouldn't care to be bothered with children. Laura took a deep breath vowing no more dreams—they'd no longer be part of her life.

    Pounding her pillow, Laura lay staring up at the ceiling but seeing nothing in the dark. Unable to get her mind to blank out the Italian, she chastised herself. I'll accept a dinner date with William. She waited for sleep to override her heartache.

10

March 2, Cella's First Birthday

Hugging Cella, Laura said, "A very special person gave you to me. When you have a lot more birthdays and you're all grown Mama will tell you about a secret promise."

Cella wasn't interested in her mama's words. In fact, knowing her words couldn't be comprehended was the reason Laura spoke them. Trista's secret was bottled inside her and she needing to mention it loud sort of eased the lump that lay dormant in the back of her mind. Laura never forgot Trista's plea or the promise they made to each other. Laura kept her word about never contacting Trista, but concern stayed with her. Remembering Trista saying Laura could ask her brother for help but Laura wouldn't consider doing so. Needing help wasn't a problem then she would have to tell why Tris chose a stranger to be Cella's mother and Laura knew she couldn't do that. No, Tris, a promise is a promise. I gave you my word.

Cella squirmed and wanted her freedom to take steps. "Okay, piccolo, little one, do your thing, you're about ready for bed."

"Bed...Mama, bed."

Grinning, Laura dropped toys in a box and pushed them into a corner. "No, darling, Cella is going to bed."

Perusing a seed catalog, the telephone rang. Laura's mind reeled, still hoping but knowing it was foolish to go there. He hadn't called and wouldn't.

"Laura," Mr. Irwin voiced, "I've been thinking over your resignation. Is there any way I can change your mind?"

"I'm sorry, Mr. Irwin, I want to stay home with Cella."

"What would you say if I could locate someone to care for your little girl?"

"Thanks, Mr. Irwin, but no. Cella's walking and beginning to talk, and I want to treasure it all."

"Then let me put it this way—if you change your mind you'll let me know first. Having you employed here at the Cloud has been our good fortune. I'll miss you."

"That's kind of you to say. I've liked working for you."

Laura made the decision to quit her job when Gretel left as planned. Laura had savings that would carry her for a couple of years and then she'd decide her next step. Laura wanted to be part of Cella's growing years—she wasn't going to change her mind.

Pushing the seed catalog to one side Laura stared out the kitchen window. She thought of Trista. My friend, I wish it were possible for you to know and see that we have a smart and beautiful daughter. I love her so…thank you.

* * * * *

End of June

Laura cleared the table putting dishes in the dishwasher. It was late. Cella was asleep. She and William were quietly talking. "Will you have more coffee, William?"

"No, no coffee or wine."

Laura suggested they sit on the porch.

"Excellent. I have something I want to ask you. I've been waiting to get up my nerve."

Laura smiled. "You bashful, William? That's difficult to believe. You are so commanding."

They were sitting on the porch swing, barely moving. William moved to sit sideways looking at Laura from the light shining from inside the house. His tone with just a shade of arrogance, he said, "I've only done this once before in my life and that was under different circumstances."

Laura knew William's proposal was forthcoming. These past couple of months William seemed overly condescending toward her and that didn't please her. Perhaps, she thought, she might be a tad oversensitive. The foremost fact being married to William Urquart with Dominic mysteriously augured deep within her heart didn't bode well. William deserved total loving support. Would William's sons accept her and Cella as a together family?

William reached for her hand. "Laura, I am a few years older than you, but we seem to be quite compatible. I have affection for you and believe you return the same. Will you marry me—become my wife and a mother for my two boys?"

The professor's voice came across as a treatise, with no inflection of feeling. Laura said nothing. Mostly, as Laura's stomach knotted because she didn't know what to do. She didn't want to hurt him; there was just no spark she hoped for one but it just wasn't there, not even a flutter.

"I've shocked you, my dear?"

"No, no…William, I'm somewhat bewildered."

Still holding her hand, he said, "I suppose I must be more explicit about our forthcoming relationship. It's been hard since my wife died, and I admit I miss her."

Laura was about to say something, but he raised his hand.

"Please, no need to say anything. My boys and I have adjusted. Now I think it's time for us to begin a new phase in our lives. I'd like it to include you."

Laura felt a jolt. William didn't mention Cella.

"Don't answer this minute, Laura, you need time to adjust. I know marrying me will be a step up for you. I will work with you and help you learn our ways. We can be a happy family."

The more William talked the more a storm began to build. "You sound like you have reservations, William, as to whether I'm qualified to be part of your little clique. No doubt you've considered what is best for Bobby and Billy and I must do the same—I have Cella to think of."

"Oh, that! Not a problem."

Those were not promising words ringing in Laura's ears. Cella is not that!

William went on. "Of course, she'll be with us. You know"—he released Laura's hand and rubbed his chin—"I've often wondered how you were allowed to adopt a baby being single. You certainly weren't mother material."

"You've just insulted me, William."

He laughed. "Really, how did you pull it off and why? Why would you take on someone else's responsibility? I know it is not yours. Everyone knows you were seen and definitely not pregnant. In fact, if it were yours I'd hesitate to…"

"What?" The storm was about to erupt into a gale. "And Cella is not an it!"

"You've got to face the truth, Laura—you with a newborn is questionable. But not to worry, I will treat her well."

Laura stood. William had just given her a concrete reason to refuse his proposal. Clenching her teeth; her curt voice lashed out—each spoken word succinct, "A step-up?" Her eyes darkened though he couldn't see them, "You have a puffed persona of self-importance and implying the mighty professor will be magnanimous in accepting me and my daughter…" Laura was on a roll. "Why the audacity of you to…to…" She was shaking. "Think to honor me to become your wife. I think not, William. It is unthinkable to have you lower your standards on my behalf."

"My dear, you must understand…"

"Understand?" she interrupted, "Oh, I do understand very well. Cella and I don't belong in your world," her voice soft and turned mocking, "I think it would be Cella and me that would have to lower our standards. Good night, William, and goodbye." Laura moved with grace and then closed the door—she did not slam it. The cicadas were chirping, yet William heard Laura turn the dead bolt, its sound echoing in William's ears.

Upset, rage simmering, Laura went into Cella's room. Seeing her sleeping daughter she calmed. Pulling the light blanket over her baby, she leaned down and kissed her.

SECRET PROMISE

Turning off the light, Laura went to bed.

* * * * *

October

Autumn leaves blanketed the landscape. Their vibrant colors seemed to surpass all others as Mother Nature proved she was in command. Laura laughed as her daughter tried to catch one of the many falling leaves floating down in the breeze.

Leaving the park and heading home, Laura stopped at Stowe's Everything Store. Winter was on its way and Cella needed a snowsuit.

"Hello, Mr. Carlsson."

"Miss Kincaid," the store owner beamed. "I've been talking about you."

"You have?" Laura, holding Cella lowered her to the floor, but held on to her hand.

"Axell was visiting when I told him my problem. He suggested I call you."

Laura's mouth curved into a smile. "Mr. Irwin?"

"Yes, yes. Forgive me. Axell and I have been friends for a long time. Please, will you come back to my office? I would like to talk in private."

Laura picked up Cella and followed the older man. She sat and lifted Cella onto her lap.

Mr. Carlsson held a box of cookies. He looked at Laura for permission to offer one to Cella. Laura nodded. Without a word from Laura, Cella said "Thank you."

"Miss Kincaid, would you be interested in helping me keep my daily records? Matt, my accountant, comes at the end of each month and is upset that I don't follow his directions. I just don't have the time."

"I stay home with my little girl, Mr. Carlsson. I'd like to help and I thank Mr. Irwin for suggesting, but…"

Not listening, Mr. Carlsson pulled down a box filled with receipts and another box filled with invoices. "It's very easy. All you have to do is put the figures in the right column for each day." He showed Laura his ledger. "See," he took a receipt, writing the amount under the proper column for merchandise.

"It looks easy enough, but I'm not able to come in and work. That's the reason I quit working."

"I know, Axell told me. That's why he thought this would be right for you and me. You can take this home and work there. Every couple of days, if you would come in, I can have the receipts and invoices delivered to you. I'll pay my bills and all you have to do is keep them listed in the ledgers."

Laura didn't hesitate. "I can do that."

Mr. Carlsson turned out a big smile. "Yes, yes, and if you have any questions, there's Matt's telephone number pasted on top of the book. He'll be happy for he's been after me for weeks now."

"I'll do my best. But if you decide to change your mind, I'll understand."

"Thank you, Miss Kincaid." He put more cookies in a bag and insisted she take them. "I'll have everything delivered to you this afternoon…about four. Is that okay?"

"Perfect. Now my daughter needs a snowsuit. We want to be ready when it snows."

When Laura got home her answering machine was blinking. 'If only," she uttered, her heart never gave up on Dominic, but it was a message wanting to sell a vacation to a sunny paradise. Her waiting message a disappointment—she clicked the recorder's delete. She scolded herself speaking out in the empty room, "Don't go there, Laura…paradise…fat chance you'll ever sail away or go to Rome again and fat chance I'd find him if I did."

* * * * *

The clock chimed ten when Laura stacked Mr. Carlsson's ledgers and papers together.

This past week, determined to do a good job Laura discovered she liked working with figures. This opportunity to earn extra dollars and remain home with Cella revitalized her self-reliance to make it on her own.

Lightning crackled and then a thunder crashed causing the window panes to vibrate. Laura went to check on Cella and found her sound asleep.

"I'm glad you're sleeping through this thunderstorm," she whispered.

Looking out the window into the dark, the rain pounding on the glass, Laura wondered if she would ever stop living in her dream world. *I wonder if it's storming where you are, Dominic.* Her eyes blurring her vision, she murmured, "Why? Why didn't you call? I believed you." Then she called herself an idiot. Trying to control her weeping, Laura dropped the curtain back in place, snapped off the light, and crawled into bed.

"Tomorrow will be better," she said.

11

October, Deluca Family Villa

Sitting on his father's favorite bench, Dominic listened to the water lap the shoreline. He leaned back staring at the full moon—it's sky cloudy. They wanted a grandson; his parents pressing him to take a wife. Dominic felt drained, hollow and lifeless. He failed in finding Trista's daughter. He kept his promise to her and said nothing to anyone. But if he could locate the child that might lessen the demand that he marry.

Dominic wasn't against marriage. First, he'd been occupied with increasing Deluca finances. Second, he'd never met anyone he felt he wanted to be bound to for the rest of his life. A heaviness centered in his chest—Laura Kincaid with her dewy green eyes. He never forgot her name; he never forgot her playing him a fool. It still rankled. Time didn't help him forget.

"Dominic," his father called, "what are you doing out here by yourself? You should have a signorina with you to enjoy the moon's shine on the water."

"Papa, let me have a little peace."

"You know Mama would be so happy if you marry Valentina Scarpello. She is a nice woman, Dominic. She will make you a good wife." His father sat down. "Valentina can cook, keep your house, and give you bambinos."

"Papa, please! I am thirty-four; I have plenty of time to marry. I have a cook and housekeeper. Listen to me," he gritted his teeth, "I am not going to marry Valentina. She is not for me."

"But your mama…since Trista go to heaven, Mama is a lost soul. It is her only hope."

Dominic's tone softened. "I'm sorry, Papa, but my getting married to Valentina is not the answer."

"What is wrong with you? You, my only son, use to be more respectful. Do you have someone you think to marry?"

"Papa," a sudden memory of Laura slammed into his mind lingering there pure and clear. Why can't I rid my memory of her? It angered Dominic so that he spoke irrationally, "All right. Let me think about Valentina."

His father's smile could have lighted the water if the moon hadn't already done so. "Good, Dominic, good. You are a good son."

"Remember, I said I will think about it."

"That will make Mama happy." He left Dominic alone with his thoughts.

"I could marry the girl and make everyone happy," he groused, "but it wouldn't be fair to Valentina—there must be mutual love in marriage." Dominic finger combed his silky hair, continuing talking to the air, "It would please Mama and Papa and make up for not finding Trista's baby. Can Valentina's love be enough?"

Dominic stood. His mind was made up. He was going to go on one more skiing trip. It would clear his mind and put his questions to rest. He had to know exactly what kind of games Laura Kincaid plays.

* * * * *

Last week in November, New York

Isabella and Lorenzo sat across the table smiling at Dominic. "I can't tell you how happy I am that you called." She raised her eyebrow, "So what gives, Dom?"

Lorenzo laughing, said, "That's my Bella—she leaves no stone unturned."

Isabella lightly knuckle knocked on her husband's arm. "You know as well as I that this unexpected visit from a guy who always says he'll call is like waiting for cows to give chocolate milk."

Dom raised his hands. "I give up. Nothing really just that I'm going up to Stowe for a ski and thought maybe you'd like to join me—as my guests."

"Stowe, Vermont? Ah, your hide-away." Lorenzo, his voice probing further, "Now it's my turn—what gives?"

Dom twisted the stem of his wine glass, hesitating, wondering if he should tell all. He shrugged, "It's about a certain woman."

Isabella leaned forward not wanting to miss a word.

"I go to Stowe to ski, but mostly to unwind. No one knows me—I need the quiet, especially privacy and Cloud Nine, a small inn, is perfect for just that." Dominic leaned back and pushed the wine glass away, "A young lady was charged to see that all my demands were met and that I was a contented guest. To cut to the quick, we had a few conversations and she seemed—mind you I stress seemed like the kind of person I would like to know better. She had this innocence about her."

"Oh, oh," Isabella butted in, "you men...innocence! What about you men?"

"End it, Bella. This is Dom's avowal."

"Sorry."

Dom couldn't hold back his chuckle. "You two are great...so I invited her to dinner and I really wanted to be with her. Then that very evening before I left to collect her I found out Trista was missing and my parents needed me. I left."

Isabella's mouth fell open. "You didn't call her and explain?"

Dom shook his head. "No. Gina and I threw some of my things into a bag and we rushed to her jet."

Lorenzo's eyebrows shot up. "Gina Escobar?"

"Si, she tracked me down and told me about Trista."

"How did Gina get into the picture, Dom?" Lorenzo's jaw thrust forward, "She's husband hunting and you're first on her list."

"Don't sidetrack him, Ren...go on, Dom," prodded Isabella.

Dominic couldn't help but smile. He was fond of his two friends, wishing he could find someone to have the same kind of relationship. "As I said, Gina tracked me down. I had no idea anything was wrong and Trista had gone off. The news scared me. I didn't think of anything except getting to my parents. I was certain when I got home I'd find her."

"You never did, did you?" Isabella's soft tone touched Dominic.

"No," raw hurt darkened his eyes. "I hired the best investigative service but they found no clues. Then one day, months later, Tris turns up at the airport. She was ill." He swallowed his misery, "And then you know she later died. Her cancer was in remission for many years, but suddenly there wasn't anything more that could stabilize it."

Isabella reached for Dominic's hand, giving it a gentle squeeze. "You never found out where she'd gone?"

"No. It's still a mystery." Dom would keep the rest of Trista's confession a secret as he'd promised. Taking a swallow of wine, he said, "So getting back to this woman, time went by and my effort went into finding my sister and catching up on my work. I didn't call her."

Isabella shook her head, remaining silent.

"After your party, I planned to head for Stowe, but my parents needed me, so again, I flew home. It was a good thing as going to catch my plane I spotted her and ran like hell to catch her..."

Isabella burst out, "Your special woman."

For a few seconds, Dominic's face warmed, and he almost smiled. "Exactly. And she looked gorgeous. She has the fairest green eyes. I can't shake them from my mind."

"Okay, I get it." Lorenzo grinned. "to make a long story have an ending, we're off to Stowe. Let's go and get her."

"Not so fast," Dominic cautioned. "I did find her and I did what any hot-blooded Italian would do—I grabbed her and planted a kiss on her rosy mouth..." Dominic's expression stilled for a second reliving the moment. "I admit it was soul-reaching if that makes any sense." Looking at Isabella, he threatened, "Say one word, Issy..." and then continued, "I knew I'd fallen, the well was so deep there was no coming out of it. She was in a hurry and said she had to go. I had to catch my plane, so I yelled out that I would call her. She waved and that's the last I saw her."

Isabella groaned, "Don't tell me...again you didn't call her?"

"Oh, I called her, all right. She wasn't there, I had just missed her." His tone mocking, "She left to go home to her daughter."

"I'll be damned." Lorenzo didn't expect that response, "married."

"And you never talked with her again?"

"Why, Issy? She's married, Dio, and with a daughter."

They could tell this woman still nibbled at Dominic's heart.

"What the hell is she playing at?" Lorenzo's sharp tone filled the room.

"My thoughts, exactly. I think what irks me most is that I was played a fool."

"Now hold on, you two," Isabella scolded. "If you never talked with her and you have no idea what happened, she could be a widow. How about that?"

A flair of hope lighted within Dominic.

"So," continued Isabella, "we go skiing."

Both men grinned.

"We'll pretend we're just going up for skiing. You and Ren can ski, and I'll do a little shopping and settle in with a good book." Isabella winked at her husband, and then looked at Dominic, "I won't be skiing because we're going to have a baby and we're not taking any chances."

Dominic's face split into a wide grin. "Congratulations. You both will be perfect parents."

"So, anico, how soon can we hit the slopes? I hope they have some good powder up there. My skis are hot."

Dominic chuckled. "I'm sure I can get reservations for the first. Will that work for you?" Dom wondered if Laura would take his reservation.

"I can't wait." Isabella was glowing with excitement. She had to meet this paragon in Dom's fantasy.

12

First week in December, Stowe

"Gretel, I can't tell you how good it is to see you. I've got your room ready." She hugged her elderly friend.

"I told Gret," Pete crowed, "that you'd be glad to have her visit."

"Of course. Wait until you see Cella, she is growing so fast and talking a blue streak." Laughing, Laura added, "Watch what you say around her as she just about repeats what she hears."

"Where is our little darling?"

"Napping. I can't wait to see if she remembers you, Gretel."

"Well, I'll make sure she doesn't forget me this time. I'll go take a peek at her."

Pete said his goodbye and then said in passing, "Ahh, remember that foreign guy that you drove to the capital…in Cloud's Lincoln," Pete scratched his head trying to remember the name.

Laura grabbed the back of the kitchen chair, she knew the guy—Dominic Deluca. She couldn't get any air; she was suffocating Dominic's in Stowe.

"Well anyway," Pete went on, "he's skiing and he brought some people with him. He isn't being so high and mighty this time. Who knows what goes on with the rich?" Pete shrugged his shoulders and closed the door.

The telephone rang. Panic thundered through Laura, she wanted it to be Dominic and she didn't. She couldn't make her feet move.

"Do you want me to answer that for you, Laura?"

"Yes, please." Laura took a deep breath.

"It's a Mr. Matthew."

Laura buried her disappointment. "Hello, Matt." She listened. "Just a minute…Gretel, I hate to ask as you just arrived but would you mind staying with Cella? I have some papers Matt needs. I'd like to take them to him. I'll be gone about an hour."

"Go, I'm glad to do something for you, Laura. Take your time. Cella will be fine."

Laura was in Mr. Carlsson's office with Matt. She was putting on her coat. Matt reached over and straightened her collar. "Don't forget I'm taking you out to dinner tomorrow night. Dress pretty."

Laura laughed. "Aren't you afraid Kathy will be angry?"

"Nope, she's the one that suggested I do something nice for you. She'd come too, but she's visiting her brother. She thinks I ask too much of you."

They were walking out of the office and into the store. Matt was right behind Laura.

Laura saw a woman drop her glove. She picked it up. "Pardon me, you dropped this."

Isabella smiled. "Thank you. I've lost more gloves, it's a wonder I don't have frostbite."

Laura pulling on her scarf, smiled. Matt touched her shoulder, "Don't forget we're having dinner out tomorrow night."

"I'm looking forward to it." Laura saluted, jauntily cocking her head.

"Me too. I'll pick you up—bring your appetite." Matt smiled and Laura, laughing, called back, "Definitely," and was gone.

* * * * *

Saturday evening, Angelo's Restaurant

Angelo's was crowded. If one didn't make a reservation, there was a long wait to be seated.

Matt and Laura arrived early.

Sitting, they sipped wine. They didn't order as Angelo came to their table and said he was fixing something delizioso just for Matt and his friend. Laura eyed Matt, teasing, "I take it, Matt, you keep Angelo's books."

"You gathered that, huh?"

Laura's smile didn't need the lighted candle to show its warmth. "So when is Kathy returning?"

Matt smiled. "The kids are anxious to come home, but Kathy is enjoying her brother's company. Since both their parents are gone, they only have each other. Jeff is driving with them, so they should be home the day after tomorrow."

Matt broke off a chunky piece of bread from a small loaf and dipped crusty bread in herbed oil. "This is worth coming to Angelo's. Try some."

Laura did and agreed wholeheartedly the flavor was fantastic with the crusty bread. Then they talked about Mr. Carlsson, agreeing he is a fine man to work for.

Angelo served a variety from his menu. The traditional antipasto—then primo pasta smothered in Angelo's famous sauce and cheese. Eating heartily—Angelo personally served each a rib steak flavored with olive oil and garlic along with seasoned vegetables: broccoli, cauliflower, eggplant, and a tomato-olive salad—all Matt and Laura's favorites and ending with gelato and fresh strawberries as they both turned down espressos.

"Matt, if I didn't know, I'd think I'm in Italy." Taking a last taste of wine, Laura offered a sated grin, "I enjoyed this feast, and I think you may have to roll me out of here. Thank you and thank Kathy for suggesting this perfectly delicious evening."

"I enjoyed your company, and I'll be sure to tell Kathy—she will be pleased." Laughing, he said, "Ready for me to roll both of us out?"

Their dining over they were walking through the restaurant—Matt stopped to talk with someone and Laura went on, and then she heard, "Why hello."

Laura turned. It was the lady who dropped her glove. Laura began to smile until she looked and saw two men dining with the lady. Dominic! Her lips moved but no sound escaped. Laura froze. She stared—her eyes became saucers. She heard Isabella say, "This is the lady that picked up my glove." The other man smiled. "Thank you. My wife loses them regularly."

Laura stood stupefied. The blood draining from her face, she stood there as if shot and waiting to fall, her mind racing with her thundering heart. Dominic...why aren't you saying something? Don't I even warrant a hello? His dark implacable expression conjured up a tight ball in her stomach. Why, Dominic, what could I possibly have done to show so much scorn? Her mind reeling with all these thoughts and she could do nothing but stand transfixed, her throat closing—she could barely swallow. Laura witnessing Dominic's smoldering hostility—she felt a vein begin to throb at her temple. I've got to get a grip. I've got to move and get away. It was then Matt came over, "Are you ready, Laura?"

Laura focused on Dominic's grim face; he merely moved his head, nothing more, though never taking his eyes off her. Unable to answer Matt, the lump in her throat constricted her breathing; Laura hadn't realized her knuckles had turned white as she gripped the vacant chair to keep from collapsing. Matt unaware of her dilemma, didn't notice one man's scrutiny—dark eyes filled with contempt. All Matt saw with indifference were three people dining. He took Laura's arm steering her toward the exit while leaning over into her ear, to some it would seem engaging, except Matt was explaining that the man he stopped to talk with asked him to go skiing. He apologized for keeping her waiting.

Once outside, the blast of cold caused Laura to shake, but she knew it wasn't the cold that jolted her. Dominic and he didn't even say hello. Determined not to let any tears fall, she used her glove to blot them.

Matt's voice was tunneled; Laura heard though her mind didn't connect. Heading toward his car Matt gripped her elbow taking her with him. Laura was numb, a heavy block of ice crushing her heart.

Matt pulled into Laura's driveway. Debilitated, feeling the crucial need to be alone or she would scream, she opened the car door. Her pulse continued to roar in her ears, and she couldn't control the slight quiver in her voice. "Don't get out, Matt. It's too cold. The porch light is on, just let me get inside before you leave."

"Are you sure? Laura?" His tone worried, "Is everything all right?" Matt noticed Laura's persona changed and didn't understand. "Are you ill?"

Laura knew she had to pull herself together, "I think I overate. Thanks, Matt. Really, I enjoyed your company and the food." Laura reached over and touched his gloved hand resting on the steering wheel. "Thank Kathy for thinking of me. Good night." Before Matt could move, Laura slipped out of the car. Matt watched Laura safely enter her home.

*****

Dominic's muscles quivered in his jaw as he tried to conceal the furor strangling his insides. He didn't want his friends to realize how seeing Laura with her husband was like getting kicked in his groin. He had it bad more than he realized.

Isabella recognized the tension between the strange woman and Dom. "When are you going to tell us, Dom?" Then Isabella's eyes flashed, "Oh my god, she's the one, isn't she?"

Lorenzo said, "Bella, leave it! I think we need a stiff drink." He flagged a waiter and ordered two whiskeys.

Isabella ignored her husband's pressure and said to Dom, "I think you ought to call her and talk. Clear the matter. Tell her the sordid game she plays isn't clever but outright vile."

"Bella! Please stop. I mean it."

"Oh shush, Hon," she waved her hand, "I'm here for Dom."

Dominic shrugged one shoulder. He took a swallow of whiskey, feeling it trail down his throat, and he calmed. "Thanks, Issy." He reached and patted her arm. "I know you mean well, but it isn't all that bad. It was the shock of those green eyes gaping at me. She didn't blink, just stared. There was no humiliation—she must have an iron heart."

"You know what I think, Dom? I think she was more shocked than you. That woman was frozen to that spot and literally hanging on to that chair." Isabella nodded to the vacant chair pushed under their table. "She saw only you. It was as if you and she were the only ones in this restaurant."

"I have to agree with Bella," Lorenzo voiced. "To me, she looked as if she was waiting for you to speak to her."

Dominic maliciously said, "I suppose she wouldn't have minded if I kissed her. I wonder what reason she'd give her husband. No doubt some outrageous lie. She excels in reacting with callous innocence."

Taking a sip of water, Isabella said, "I have to say this whether you like it or not, she doesn't appear to be any of those things you're accusing her of. She seemed utterly devastated when she looked at you. Are you sure about her, Dom? Really sure?"

Dom bridled at Isabella's defending the green-eyed tramp. "Dio, Issy, she has a daughter. I'm not mistaken." Dominic had hoped that perhaps as Issy has suggested Laura was a widow. It wouldn't have mattered because he wanted her so much in a way he didn't understand himself. He laughed.

Lorenzo's unsinkable spirit, eyed his friend, "Are you going to share what's so funny?"

Dominic wasn't about to confess how this heartfelt shredded, so he grinned. "I wished I would have had a date with me. I must have looked pathetic."

"Ha! You're speaking gibberish. Isn't he, Hon?" Not waiting for her husband to agree, she went on. "Dom, is there something between the two of you? I don't know what it is, but are you certain you want to pass up this opportunity to just talk with her and ask her why? That way you can put it to rest. Besides"—now Isabella grinned—"I'm curious. Want me to investigate?"

"Bella!"

"There you go again, Husband. At least this time I'm asking."

"I'll think about it, Issy." Dom looked at Lorenzo. "How about we ski tomorrow? Early?"

"Now you're talking my language."

* * * * *

SECRET PROMISE

Gretel left a light for Laura. Still shaken from seeing Dominic she went to check on Cella before hurrying to her bedroom and unleashing her choked-up sobs.

The water collecting under her lids rolled down her cheeks. She fell on her bed pushing her face into her pillow. Never could she remember feeling so bereft.

How had he come to despise her? Despise her he did. Try as she might to recall every incident or conversation with Dominic, she came up empty. She not only saw—she felt it. It was as though he wanted her to have no doubt about what he thought.

Laura turned over bringing her pillow with her covering her face. Racking her brain she wondered if it could have been when he kissed her and she returned his kiss—did he find it repulsive? What did I do, Dominic? I don't know. Laura couldn't hold back her choking tears. She dug her nails into her palms feeling pain matching her heartache. She could no longer deny telling herself it was mere friendship between them. She felt his magic, black though it was. Now without question, Laura knew it was only her dreaming and dreaming and dreaming that built hope that there could be more. She sobbed until she had to catch her breath.

Just when she thought she was getting on with her life, the ski season opens and Dominic decides to come to the Cloud. There are hundreds and hundreds of places to ski—why...why come back to Stowe? She didn't know the answer. She lifted her head, reached for a tissue, and whispered into the dark room, "I'm stronger than you suspect, Mr. Deluca. Take your self-importance and go back to Italy." Still, tears rained as those same words repeated again to convince her Dominic meant nothing to her.

Laura lay in the dark hearing the clock strike one. Sleep wouldn't come—she hurt, she hurt so bad trying to figure it out. The clock struck two.

Laura slammed her fist on the bed before pushing the quilt away. She was going to get answers directly from Mr. Black Magic. Slipping on her slippers she quietly headed toward the telephone and dialed Cloud Nine's number.

"Please connect me to Mr. Dominic Deluca's suite." She used her best authoritative voice; she didn't want to lose her nerve.

Dominic picked up on the first ring. Laura realized he also wasn't sleeping.

"Dominic," her voice a lifeless monotone, "this is Laura Kincaid." She took a gulp of air. "I would like to meet with you for just a short while if you will."

Dominic's body stiffened in shock, yet his heart was pounding. His mouth dropped open; he was too stunned to speak.

Laura's tone challenged, "If you haven't the time, I quite understand. But know this—I'm asking just this once and no more." She was angry. "And if you agree, I expect you to honor your word."

"Si, Signora." Dominic's furor was ready to explode. "How dare you of all people question my honor? I am onto your game and I want answers. I will meet with you. Where do you suggest?"

Laura covered the telephone with her hand, Games? Her nerves clawing at her, she said, "We can meet here at my home."

Dominic was flabbergasted. Meet in her husband's casa? Has she no shame? Why she uses her own name and not her husband's must be another game. Modulating his disgust, said, "I would not like that. Is there not somewhere that will not be too inconvenient?"

Hearing Dominic's chilly monotone, Laura evenly replied, "As you wish. There is the Snowball Diner about a mile north of the inn. Will you need transportation?"

Dominic grimaced. This woman will even use her husband's car to make a rendezvous. It sickened him, but he'd meet and tell her exactly what kind of a contaminated person she was and not to bother ever contacting him again. "I have transportation. What is the time?"

Laura hedged, then came out and told it like it was. "I'll put my daughter down for her nap around noon. Will one o'clock work for you?"

Thick with revulsion, he replied, "That will be fine."

"One thing more, Mr. Deluca, I expect you to keep your word, this time." Laura hung up.

Dominic purposely arrived early. The Snowball was crowded. Fortunately, he located a booth in a corner. It was perfect. He could see parking and watch for Laura's arrival.

A cup of coffee, untouched, cooled. His nostrils flared—hardening his features. The chill surrounding his demeanor appeared colder than the air outside. He said nothing, sat, and watched cars enter the lot. He was disturbed by his actually looking forward to Laura's arrival. Though bristling, a strange surge of caring for her engulfed him. He assumed it was because of their kiss when she melted in his arms.

"Warm your coffee, sir?"

Dominic eyed the waitress, "Pardon?"

Holding the pot of coffee, she smiled. "Coffee?"

"Oh, sorry. No, thank you. I'm waiting for someone. Later will be fine."

Laura drove in, squeezing her little clunker into the only open space. She sidestepped to edge out and about slipped, but her arm was grabbed and held her to get her balance.

Surprised, she laughed.

"You know, Miz Kincaid, I can arrest you for parking too close to other vehicles. That isn't a parking space."

Laura laughed, "Is that right, Deputy Kolski? You can't arrest me you're not in uniform."

Joe's grin lighted his eyes. "You got me there."

The wind blew at the hood of Laura's parka sending it back off her head. The sunlight caught her hair bringing out reddish highlights. Unaware of the pretty picture she made with her reddened cheeks, she gripped her purse and started to move, slipped, and Joe grabbed her arm again.

"Easy, I won't be responsible for broken bones."

Getting her balance, Laura moved away. She waved heading for the diner. Glad to have a bit of diversion before confronting Dominic. She hoped that he'd keep his word and show up.

All that had transpired between Laura and Joe was viewed by Dominic. His face became a dark mask—he was roiling as he watched Laura flirt. Her was smile so broad the day didn't need sunshine to brighten the day. Dio, she has no shame. He scrutinized the sway of her walk. She looked beautiful wearing gray corduroy pants stuffed in her boots. Her pink parka set off her rosy complexion. Dominic's eyes blazed murderously. So much so that when the waitress was about to approach him, she backed away.

Laura entered and didn't see Dominic right off as she hung her coat on a peg.

"Hey, Laura," the call came from the kitchen.

Laura offered a big smile. "Hi Mickey."

"I've got your favorite—split pea with ham."

"It's the best." She spotted Dominic glaring.

Stay calm; she told herself, you called him. Don't let him get to you. Laura went to meet the man that she couldn't forget.

Dominic stood, saying not a word.

Laura slid onto the booth. Dominic sat across. Her insides were jumping; she only hoped her nervous condition wasn't noticeable. All she could think of at the moment is how good he looked even with his scowling. "Hello, Dominic…" Before she could continue the waitress brought over a bowl of soup and a glass of milk.

"Thanks, Gladys. This is perfect."

The waitress looked at Dominic. "Will you order?"

"Not at this time, thank you." He said that all the while looking at Laura. Gladys shrugged and knew to go.

"How are you, Dominic?" Laura eyed his monstrous glare. He still didn't answer, just continued to stare.

Biting her lip she tried to look away but it was impossible. "I can't believe I called you," she offered.

Dominic still made no effort to talk.

Laura cleared her throat. "I guess it's up to me to talk since I asked you to meet with me." Determined not to let his silence visibly shake her, she lifted the soup spoon, and then slowly replaced it on the table. "I called you last night as I'm bothered when seeing you at Angelo's you didn't say hello. Why? What have I done?"

Dominic's scorching look and in a soft simmering voice asked, "Tell me something, Signora, what kind of games do you play? Do you take me for a fool? Dio, you have a daughter!"

Stunned by his venomous tone, Laura sat back and now it was her turn to stare—her face paled. She couldn't speak.

"So your answer is to remain silent?"

Laura chewed on her bottom lip. Anxiety stabbed in her gut; He doesn't like children. She had no intention of cowering. She augured deep inside of herself for courage. She wasn't employed at the Cloud, so she could say what she pleased. Smartly she charged, "Playing games? That's what you are doing and have done since I first met you. Yes, I have a daughter." She couldn't help beaming, "I'm the luckiest mother in the world as she is the sweetest little girl."

Dominic sneered. "And the father, is he lucky to have you?"

Laura had no idea what initiated Dominic's thinking or what he thought he knew, so when she answered, she heaped more suspicions and contempt to his list about her.

Her raspy chuckle raised Dominic's ire. "Husband? I have no husband. I've never married. Though it's not what you think. You see…"

Dominic spewed words between clenched teeth. "I don't want to hear your lies. I regret that I ever took the time to think of you. You played me a fool but I'll make this clear, Miss Kincaid, not ever again! I would sterilize my mouth to cleanse it from kissing you if I could. Tell me, does your suggestive innocent acting bring you into contact with many men?" His black eyes clawed at her like talons, as he continued to spit out his rage, his quiet voice filled with venom, "I've never known another woman with your talent to lie, and parade your despicable actions without remorse. I feel for your poor daughter and what she will have to endure."

Laura bared her fury, "You listen to me," her voice low but obviously wanting to shout, "you pompous, overbearing snob," she leaned toward him wanting to make sure he heard every word, "I don't care what you think of me and I won't defend myself because it's not necessary. So be it." She seethed, her eyes narrowed, her face paled, "But when you mention my daughter and have the unmitigated gall to suggest that I am a poor mother or that she will suffer because of me, you go too far. You, Mr. Deluca, are brain thick," her defiant stare brooked no interference, "and that makes you a complete dullard. You, Mr. Know-it-all," her voice pushed low so as not to shout, "haven't a clue as to what you're talking about." Disdain dripped from her tone, "You aren't the man I thought you were." She moved to leave, but Dominic gripped her wrist, holding her in place.

An unexpected ember ignited traveling from his fingers up his arm and into his beating heart. The impact was compelling. He released his hold as though scalded. Hiding his tremors he allowed his curt voice to lash at her. "I haven't finished."

Stunned, Laura felt the odd feeling of needles dancing over her skin—Dominic's electrifying magic. She bit her bottom lip slowing the momentum it stirred. Laura's green eyes glittering, she said, "As far as I'm concerned you are more than finished."

"Oh no, puttna, there is one thing more. Do not ever ever telephone me again." His voice held malice as he bluntly announced, "Now you can leave."

Laura was really shaken, but she'd be damned if she'd let him see. "Have no fear, Mr. Deluca. That works both ways." Standing, she looked down at him in antipathy. "You have always been arrogant. You believe only you are honorable and," her voice softened, "I once thought you were noble." Unblinking, her long lashes framing her fired-up green eyes, added, "Now I know you for what you are—a man who believes only he is the owner of high moral standards. Well you're wrong. Goodbye, Dominic."

Laura went for her jacket. She reached into her purse and dropped some cash on the counter. Loudly, on purpose called out, "This is for my soup and milk, Gladys. Thanks." She hurried out the door not looking back.

Dominic's furor spilled over. He saw her drop money on the counter for the bowl of her favorite soup and glass of milk when she knew that he would not like it. He felt a quirk of admiration because she knew he would not like her paying. She continued to bother him. The jolt he experienced when he touched her. There was something about Laura Kincaid. That innocent ploy of hers still got to him. Dominic would never admit that it was lust, or worse jealousy. The thought of any man touching her riled him. He eyed the glass of milk, innocent? Oh no, he knew better. He dropped a ten dollar bill on the table, slipped into his ski jacket and left.

13

Laura clamped her lips to keep from screaming. Her boots felt like lead as she tried to hurry to her car. Acid welled in her stomach. She was careful leaving the parking area. She'd not cause an injury to anyone. Too, she didn't want to give Dominic any satisfaction that his words were tearing up her insides. Laura eased out onto the highway. A side road a half mile from the diner is where she pulled over.

The blood drained from Laura's face. She gripped the steering wheel, shaking. She'd felt the spark. It felt as if lightning buzzed through her from him. Warm tears fell as her sobs echoed in the silent surroundings. Trista, Trista—are we both doomed? The spark works only for us? Laura rested her head on the steering wheel. Between sobs, she moaned, "Why, Dominic, why have you condemned me without letting me explain? How can you even think that I am immoral?" Unleashed fury, Laura screamed, "How dare you!"

Her face swollen and red from crying she pounded the steering wheel. "Enough," she shouted out, "I've had enough…I will stop this stupid dreaming." Laura mopped her tears and then shifted forward; she was going home to her daughter.

When she opened her kitchen door, Cella came running. Her sweet welcoming smile filled Laura's heart.

Gretel noticed Laura's puffy red eyes but said nothing. "Matt called and said he would be bringing you some papers tomorrow, but he didn't know the time."

"Thanks, Gretel. I'm going to be here so it doesn't matter."

"Then if you don't mind, tomorrow morning Pete will pick me up."

"By all means, Gretel. I apologize if I've taken advantage of your goodwill."

"That's silly. I don't mind at all."

Laura reminded herself, I've got it all right here. It is a good life...mine and Cella's."

* * * * *

Dominic charged into his suite throwing his jacket on a chair, it slid to the floor. He left it. His growl ascended to a murderous roar but he wasn't able to bellow out his frustration because the tap on his door brought him back to good sense.

He opened the door and Isabella waltzed in, her smile quickly disappeared. "Oh oh, I'm visiting at the wrong time."

Dominic dragged his hand through his already messed hair, his words clipped, "Not now, Issy."

But Isabella wasn't one to heed his warning. She closed the door and picked up his jacket—giving it a shake and putting it on the chair. Moving over to the other one, she sat.

Dominic couldn't hold back a snicker. "Issy, you are one of a kind. But really, I'm not in the mood for company. Where's Ren?"

"He's skiing. He said he came to ski, waved goodbye, and took off." She kept her eyes aimed at Dominic. Her tone gentled, "You went to see your friend, right?"

He nodded. "Big mistake. I had Laura pegged as a nice and sweet lady," he went on sarcastically, "oh how wrong I was. Talk about a fool, you're looking at one."

Isabella thought he'd got it bad for this woman, but she kept her thoughts to herself for if Dominic knew what she could see he'd be furious and toss her out of his suite. "Tell me, Dom, what happened? How did you arrange to meet?"

He smirked. "She called me last night at two in the morning to be exact and said she wanted to talk. She had the audacity to suggest I meet her at her home. I thought it crass to invite me to her husband's domain." His face pinched tight, "We met at a diner and she unflinchingly admitted she never married."

"But...a daughter...oh, I see."

"Not only that, she flaunted about being a single mother. How could she?"

Dominic's fists locked with suppressed rage. "She has no shame. Why does she even brag about having a child? I could only think her a puttana."

Isabella's eyes were transfixed with horror. "Please, Dom, tell me you didn't say that to her."

His brows furrowed. "Of course, I did, but I don't think she knew what it meant. Issy, why am I obsessing over this woman?" Not waiting for an answer, he went on, "I hate being made a fool. Never has anyone accused me of being anything but honorable and yet, that cheap green-eyed flirt sharpened her claws on me." Dominic paced the room.

"Didn't she explain? I mean why did she want to meet if not to clear up any misunderstanding?

He laughed, but it was a cruel sound, "Oh yeah, Laura dear, wanted to know why I didn't speak to her at the restaurant. Also, what did she do that has angered me?" He sneered, "As if I'd have anything to do with her kind or that it mattered."

"Take it easy, Dom. If it's meant to be, it will be."

"You've got to be kidding! What have you been drinking?"

"Hey, I'm a woman, if you remember. I know that we have our idiosyncrasies, but along the way, there's a reason for them. I can't believe you misjudged this...Laura. You're way too sharp. In fact, one of the things I admire about you is you're a good judge of character."

"Well this time, Issy, I failed." He plopped down on the sofa. The same stinging heat raced through him as he remembered touching Laura—the sensation causing his heart to take a perilous leap—but to where? Dominic simmered; Laura Kincaid is dead. Fini. "I'm going to put all of this behind me, Issy. In fact, you're the first to know, I'm getting married."

"You're what?"

"I've decided to marry. My parents have been after me to marry Valentina Scarpello. I think it's time. When I return I'll have her set the date."

"You can't be serious, Dom. Truly, you can't just agree to take vows unless you're in love."

"Issy...Issy, you're a romantic. And I realize that you and Ren have an ideal marriage, but," his short bark of humor lacked laughter, "I'll have a wife that I can trust." A painful knot tied his insides, "Besides I have loads of contracts to keep me busy, along with Deluca holdings. When Valentina becomes a mother she'll have enough to keep her busy, too."

"Dom, you can't mean it, you can't. You must have love in marriage or you'll find you can't endure the years ahead." Dismayed, Isabella said, "What about Valentina?"

"What about her?"

"Oh, Dominic," she admonished, "I've never known you to be so insensitive. Isn't she entitled to a husband with feelings?"

"I'll have feelings for her when the time comes. Leave it, Issy. I mean just that, leave it!"

Isabella got up. She went over and leaned to kiss Dominic's cheek. "It's only because I love you, you know."

Dominic offered her his first warm smile. "I know, and I won't tell Ren if you don't." He walked her to the door. "Are we still on for dinner tonight?"

"Absolutely. If Ren is too tired, then there will be just you and me."

Lorenzo stuck his head around the corner of the opened door. "I heard that. You, anico, will not steal my wife—get one of your own." Little did Lorenzo know how fitting that comment was.

Dominic closed the door on his friends. Inexplicable feelings of emptiness clamored through him starting at the top of his head and slowly winding their way down his lean muscled torso to his toes. Motivated to expunge those irritating feelings he readied to shower in hopes the water might cleanse away his undeniable yearning for a green-eyed scarred witch.

He studied himself in the bathroom mirror. He looked haggard. He determined it was mostly because his being unable to find Trista's baby and hating to admit the jolt of finding Laura Kincaid a tramp. Men don't cry but that's exactly what Dominic felt like doing. He dropped his robe and stepped into the shower. There was no way to tell if those were tears running down his face or shower spray flowing over his body.

Toweling off Dominic pulled the terry robe around him.

He made his decision, there was no retreating—he was going to settle down. Yet he felt no pleasure. Dio, he was going to get married; shouldn't that stoke some kind of flame and send his spirits soaring? Instead bitterness invaded his mind, upset and telling himself he can do it and he will to end the torture. He'd be a good husband and marrying will bring joy to his parents.

* * * * *

Laura finished putting away folded laundry. Cella sat in her high chair mangling a cracker.

Laura sat at the kitchen table, her elbow on the table resting her head on her palm, staring out at the snow drifts. The ticking of the clock competed with Cella's sing-song words mixing letters and numbers together as well as adding her own gibberish.

Yet her daughter's sweet resonance didn't avert thinking of Dominic's appalling conduct coming to the forefront of her thoughts. His righteous anger stunned her already bruised heart. Laura had watched his luscious mouth—his tender lips she'd longed to have to touch hers again as they contorted grotesquely while spewing vile words telling that their kiss was a mistake. Blood pounded in her temple remembering his saying that he would disinfect his mouth if possible. That kiss she treasured and cherished while hungering for more meant nothing to him. He called it a nauseating incident.

Derision burned through her wondering how he could think her immoral. Puzzled over why it should matter when his disdain for her was so obvious, yet it did. He had offered no explanation for never contacting her since leaving two years ago. No apology for his rude manners, jilting her, and causing her humiliation. Yet he reenters her life filled with rage and asserts that her actions were an abomination. How could she have ever considered him an exceptional man? Arrogant? Yes, he definitely was that. Laura's mouth turned up at its corners—it had been part of his charm. She realized how silly and naïve she'd been and how she had secretly lived with him in her private dream world.

A true romantic, Laura's unseen burning desire to find a love that melded their souls together with a love that would find its way into both their hearts and last until death parted them. She fantasized that spark Trista Serrano claimed a must was there with Dominic. Now facing reality—grappling at her foolishness, she shed no tears for she had cried herself out last night. Even her wrath over Dominic lessened. Laura would not allow his unjust attitude to stir more havoc in her life. In the wee morning, unable to sleep Laura reflected on all that transpired. She had to come to grips that Dominic wasn't worth the heartache when he automatically believed her to be an unwed mother. Too, that she would do something immoral. Dominic, as a decent human being you are a zero. Adamant, Laura vowed no longer would any man get a piece of her heart.

The doorbell rang, startling her. She knew it was a stranger as friends used the back door.

Cella was struggling to rise. Laura took her with her to answer the bell.

Peeking through the window, Laura frowned.

Holding Cella and taking a deep swallow of air, unlocking the door, she smiled. "Hello."

"I know I should have called to see if you have time for me to visit, but I didn't have your number," Isabella explained.

Laura recognized a fib when she heard one. Curiosity made her open the storm door and invite Isabella into her home. There was a connection to Dominic and Laura wondered why she lied and why she was visiting. "Won't you come in?"

Isabella offered her best smile. "Thank you." She looked at Cella. "You have a beautiful little girl."

"I think so."

"I'm Isabella Mancini, my friends call me Bella. Perhaps you will too. I know you're Laura Kincaid, Dominic's friend."

Perplexed, Laura said, "You're under the wrong impression."

Isabella paused, and then said, "Oh."

"Will you join me for a cup of coffee?" Laura led the way to the kitchen. "You can hang your coat on the tree if you will."

"Hang coat." Cella wanted down. Cella ran and got her teddy bear giving it to Isabella. "Whisper," she said.

Isabella took the teddy from Cella. "Teddy bear is very nice."

"No...no," Cella corrected, "Whisper."

Laura had to smile. "Whisper is the teddy's name." Cella took back her teddy and ran into the other room giving Laura a chance to explain. "When I put Cella in for her nap, I used to tell her to whisper so we wouldn't wake teddy bear. She began calling it Whisper."

Isabella, taken in by the warmth of the story as well as the woman, smiled. "Please forgive me for intruding. I lied, you know. I did get your address from the phone book. I thought if I telephoned perhaps you'd tell me not to come. I had to."

Just then they heard Cella whimper.

Laura moved in haste finding her daughter tangled in her little blanket. She'd pulled it off the sofa and it covered her head. "There you are, baby, it'ss okay now."

Picking up her daughter, she said, "I think you and Whisper should take a rest."

"Okay, Mama. Whisper to sleep."

Laura returned to the kitchen.

"How old is your daughter?"

"Twenty-one months. She's precocious." Laura chuckled. "She tries repeating just about everything she hears."

Isabella hesitated but couldn't keep her news hidden. "I'm going to have a baby. I envy you the joy you're already sharing."

"Congratulations. Do you want a boy or girl?"

"Neither Ren nor I care. We're so excited."

"I can imagine. I wouldn't give up my daughter for"—Laura grinned—"as the saying goes...for all the tea in China."

Both ladies laughed, and the mood was pleasant. Laura poured coffee and settled down to visit.

Isabella took a deep breath. "I know this is not any of my business, but I can't let Dom make the mistake of his life."

Laura's pride concealed the turmoil suddenly escalating within her. "What Dominic Deluca does or doesn't do is no concern of mine."

Isabella wasn't one to let matters rest. "He cares for you. He won't admit it outright but every word that comes out of his mouth tells me. If he knew I said this he'd be furious." Isabella grinned. "His ranting and raving about you proved to me that he has a monstrous jealous inferno burning inside of him."

Laura's bitter laugh reached her eyes. "Trust me, Dominic cares only for Dominic."

"You're wrong. Dom is the kindest and most honorable man I know, other than my husband."

"In my opinion, he doesn't measure up to your accolades."

Isabella's voice softened. "Don't you care just a little for him?"

"It doesn't matter. Not anymore."

"Are you sure?"

Laura hedged answering by asking a question. "You're Italian, aren't you?"

Isabella nodded.

"Dominic called me a puttana. I presumed it wasn't a compliment. I was right, wasn't I?"

Isabella would have wrung Dom's neck if he had been with her this minute. "It isn't a nice word. You're right, but Dom was wrong to say that about you."

"Well, I thank you for that…I guess."

"Laura, I saw Dom when he returned from seeing you. He was enraged, but not from disliking you, it was jealousy. He assumed you married, and then when you said you weren't, it upset him. One doesn't become pregnant like Mary Magdalene. He didn't think you were that kind of woman."

Laura stood, her lips thinned with disgust. "How dare you? That kind of woman? And you have the gall to repeat it…to come into my home and infer that I have done something immoral. What is it with you Italians? Are you all so smug and perfect that only you have the charter on morality? I think you should leave."

SECRET PROMISE

Isabella had no intention to leave just yet. "Please, Laura, forgive me. I only repeated what Dom said. I didn't agree with him. In fact, I tried to have him see there might be another side. But I believe his jealousy over your having been touched by someone…well, he's a man, and as sorry as I am to say it, this time he's a complete idiot."

That brought a smile to Laura. "Dominic is your friend. It's admirable of you to come and think to mend our differences but it will not happen. He said ugly things about me and accused me of being immoral. I will not forgive him. I will admit I lived in a dream thinking of him and hoping that we'd be more than friends. I see now that was preposterous thinking. I'm also an idiot. I could never measure up to his privileged society."

Matt chose that moment to knock at the back door. He opened it without waiting for Laura to answer. "Hey, Laura, okay for me to come in?"

Laura opened the door wider. "Certainly. Come on in."

Matt looked at Isabella.

"Matt, this is Isabella," she hesitated, "my friend from the inn."

Matt smiled. "Hello Isabella from the inn."

They exchanged greetings and then Matt said, "I brought you some more papers. Are last months finished?"

"Yes, all in order. I'll get them."

"Never doubted it for a minute." Matt hefted the box under his arm, "Thanks, Laura."

"Thanks for coming. By the way did Kathy make it home?"

"Oh yeah, I almost forgot. Kathy wants you to meet Jeff. How about coming for dinner Saturday night?"

"I'll have to see if Gretel has plans."

"You know Cella is as welcome as you are. Give Kathy a call, will you—one way or the other."

"Will do and thanks for thinking of us."

Matt said his goodbyes and left.

Isabella remembered Dom glaring at Laura when they were at Angelo's. Another piece of the puzzle fell into place. Laura wasn't on a personal date. Isabella decided she had to convince Laura to see

Dom one more time. She had to try to arrange a meeting. These two belonged together.

"Laura, please won't you help me with Dom?"

"No!"

"He's going to make a mistake that will destroy any hope he'll have for happiness."

"Isabella...Bella, I know you mean well, but there won't be anything between Dominic Deluca and me...ever! If he had any feelings for me at all he would have asked me for answers rather then assume the worst. I haven't the faintest idea what he's going to do to destroy his life, but it's not my concern."

"He's going to marry."

Thunderstruck, Laura gripped her hands to keep them from shaking. She bit into her bottom lip before turning away to hide the wrenching kick to her heart.

Isabella caught Laura's shock. Laura's face paled before turning. "We can't let him do that, Laura."

"It's not any of my business. And don't say we. If you think it necessary to take a message to Dominic, tell him 'The puttana wishes him well'."

Isabella pleaded. "Laura, in his rage he said things he shouldn't, but there's not one scintilla of doubt in my mind that he cares for you...very much. I believe his stupid pride overrode his heart."

Her nerves calmed, Laura turned, "Please, what's done is done. Dominic Deluca is an arrogant ass. He isn't noble or trustworthy. His word isn't worth a pile of doggie-doo. I'm asking you to quit. I have my daughter to raise and if some man does come along that can accept my child, then that'll be a little more icing in my life."

Isabella rose. She knew when to stop. "I'm saddened as I just know in my gut that the misunderstandings between the two of you can be rectified." There was a final look of mute appeal before Isabella softly said, "I'm sorry."

"That's life. I've accepted mine. I have good friends and I have my daughter. A great blessing crossed my path and I've become the mother of my precious tesoro. You will soon know what I mean—especially when you hold your baby the first time in your arms."

Isabella's warm smile lightened her mood. "You use the word tesoro, so you must know it means treasure. How did you come to use it?"

Laura, careful of her words, remembering her promise to Trista, said, "I vacationed in Italy and learned some of the words. Tesoro was used by a mother to her child. I never forgot it. That word says it all, don't you agree?"

"Definitely. I'll probably be using it myself."

Isabella's eyes watered. "Please, I'd like to be friends. You are one special lady, Laura. Do you mind if I keep in touch?"

Laura thought of Trista and the results of their meeting—no contact. "I'd like that." Then Laura did something she never did before, she explained. "Bella, my daughter is adopted. Her mother gave her to me as it was impossible for her to keep her. You see, the way I look at it I must have a special star over me to have received her gift."

Isabella embraced Laura. "I'm honored to know you."

Laura opened the front door. "Watch your step, it's icy."

Isabella waved goodbye.

* * * * *

Isabella wrung her hands so tightly that her knuckles lost color. She pressed her lips together while glaring at Dominic as he ranted at her.

"You have gone way way too far, Issy. You have the audacity to inform me that I am wrong and that Laura is every bit a lady. You don't know her!"

"Dom, calm down."

"I am calm. I am so calm I'm ready to push you into a snowdrift and leave you there."

"Hold on, anico, you are talking about my wife." A lopsided grin appeared. "On second thought, I might just do it for you."

Isabella was not to be deterred. "If you would just listen, that man you saw her in the restaurant is her boss. She works from her home. He is happily married, and I was there when he said his wife wanted Laura to meet her brother."

Dominic's jaw clenched, his eyes narrowed. "What's that got to do with me?" Although his heart was hammering, he hoped its beating wasn't visible.

"Just, Dom, that you might possibly have misjudged her. You may have jumped to idiotic conclusions." Isabella's voice softened, "Perhaps you have affection for her and don't want to admit it. Perhaps that's why you didn't give her a chance to explain away your accusations."

Dominic's temper was on the verge of exploding; his sarcasm eddied around his friend. "Don't go there, Isabella. I mean it. I am getting married. There are no feelings for that little puttana. Now please, I ask you...no, I'm really begging you, don't mention her to me again."

"If you weren't our dear friend I would never bother to ever speak to you. That you would label that horrid word upon her is unforgivable." Isabella stuck out her chin defiantly, "You have my word I'll never speak of Laura or her adopted daughter ever again in your presence." Isabella eyed her husband knowing she gave Dominic one more shot across his bow. Smug, Isabella, grabbed her husband's hand, "Let's go, Ren. We have to pack if we're leaving first thing in the morning. Rise and shine, Dom, we'll have breakfast at six-thirty."

Dominic's dark eyes shot up, he was about to say something but Isabella didn't give him the opportunity, she was literally pulling her husband out the door.

Dominic slouched in a chair. His stomach in knots and he knew he couldn't untie them, not after he'd accused and insulted Laura. He rubbed his whiskered jaw. *There's no turning back. I gave my word to marry Valentina to Papa. The wheels are in motion for the wedding. As for Laura's innocence, I did jump to think the worst of her. I've never obsessed over a female as I have Laura.* He slapped his leg and his laugh was bitter because he had to admit jealousy built within him where Laura was concerned. *Too late, best leave and marry and continue to hunt for Trista's baby. I've got to find her little* girl. Dominic rubbed his eyes—never had he ever felt an acute sense of loss. Pulling out his suitcase he began to toss in his belongings.

*****

Deluca Villa, Italy

"What's the matter, Son? You should be happy. Valentina, she is coming. She will make a good wife. Your mama is smiling once again."

Dominic's heart felt as though it was encased in a fifty-pound cement block. So many regrets; he didn't want to marry Valentina but he owed his parents. He should have been more astute about his sister's comings and goings. All he did was warn her about Antonio. He blamed himself for not being there for her when she needed him most. The least he could do now is please his parents.

Dominic's father looked out over the lake. His son wasn't talking. "Mama is pleased. She is looking forward to when you have little bambinos."

Dominic reached for his papa's shoulder—his fingers meeting his bony body. He knew there was no turning back. He'd do it. He had made this rash decision because of that green-eye liar. But Issy said Laura is innocent…what have I done? Laura didn't lie. Dominic realized he'd been right about her in the very beginning but let his temper lead him to think the worst—now he was going to punish not only himself but Valentina too.

"Papa, I will talk with Valentina. I will not go back on my word. But we both must be sure. I have work that will keep me away. I don't know her well enough to believe she will accept that."

"Don't worry, Mama has told her how wonderful you are. Valentina has been coming to visit Mama once, sometimes twice a week since Trista died. She has been a great comfort." The old man rose from his bench. "I'm going to go. I will tell Valentina to come here."

"I think, Papa, it would be better for me to greet her at the house."

The old man's face creased with a smile. "She is coming now. I will leave you."

Dominic saw her coming down across the grass, walking with long, determined steps. Valentina wasn't smiling. Dominic walked to meet her with his father.

Mr. Deluca held out his hand to her. "Ciao, Valentina."

Valentina took his outstretched hand, but all the while she was glaring at Dominic.

"I'll leave you two." Dominic's father all smiles walked off.

Dominic was about to kiss each of Valentina's cheeks but instead reached to take her hand. She pulled it back so fast as if he held a hot poker. "Dio, are you mad?" She gritted through her teeth.

Having dropped his hand, he semi-smiled. "I don't think so." He moved to return to the bench. "Come, sit with me."

"You must be out of your mind. You dare to think because you are the great Dominic Deluca that I will jump to marry you?"

Dominic's breath caught in his throat. He took in her rage—its color heightening her olive skin to a warm glow. The heavy cement block he'd been hauling disappeared as Valentinas' agenda became clear. Dominic couldn't help but smile and suddenly the gloom of his day vanished.

"This funny to you?"

Dominic's tone gentled, "No, not funny at all. My parents have jumped that you want to marry me." He held up his hand to stop her from interrupting. She tightened her lips so she would not speak. Dominic motioned for her to sit with him. She did leaving space between them.

"Well?" Valentina's sarcasm was evident.

Dominic looking at a vibrant woman whose eyes focused on him like a hawk, said, "Valentina Scarpello. I remember you as Trista's good friend. Since Tris died my parents have been after me to marry…wait, please let me finish, and then you can talk and I'll listen." Dominic combed his hair with his fingers, he didn't want to be blunt, yet he wanted no misunderstanding. "As far as I knew, you and Mama have agreed that our marrying will solve everyone's heartache and most importantly, we will be family. I have no idea what either of my parents has said to you, but when they encouraged me to propose, I couldn't add to their heartache. But I did say that first you and I would have to talk. That's it."

Valentina's voice softened. She even smiled. "I apologize. I was under the impression that you were the one making arrangements and not consulting me. Naturally, I was furious."

"As you should be. In fact, I'm embarrassed to have put you in this predicament, but I will admit that I never for a moment thought you didn't want to marry me."

"Surprise surprise, Mr. Deluca."

"You know someone accused me of being arrogant. This proves it."

"Perhaps this all started because I came over to visit your parents, and they got the marriage idea. When Trista died, I felt sorry for your mother. She was always so sweet to me. I guess I filled that empty space in her life, but it was not my intention to have her conjure us marrying." She shook her head. "I guess I did more damage and hurt by trying to ease her pain."

Dominic reached for Valentina's hand. "No, in fact, you've helped her out of her depression."

"Yes, but when she hears that there will be no wedding bells between the two of us, will that depression return?"

"Let's hope for the best." A pensive look crossed Dominic's face. "About my sister, did she confide in you? I mean about her plans? Who she was seeing? Did she have a favorite place to go when she wanted to be alone?"

"Those are a lot of questions."

"Please, anything you can tell me. Tris disappeared for a while and my parents were frantic. I'm trying to find where she went. If she was alone or with someone."

Valentina shook her head. "Trista was going with Antonio Rossi. I tried to tell her he was using her. He doesn't have an honorable bone in his body, but she wouldn't listen. She was in love and insisted he felt the same. I didn't see her for some time. She stayed in Rome most of the time and I stayed here. She telephoned me one evening, and she sounded miserable. I asked if she had a falling out with Antonio.

She called him a swine and said that it was over. I asked if she really meant it as I couldn't have been happier for her. She assured me that it was and that she needed to get away. She asked that I keep an eye on her mama and papa. To tell them she was with friends and would return when she was over her holiday. I asked where she was going, but she was evasive. I asked what was wrong and she said not to worry. She had everything figured out. I told her to call me and she laughed. We said goodbye and that was that. She never called. I have no idea where she disappeared to or with whom." Valentina looked at Dominic's pained expression. "Tell me what's wrong. It's about Trista, isn't it?"

He nodded. "I made her a promise so I can't tell you. But I wish I could." He took Valentina's hand, "Marry the man you love, Val. Be happy and work out any misunderstandings. Listen to each other, and if there is question, use patience."

"You sound like someone should have given you that advice."

"Someone did, but I didn't listen."

"Ah, the love bug has struck the mighty Dominic Deluca. Did it really hit you or just whiz by? Too late for you to catch it and offer marriage?"

"I don't know. I know I made an ass of myself."

Valentina laughed—tears rolling down her cheeks. "It does my heart good to hear you admit you can be a jackass. I used to watch you and think you were wonderfully perfect. Trista and I agreed you were handsome but then she would add, 'But he's my brother.'"

"You are a special lady, Val. I wish you every happiness."

"Thanks." She kissed his cheek. "Now I think it's time we went up to the house—we're going to create some heartache. I do feel bad for your mother. She's counting on me marrying you."

Dom smiled, its warmth reaching into his eyes. "I suspect it is only to make you a permanent part of her family."

"You think?"

"Si. So let's do what we must do. It'll work out after they rant and rave at me. They'll probably call me a jackass, too."

* * * * *

SECRET PROMISE

Last week in January, Rome

Dominic leaned back in his chair; his desk layered with papers. He had work that needed his attention, but his mind persistently traveled to Stowe visualizing green dewy eyes and golden brown hair splashed with red highlights.

Uttering, he said, "How could I have belittled her? Why did I jump to conclusions and condemn her? I'd give anything to see her warm smile. I've got to end this madness." He picked up the telephone and dialed her number—he never forgot it.

His heart was pumping; the connection was clear and passed on without difficulty. One ring…two rings…three…

Laura was drying Cella's fingers smeared with jelly. "Hello." Her melodious voice beamed through the lines all the way to Rome.

Dominic swallowed, saying nothing for a second. "Signorina? Laura…?"

Laura's stomach tightened, and she gasped. "Dominic?"

"Si…caro…"

Laura was shaking, anger came to the forefront and all she could think was not again. Dominic heard the click—its sound a gigantic click echoing in his ear. She said his name and not another word. She ended the connection. Devastated, the pencil he held snapped and he threw it on his desk as his phone started ringing, but still he didn't move, but with a smidgen of hope he thought she might have second thoughts…just maybe. Dominic answered. It wasn't Laura but the call changed his life. He was moving to London.

14

March, Stowe

Laura carried in the receipts and invoices for Mr. Carlsson. He smiled and said he'd take them back to his office. "Matt isn't here."

"Thanks, Mr. Carlsson. I don't have to see Matt right now."

Mr. Carlsson returned with a cookie for Cella. "Hello, Cella. How are you today?"

"I'm good."

Handing her the cookie, he said, "Come with me and I'll introduce you to another little girl, my granddaughter—she likes cookies too."

Sitting at the children's table were two little girls smiling at each other while each ate part of their big cookie—one blond and the other one with raven curls.

"Sage never meets a stranger," said Sage's mother to Laura. "I'm Eve Durand. I know who you are; Laura Kincaid as my father sings your praises."

Laura's smile lighted her face. "You have wonderful parents."

The children finished their cookie and started to rise. Laura said, "It's time to go."

Eve didn't want to lose Laura's company. She no longer knew many people and with her parents busy, she wanted to get out of their way. "Laura, if you don't think me too forward, how about joining me for a cup of coffee? There's the diner down the road and I remember they have jump seats for children."

Laura smiled. "I'd like that."

SECRET PROMISE

They were seated in the corner booth. The little girls eating ice cream.

This is the booth that Dominic called me a whore. Laura blinked back tears hiding under her lashes. She bit the inside of her jaw and took a noticeable deep breath.

"Is something wrong, Laura?"

"No, no, well…I just thought of something unpleasant. Sorry."

"Hey, don't apologize. I have lots of those moments." Eve sipped her coffee. "You haven't always lived in Stowe?"

"No. I'm from Maine. My parents died and my grandmother brought me to live with her."

"Of course, Mrs. Kincaid. I remember her…how is she?"

"Gran died a couple of years ago."

Eve reached for Laura's hand. "I'm sorry. You can see that I haven't been back for ages."

"So how about you? Your life has to be more interesting."

"I went off to college. I wanted to be a doctor, but to be honest, I couldn't cut it. It takes more than desire, it takes perseverance. So I switched to American Lit."

Laura laughed, "The Poets, right?"

Eve nodded. "I've got my favorites."

Their sleepy little girls closed their eyes. "If you don't mind, Eve, let them nap and we can visit a little longer. It isn't often I can enjoy adult conversation. That's if you can spare the time."

"I'm not in any hurry. In fact, I think my parents are happy to see me get out from underfoot. The store keeps them busy and they have their system for each day."

"Your father gave me a job I can do at home. Matt is as nice as your parents."

"I remember Matt. He was sort of a book-end in school. Didn't socialize much."

Laura laughed. "His wife Kathy is very kind. He found his ideal."

"So you've found your ideal too."

"Never happened."

"I'm sorry, Laura, I just thought because you and your daughter are so happy."

"I guess this proves that your father doesn't gossip." Laura took a drink of water and looked at Cella and Sage to make sure they were really in dreamland. "Cella is my adopted daughter. I'm a single mother."

With a broad smile, Eve said, "Good for you. Aren't you the lucky one?"

"I am. Cella is the best thing that ever happened in my life. She's mine!"

"Of course, she is. I know how you feel, Laura. Sage is the best thing that's happened to Paul and me. Children are pure joy."

"So it's your turn. You left Stowe for college and never looked back, right?"

"Something like that. I didn't come home often. Then the longer I was away my life changed. I worked in a coffee café near the hospital—ten till 2:00 a.m. And lucky for me as that's where I met Paul."

"Love at first sight?"

"For him." She laughed, and the soft sound floated around them giving Laura goose bumps. "The more I saw Paul the more I realized what a great guy he is and I wasn't going to lose him. The rest is history."

"Is he here with you?"

"No, he's attending a medical seminar in New York and it gave me a chance to visit and have Sage meet her grandparents. Paul will come up and then we'll go home together. We live in Florida."

"That's a different way of living from Stowe."

"You can say that again. I like living there as the weather is almost perfect, and when it's not, we pack up and go off if Paul's schedule permits. Have you been to Palm Beach?"

"Heaven forbid." Laura chuckled. "I've only read about Florida's lifestyle."

"Our home is lovely, but we don't rank up with the elite. It's because of Paul being in the medical field that we are invited to some of the island's galas. Paul's brother, Gabriel, is really into the swinging set on the island. He has an art gallery and is acquainted with many of the Islanders."

"It's certainly another world from Stowe." Laura eyed the sleeping girls crunched in the jump seats. "I think we better have mercy on our darlings and be on our way."

"Yes," agreed Eve, "but let's do this again. I have so enjoyed visiting. I feel as if I've known you longer than just these few hours."

"Me too." They gathered their girls who woke but were too sleepy to put up a fuss. "When you have extra time, Eve, come over—the girls can play. I'll fix lunch."

"It's a date. I'll call."

Laura mentioned that it was Cella's second birthday in two days…if Eve could…she suggested they come and share some of Cella's birthday cake.

Eve jumped at Laura's invitation. "You've given me an ideal reason to sneak away from the store."

"Thanks. We'll look forward to seeing you and Sage."

Eve teased, "We'll sing 'Happy Birthday,' won't we?"

Laughing, Laura said, "You can count on it."

15

March, London

Dominic stood looking out at the serpentine—its winding course adding beauty to the park. The beautiful day brought many walkers. He wished he could be among them but taking the opportunity to accomplish many of his plans, he now had to put his heart into making a go of this firm.

The telephone ringing brought him back to the reality of getting to work. He heard his secretary take the call. "I'll see if Mr. Deluca is available, one moment please."

Margo Selan stepped into his office. Her lithe figure in her form-fitting suit swayed as she walked. She beamed a smile at her boss. Dominic noticed her blond hair twisted on top of her head, making him look taller than her small frame. "Mr. Deluca, there is a call from Mr. Lorenzo Mancini, will you take his call?"

Dominic's face lighted with a bright smile. "Anytime Mr. Mancini calls he is to be put through to me immediately."

"Yes, sir." She glided from his office and closed the door.

"Hello, Ren." Dominic's voice was cheerful. "How did you find me?"

"Ciao, Dom. You've got to be kidding. You've made all the papers' business section headlines. I never thought I'd see the day you'd take on a floundering corporation."

Dom leaned back in his chair, laughing. "I know but circumstances fell my way, and I couldn't turn down this challenge."

SECRET PROMISE

"May I ask what you did with Deluca Rome Properties? You used to complain about having too much on your plate."

"I brought them with me."

"I still can't believe it. Bella insisted I call and see if you'd lost your marbles." Lorenzo chuckled. "But I can tell you're feeling in the pink even with all that fog out your way."

"Don't kid yourself, Ren, I've got a view to die for and it's a beautiful day."

"So tell me why? Why take on the load?"

Dom leaned forward on his desk. "Besides letting dozens of talented people keep their jobs I want to do something I've long thought about and this fits well into accomplishing some of my dreams. I've cranked out so many degrees and didn't put them to use. But now"—Dominic's voice became animated—"I'm going to expand into civil engineering—do you realize the areas I can work in? There are roads, airports, rail systems, factories, urban planning, and design landscaping. There's no end to where I can take this firm. Not just England, Ren, but here in Europe, the Americas," laughing he went on, "any place on the globe."

"And you're just the man that can do it."

"Thanks, Ren, coming from you that means a lot."

"So this looks like there won't be any more quiet holidays with you up in Stowe. Do you mind if Bella and I make use of your hide-away?"

Dominic was silent for a moment. His guilt never left him for the way he treated Laura, his Laura. "Why would I mind?"

"I had to mention it, Dom…Bella insisted."

"Tell Issy, no problem. By the way how's the mother doing?"

"Getting rounder and telling me the next baby is on me. It can't happen fast enough for either of us. We're going to have a son, Dom."

Dominic swallowed his envy. "No wonder you're walking on air. Whatever you do, don't forget to keep in touch and let me know when you become a bona fide padre."

"Will do, Dom. And don't forget us. You know we'd love to see you anytime."

"That goes for me also, Ren. Give Issy my love."

Dom hung up the phone. He didn't have time to mull over his conversation with his friend or think of Stowe that reminded him of a certain green-eyed woman. His PA glided in with a stack of folders.

Margo hadn't been certain she was going to continue to work with the firms' new owner. She'd been offered a position with an increase in salary, but when she got a look at unattached Dominic Deluca—tall, handsome with eyes that told you he appreciated women and the power he exuded in his very suave manner, she knew she was right where she wanted to be. Margo Selan would work toward becoming Margo Deluca. And when Margo set sights on a target, she always hit the bull's-eye.

16

March, Stowe

Cella and Sage were sound asleep on a quilt spread on the floor.

Eve glanced at the two little girls in dreamland. "They are special, aren't they? And they were taken with each other"—Eve grinned— "just like you and me. I'm so glad we met, Laura."

Laura's voice held a tinge of melancholy, "I've never had a close friend since moving here. I mean, I have lots of friends, but not one I connected with as I have with you. I'll miss you."

"Then there's only one solution, Laura. You must come to visit us in Florida."

Laura almost dropped the plate. "You've got to be kidding."

"Why?" Eve raised an eyebrow in question.

"Well…because," Laura hedged.

"Nonsense. You're allowed to leave the state, aren't you?"

Laura laughed. "The only time I left Vermont was to vacation in Italy."

"See, you can do it." Eve grinned. "And you won't have to cross an ocean. By the way, where in Italy?"

"I took a tour. We covered so many places…unbelievable, but Florence—Michelangelo's *David*, continues to blow my mind. To actually view his magnificent talent—I will never forget how awesome. But Rome was magic."

"Ah, those Italian men are a handsome lot. Meet a young man, perhaps?"

"Oh yeah, he followed me all the way to America."

"You're being funny. But never mind; promise you'll visit Paul and me in Florida. We'll have you view the male populous and they'll automatically be drawn to you with your sweet disposition."

"You're putting me on, Eve."

"The devil I am. Tell me, Laura, isn't there someone that you've cared for that rang your bells?"

Laura leaned her elbows on the table. Her eyes gave her away—they didn't tear up, but they glistened.

Eve's soothing voice probed, "Tell me, Laura. You have my word this remains between us. Sometimes it's good to let go to someone—ease your hurt, maybe?"

Laura didn't hesitate. It was a though she was waiting for someone to share her broken dream. "His name is Dominic. I had this thing for him. It wasn't reciprocated." She took a deep breath, "I worked at Cloud Nine and he was an important guest and I was to see to his every demand. He was arrogant and handsome. Then one day he asked that I drive him to Montpelier."

"He couldn't drive?"

Laura smiled. "Oh he could, he said later that it was an excuse to spend time with me. Anyway it was a pleasant trip. We even stopped to ice skate—it was wonderful." Laura closed her eyes reliving that time they skated close together—laughing. "He invited me to dinner that night. I was literally on cloud nine, very excited. I dressed in my finest and waited for him and I waited and I waited and I waited. He never showed."

Eve's mouth fell open, "You mean he didn't telephone and say why?"

Laura shook her head.

"So what did he say the next day?"

"Nothing. He had departed that night without checking out. In fact, some gorgeous woman came for him and that was that. I never saw him again."

"Well lucky for you…he's not only a jerk, but a rude one."

"I know, but still all I see is his tall, powerful frame, his black hair that he let grow—it reached his collar. God, Eve, he's so handsome and his accent is fabulous. He has hidden charm."

"But Laura, if you never saw him again."

"Oh, I did. I escorted one of the Cloud's esteem guest's child to the airport. I got the child on his way to Paris and had to hurry back to the limo as it was parked in a no-zone. Suddenly someone grabs me and wraps his arms around me and gives me a kiss that to this day I can't forget. He wanted me to stay and talk but I couldn't and he must have had to catch a plane so he yelled as I moved on that he'd call me." Now tears rolled down her cheeks. "I was so sure the he would. Again, I waited and waited and waited."

"Oh no, not again?"

Nodding her head, Laura answered, "Again. No call. So time marches on and it was sometime much later Matt takes me to Angelo's. You know that fabulous Italian restaurant."

"Wait, are you telling me you were on a date with Matt, Dad's accountant? Matt?"

That made Laura laugh. "It wasn't a date. His wife suggested Matt take me out. Now do you want to hear the rest?"

"Of course. Sorry."

"When we were leaving Matt stopped to talk with someone and I moved on toward the exit and there was Dominic with another couple. The lady spoke to me and it was then I saw Dominic. I froze and stared waiting for him to say something but he just glared and barely nodded his head in recognition." Laura rested her forehead on the palm of her hand before looking at Eve. "Remembering that night still shakes me; the dislike from Dominic so obvious—to me anyway; so then Matt came over to get me and we left."

"Neither of you spoke?"

"Not a word. To make this long story shorter being unable to sleep I called Dominic at the Cloud hoping to get answers. I asked him to meet with me."

"Did he show up this time?"

"I'll say he did."

"So what were his reasons for never getting in touch with you? Surely you deserved some answers."

"I'll admit I was nervous and didn't want him to think I cared all the much so I thought to play it cool and get my answers. But it never happened. I can still see his sneer and it shook me. He was cruel. He attacked me and I fought back and told him he was a pompous ass and walked out and never saw him again."

"Good for you."

Laura plunged on, her pride visibly gone. "Yeah, but I still can't get him out of my mind or my heart. It was that kiss, it was powerful."

"You've got it bad."

"I know. He telephoned a couple of weeks ago and I wanted to scream with joy, but I hung up. I'm not up to anymore broken promises."

"Oh Laura, I'm so sorry. You deserve better than that guy."

"His friends are as nice as can be. They pitched good words about him to me, but it's too late. How do I know that if we did settle whatever is bothering him that he would accept Cella?" Laura shrugged a shoulder, "Anyway, the last I heard he was about to marry."

"Poor woman."

Laura laughed. "You're good for me, Eve."

"If you mean it, promise you'll visit us in Palm Beach. Please, Laura. Think of Cella—we have a pool and she can learn to swim with Sage."

"I promise to give your invite serious consideration. We might surprise you and," Laura laughed, "you'll be sorry when two strays show up on your doorstep."

17

January, London

"Dom, do you think you can get to those contracts from Finance?" Margo wore a light blue wool form-fitting dress that followed the curve of her figure.

Dominic watched her cross his office thinking she's one classy lady. He smiled and didn't realize he set her heart racing. "I'll go over them this evening and have them ready in the morning."

"Don't you ever slow down, Dom?" She leaned over and let her breast brush his shoulder. "When have you had a decent meal? I notice paper plates and boxes in your waste bin each morning."

Dominic leaned back in his chair, his dark eyes giving her the once over, noticing the outline of her breasts. "If you're not doing anything at six o'clock when we close shop I'd be pleased if you'd join me for dinner. It'll be quick as I have to get back and finish up some work. Can you make it?"

You, Mr. Deluca, have no idea how long I've been waiting for you to take a good look at me. You, sir, are going to be hooked; all I have to do is be careful while I'm reeling you in. "I accept though you should know I'm starved—will you leave me enough time to enjoy all of my dinner?"

He beamed a smile at her that to Margo could have lighted Parliament. "I think that's a possibility."

"I'll be ready at six. Just open that door over there, no need to knock." She sashayed back to her office hiding her satisfied smirk.

Dominic rubbed his whiskered jaw. He thought that if this dinner ended well, he might invite her to join him on his trip to Palm Beach next week. The museum and parkland in the offering require on-site inspection. He wanted the contract as it would be his first step in America for his firm. Too, with Margo, he'd make it a mini-vacation.

18

February, Palm Beach

Laura luxuriated on a soft toweled lounge watching Cella and Sage splash in the pool wearing plastic water wings. "Thanks, Eve, for insisting that I visit. I never conceived warm sunshine and swimming on the sixth of February with Stowe covered in snow."

"I'm glad I didn't give up on you." She looked at the girls kicking their feet and moving their little arms. "Sage is excited to have Cella to play with. Aren't they cute?"

"Sage so blond and Cella's hair just the opposite.' Laura thought of Trista and quickly put it out of her thoughts taking a taste of perfect iced lemonade served by Eve's housekeeper. "I always thought Vermont had it all but Florida is an unbelievable paradise."

Eve wondered about Cella's parents but would never ask. That was personal territory and she noticed Laura change the subject. "I think we better haul our girls out of the water before the sun turns them to toast." Eve eyed Laura. "You better come in too, you're getting a light burn, and you don't want to start peeling."

"Eve, please…I don't think I should attend that charity ball."

"You are coming, Laura. Gabe is going to be your escort. Paul made the arrangements and we don't say no to my husband." Eve grinned. "You're not reluctant to go with Gabriel because he's gay, are you?"

"Heavens no! I should think he'd be reluctant to go with me."

"Gabe said to tell you that you'll improve his image. He's a sweetheart, Laura, and not because he's Paul's brother. He really is a fine gentleman."

"I never doubted that for a second."

"I'm glad that's settled. Let's gather our little chubbies, give them lunch, and put them in for naptime. Then we're going to my closet and find you a luscious gown to make Gabe wish he was straight."

Both ladies giggled.

* * * * *

Six days later, night of the charity ball

Stunned, Laura stared at the woman in the full-length mirror decked out in a satin sheath gown. Its emerald color highlighted her green eyes. *Eve's gown makes me look pretty.* Laura was surprised and thrilled. The gown's transparent Chantilly lace—its lighter overlay with its intricate design complemented her long willowy form. She couldn't believe it was really her. She smiled while turning right and then left. She felt sexy. Pleased that Mrs. Ames, the housekeeper, willingly plied her talent with a needle so that between the two of them they added fitted lace sleeves with the same delicate lace formed around her breasts encasing her shoulders and hugging her neckline. Laura studied the gown's soft folds. It was the most magnificent gown she'd ever worn.

Eve tapped on the door, walking in she stopped and stared. "Oh, Laura, you are Cinderella."

Laura filled with unknown radiance, burst out, "I know this sounds vain, but I've never felt pretty in my life and now look at me."

"The gown is you, Laura, and I like what Max did with your hair and makeup. You glow."

"I never thought to wear my hair up and curled." Grinning, Laura said, "I feel glamorous."

"And you are."

"All because of you, Eve. I can't thank you enough."

"I'm just so happy you and Cella are visiting." Holding out a pair of emerald earrings, Eve said, "Try these on, they will match the sparkle in your eyes. Wait until Gabriel sees you, he's going to flip."

They both laughed.

"You look beautiful, Eve. The colors in your gown change as you move. The lavender colors blend that I can't define exactly what color stands out the most."

"I thought it gorgeous when I first saw it. I love wearing taffeta, it announces that I'm coming into the room and also it makes me feel young."

"Has Paul seen you? Won't he be jealous?"

"That's the idea. I want to keep him interested."

"So that's how it's done. I'll have to remember that when I find myself a guy."

"Laura," Eve turned serious, "you'll have no problem if you let yourself go. You've got to give up on that Italian. Promise that tonight you'll dance and enjoy the ball."

"I've been meaning to ask you what the charity is for."

"The Islanders have set up a committee to raise money for a museum setting in the middle of the green. It's a big project and they've gotten many bids on it, but from what I understand they want this architectural firm in London to take it on. I haven't been following it closely as six of the Islander's elite are totally in charge."

"I'm attending their ball, how much am I to donate?"

"No, no. Gabe is your escort, the men handle the donations. Not to worry."

"If you say so…are you sure?"

"Laura, they collect thousands of dollars from each of the male guests attending. That's why I'm glad the men handle the giving and we women get to dance and enjoy the evening." Eve checked her gown in the mirror, "Come on, our men are waiting."

Paul and Gabe both offered a soft whistle when the ladies descended the stairway.

Paul went to Eve and kissed her cheek. "Hello, Wife beautiful."

Gabriel put out his arm for Laura. "You are a vision of loveliness. Your pumpkin waits."

* * * * *

Dominic entered the ballroom with Margo on his arm. Jack and Diane Russell preceded them, forcing them to stop and be introduced to more of Palm Beach's privileges. Dominic was used to mixing with influential people. He felt Margo's fingers tighten on his arm.

After several introductions and sipping champagne, the ballroom opened for dancing. Stepping into the room's exquisite décor with its crystal chandeliers reflecting the polished parquet flooring and with mixed flowers everywhere—it was like entering a lighted garden. The doors were open to the patio and if one stepped out the Atlantic's gentle waves, lapping a short distance at the shoreline, added to the ambiance.

Dom asked Margo to dance. The music was smooth and slow. The singer's mellow voice carried across the room.

Margo was in heaven. This is the life for me and this man is going to give it to me.

Dominic leaned into Margo's ear. "Happy to be here?"

"Yes, very very much."

Dominic smiled as he moved in step with the music.

Margo looked up, her eyes soft telling him she'd welcome any advances from him if he wanted to take this evening to a more intimate level.

The evening seemed to fly. Dominic danced with Diane and Margo danced with Jack and some of his friends. She was having a glorious time. She looked about for Dominic and saw him talking with three men; he was holding a glass of whiskey. She saw him laugh. She whirled around and smiled at her dancing partner.

Gabriel winked at Laura. They were doing the foxtrot and bumped into a couple.

"Sorry," said Gabe.

The man grinned. "No problem if your lady will save me a dance."

Laura smiled. Gabe, always the gentleman returned, "And if your lady will also honor me?"

SECRET PROMISE

Margo didn't want to dance with the tall thin man. She wanted to get back to Dom. "Perhaps," she replied. Her partner looked at Gabe raising an eyebrow.

Gabe grinning danced away.

Laura squeezed Gabe's hand that was holding hers. "I don't think she dances very well, anyway."

Gabe laughed. "Do you suppose her perhaps answer means bug-off?"

Laura laughed with him.

Gabe and Laura moved to the outside of the dance floor. Laura's profile was on the sideline and it was then that Dominic saw her. One of the men asked him a question, but he didn't answer, he stared and stared. Gabe danced Laura further down and soon Dominic could see her face. The shock hit him full force, his fingers tightening around the glass. Laura? Here? He was visibly bewildered.

The man nudged Dominic. "I say, if you want me to introduce you I can arrange it. I don't know who she is, but I think she's Dr. Durand's guest."

Dominic concealed his inner turmoil. "No. No thanks. I thought she looked familiar. I'm not sure." Dom swallowed some whiskey and felt it travel to his stomach. He had to get back into the conversation. "I'm not much good with a golf club, but I'm willing to go eighteen if you can put up with me." He forced a smile, but his mind was on the emerald-gowned woman dancing with a glowing smile on her beautiful face. A face with lips he kissed.

Margo walked over and touched his arm. "Dom, Jack, and Diane would like us to join them for a light supper. I'd like it too if you don't mind."

Dominic always considerate made excuses after setting a tee time and with Margo clutching his arm they walked toward the dining buffet. He tried to seek out the woman in the emerald dress; because of the crush, it was difficult.

Paul suggested they sit on the patio. "Gabe will know where to find us. Don't say anything," he whispered to the ladies, "but I think he's drumming up a little business."

Eve shook her head, but her eyes sparkled.

"I'm glad he doesn't think he has to sit me."

Paul intervened, "Gabe is one guy that you won't get rid of until he delivers you safely back home. He won't even trust me to take you home."

Paul led them to a corner table on the patio. "If you, ladies, will excuse me, I'll get us something to munch on. Champagne?"

Eve answered, "Absolutely."

Lowering her voice, Laura said, "I've never had champagne. This is definitely a fairy-tale evening." Looking about, Laura added, "The stars are brighter and the air pure with a tinge of salt. It's so unbelievable." More to put in my memory box. A pool and cabanas were away on one side.

Laura teased, "Eve, want to go swimming?"

Before Eve answered, Paul returned with a waiter carrying a tray with finger food and champagne.

As Paul seated, Laura asked, "Do you think it's all right to walk to the beach to view the ocean?"

"You may walk anywhere on the property, Laura, it's open to guests."

"Laura wants to go swimming," Eve teased back.

It was then Gabe joined them. "I knew I'd find you all hiding out here in a corner." He pulled out a chair and plunked down next to Laura while reaching for one of her finger sandwiches.

Paul asked, his voice low, "Have you made any good contacts?"

"You know, brother, you don't have to tell on me."

The four of them giggled like school kids.

Gabe reached for Laura's hand and squeezed. "I hope you won't mind, Laura, but I offered your charming person for charity."

Eve looked at Gabe. "You what? Without asking?"

Laura didn't want any hard feelings between Eve and her brother-in-law, so she quickly said, "I don't mind…if it's for charity. I should do my part."

Paul shrugged. "Okay, bro, what have you concocted?"

"Well, you know the tickets for this ball were sold for the benefit of building the museum. At five thousand a head we still require more donations and other means to achieve our goal."

"I know, Gabe, just get to the point."

"We've decided to hold a raffle."

Eve jumped in. "A raffle for Laura? Are you mad? How could you?"

"Hold your horses, sister-by-marriage, it's all legit. She doesn't have to leave the ballroom."

Doing her best to hide her upset, Laura nudged Gabe. "What do I have to do? I can't sing."

"Not that bad, Darling. We are taking ten single ladies and we are going to auction off one dance with them. It's going to be a waltz or some other reasonable music and will last no longer than three minutes—five tops. It'll be fun and with the tickets sold tonight and this dance auction we figure we'll have several million more in our kitty. What do you say, Laura?"

Laura shook her head.

"You mean you won't?" Gabe was disappointed.

"It's not that. Don't you see no one will bid that kind of money to dance with me? It'll be humiliating not only to you and me but what about Eve and Paul?"

Gabe broke out into a big grin. "Not to worry, my dear, I've got you covered. I will bid for you. Guaranteed."

"Are you sure, Gabe? Do you really want me to do this?"

"Without question. I want to show off the most elegant lady at the ball." He looked at Eve, "Oops! I meant to say the most elegant single lady at the ball."

Paul took a taste of Eve's champagne. "You covered yourself well that time."

"Yeah, I did. I'm a fast thinker. And you know I love you, Eve."

"Yes, Gabriel, I know that for sure." She picked up her small purse, "What do you say, Laura, we retire to the powder room and repair our faces? Let's leave these two connivers to themselves."

They were in the powder room. Eve and Laura found a vanity to share.

An older lady glanced up at a blond and spoke with a bit of clout, "You're from England, aren't you?"

Margo smiled. She was in with the very rich. They could say or do anything and she'd be agreeable. "Yes, London. I'm here with my boss, or I should say, my soon-to-be husband."

"Oh. I wish you happiness." The woman rose and left.

Eve and Laura peeked at the blond as she checked her teeth for lipstick. Then she literally stood, checked herself in the full-length mirror, and left.

Eve waited until they were alone and concerned and asked, "Laura, are you certain you don't mind being auctioned off?"

"How bad can it be? Especially when I know I won't be left standing there without a bid. Gabe assured me he is going to bid for me."

"And he will."

"Then we'll grab the tiger by the tail and follow through." Laura blotted her lips.

Laura stood on the band's decorated raised deck with nine other ladies. She discovered she was the oldest. *I'm going to kill Gabriel Durand when this is over.* She bit her bottom lip, her nerves taut, and then worried did she smeared her lipstick.

The recessed lighting shined down on the girls as the chandeliers dimmed making it impossible to see who was bidding for their dance. The girls were tittering and whispering among themselves. Laura felt out of place.

"Ladies and Gentlemen. This evening we are going to try something new. In the old days, women would pack a picnic basket and cowboys would bid to share the makings." People laughed. "So tonight, so that we may add to our museum building fund—these charming ladies have agreed to dance with the man offering the highest bid for the pleasure of dancing with her. Are you game?"

There was loud applause as well as laughter.

"We will begin with this young lady. We will call them Volunteer Number One and so on. Now, gentlemen, let's remember this is for a charitable cause. We'll start the bidding at ten thousand."

Laura felt her legs wobble. She couldn't believe she heard right. She worried about Gabe paying ten thousand dollars to dance with her when he danced with her for free.

The first bidding went for thirty-five thousand dollars. The second bidding went for thirty-five. Laura caught on; no one would allow embarrassment toward the ladies. She felt relieved.

Laura was Number Eight. It was her turn. Though nervous she knew Gabe would claim her. The bidding began—twenty-five thousand, thirty thousand, and thirty-five thousand. Laura sighed, she made it. Then she heard forty thousand, another bid for fifty thousand. She heard whispers. Sixty thousand was the next bid and then sixty-five thousand. What is going on…Gabe, what are you doing to me? The next bid, Laura recognized Gabe's voice, "Seventy thousand dollars."

"Going once," and then the next bid came in; the bidder's voice strident and clear, "One hundred thousand dollars."

It wasn't Gabe's voice. Laura's stomach knotted. She twisted her fingers as her body quavered and she did her best to still it. Dominic? Surely not yet she knew that deep melodious voice, it haunted her. How? Dominic in Florida? No, no way. I must be going crazy. It has to be my imagination.

There was loud applause and Dominic turned on his charm—his smile, saying "It's for a good cause, is it not?" More applause didn't stop his words floating up to her.

Oh my god, it is Dominic. I can't do this. I can't.

"Ladies and Gentlemen, we still have two more bids. Let us continue and then the gentlemen may collect their dance." Bids for the Numbers Nine and Ten ranged up to sixty thousand. The auction deemed a success, applause again as the men went about claiming their dance. Voices and laughter followed the excitement.

Margo, bewildered, reached for Dom's hand, but he moved it out of her reach. "Why, Dom? Surely you'll get this contract without having to take part in this dancing exhibition."

His voice gentled, "It's not for the contract, Margo. I owe the lady an apology, and it's important that I tell her." He looked down at her. "When the dance is over, we'll find Jack and Diane and leave."

Margo nodded, but she wasn't happy. For some reason, this woman had some kind of hold on Dom, her Dom and there was no way she was going to lose him to the bitch in the green dress.

* * * * *

Laura stood with Eve and Paul. Gabe stood on her other side, his hand lightly touching her back above her waist hoping to give her support. She knew there was no escape. If she tried to sneak away it would insult her friends. Nervously, she intertwined her fingers waiting for him.

Dominic walked toward her. Eyes were watching him—wondering why he'd bid so much to dance with this unknown.

Eve leaned toward Laura whispering, "Oh my god, Laura, he's gorgeous."

Laura's eyes stayed on Dominic. He stood apart from other men even though they were all wearing tuxedos. It seemed as though he was on slow speed and it was taking him forever to come for her. His stride-smooth, his facial expression—determined. Laura's pulse raced, her emotions in pandemonium seeing Dominic's powerful aura of self-assurance.

Squeezing her fingers and digging her nails into her palms, Laura eyed Dominic's black silky hair. His olive skin against the white of his shirt and his broad shoulders filling out his jacket wreaked havoc within her. *He is more handsome than I remember.* She heard Gabe say something to her but she didn't have a clue to what he said. Dominic was looking at her with those unforgettable long lashes and golden-black eyes. Laura's pulse battering—she straightened her spine and dug deep for courage to carry off this dance.

Dominic stopped and nodded to Eve and the Durand men. He held out his large tanned hand, his eyes intently on Laura, "Signorina, this dance is mine, I believe." His deep velvet voice caused her heart to double beat.

Laura gave him her iced hand—it seemed lost in his warmth penetrating through her gloved hand—unable to say a word as a sudden jolt zinged through her. She started to move and then stopped. Dominic looked at her and she said, "I'd like to introduce my friends—Dr. Paul Durand, his wife Eve, and my escort Gabriel Durand." She calmly said to them, "This is Dominic Deluca," then softly added, "This man that knows I have no wish to dance with him."

Not the least inhibited, Dominic returned with a smile that reached his eyes, "Caro, I would have bid as high as necessary to dance with you." He looked at the three people listening and said, "A pleasure to meet Miss Kincaid's friends." Then taking Laura's iced gloved fingers placing it on his arm and holding it there led her onto the dance floor with all eyes watching, especially Dominic's secretary.

It wasn't a waltz; the band was playing a ballad as the singer crooning softly It Had To Be You. Dominic smiled down at her. His voice deep and caressing, "The song is perfect, Caro for our first dance." Dominic felt as if the gods were on his side this night. His mellowed voice whispered, "I wish we were somewhere other than here." When Laura remained silent and her body starched, Dominic softly said into her ear, "Smile or people will think you aren't pleased to be in my arms."

Laura's throat shut down forcing her to take short breaths as she looked up at him.

Dominic drank in Laura's magnificent green eyes that she quickly dropped away from his steady gaze. She didn't relax as he brought her closer into his arms. Her heart pounded remembering his cruel words.

Dominic never wanted to let her go but most important he owed her his deepest apology. How could I have been so dense? His voice a husky whisper, he put his head down next to ear and whispered, "I was so wrong, caro mia, I beg your forgiveness." Hearing his words Laura's misstep that he smoothly corrected as his lips touched her forehead. "I was a fool," he whispered. She felt the movement of his lips near her hairline causing electrified goose bumps. Dominic searched her face wanting to see her acceptance for his apology but she had closed her eyes. "Laura, look at me, please." He wouldn't give up. He embraced her more—pulling her closer to him.

Laura was lost, her emotions clashing between joy and pride. She wanted to run from this man whose words bruised her, yet feeling his body heat and smelling his cologne she swayed in his arms taking her back into her dreams. His kiss—his mouth on hers—she moved unconsciously closer to him.

"Dio, caro, if you look at me with those dreamy green eyes I can only hope that you will forgive me. Please, Tesoro mia."

Laura jerked away, but Dominic held her to him. She flushed. "I must be out of my mind." Her voice raged out in smothered whispers.

Tension was paramount as the music continued. Dominic wouldn't release his hold as much as Laura tried to pull back. "No, Signorina Laura, I cannot let you go." His breathing increased as his thighs brushed against hers. His tone was seductive as the heat between them rose. "Stay, please."

"Dominic," she entreated, "I…I can't."

Dominic danced them toward the open doors out onto the patio. "I don't want to cause a scene and embarrass you," he urged, "we must talk."

She nodded, following his dance steps out into the sultry night air. Dominic continued to dance until they were near the walkway that led to the beach. He stopped, putting his arm around her waist not allowing her to move from him and taking her down toward the ocean.

The moon's reflection shimmered across the sea offering a silver glow; neither seemed to notice. Dominic stopped, "A moment, please."

Stunned, Laura stayed still as Dominic removed his jacket and put it on her shoulders. There were other people about but no one paid attention; each with their own rendezvous in mind.

"Walk with me?"

Mystified by her own actions, knowing she shouldn't be out here with him, her stomach churning, she pulled Dominic's jacket closer to her. She could smell his scent thinking this must be what a volcano goes through before erupting.

They followed the cement walk. The noise from sand grinding under their shoes joined in with the sound of the surf.

They came to a bench. "This will do, Dominic."

"You look beautiful—your gown matches your eyes."

Gripping his jacket, her voice quaking, "What...what do you want from me?"

Dominic put his arm around her shoulder and gently held her against his side as they looked out over the Atlantic. Far off a cargo ship, its lights discernible, added to the eerie glitter. "I beg your forgiveness, Laura. I was so very wrong." She could feel his hand tighten. "Do you remember Isabella...Lorenzo's wife?"

"I do, but what has?"

"Let me explain," he softly interrupted, "she told me my problem with you—that my behaving like an idiot is because I am jealous. And she also added that I am a total chooch—that's jackass in my language."

Laura turned and trying to see him in the moonlight. "She said that to you?"

"Si."

"Jealous? You jealous about me?" Her shocked tone left no doubt that Laura didn't believe it. Laura laughed. "Why would she say something so ridiculous? Now jackass, that I understand."

Dominic knew this was his only chance to convince her about his feelings and he'd plead if he had to. "Because, tesoro, it is not ridiculous." He took one of her hands, rubbing his thumb on her wrist through the glove opening. "I've never met anyone like you—your innocence is a gift. I savored your friendship and wanted more. When I kissed you my feelings for you felt like a lightning strike. I could have flown back to Rome just on the elation I felt." He chuckled, "I wouldn't have need of an airplane." He kissed her knuckles through her gloves and still felt static. "Did you feel that?"

Laura nodded.

"I couldn't forget your soft luscious returning kiss and my world opened. It was beautiful again. Later when I telephoned that very night and found you had a daughter, I assumed that you were married and kissing me meant nothing to you." Dominic leaned over and brushed Laura's forehead with his lips—she felt his hot breath move the wisps of hair, and she shivered. Dominic continued, "I was angry at you and everyone around me. It wouldn't go away so I returned to Stowe to confront you hoping it would give me peace. It shocked me when you said you weren't married and yet you had a daughter. I was filled with rage, not because you had a little girl but because another man had touched you. I wanted you to be mine, tesoro…only mine."

"Dominic, you talk in riddles. Remember when you first invited me out to dinner and you never showed? I waited for you." She choked back her despair. "And I waited. You didn't have the decency to call."

"I do remember that day and night. An emergency; my sister was missing and it was a family crisis. I had to go. I can only say the worry over my sister and my parents was my primary concern and not my personal want."

"Yet when you finally returned and I saw you in Angelo's, you didn't even say hello. I was the one making contact when I telephoned asking to see you"—her voice cracking—"you didn't ask me anything as your mind was already made up." She threw his words at him like tossing stones. "The name calling and the insults. How could you think that of me? Why?"

"Because it is as Isabella says, I was a jealous fool and I still am." He embraced her to him, "Who is the man you are with?"

Laura's light giggle floated in the air surrounding him. It warmed him to think she just might forgive him. "Dr. Paul's brother, Gabriel. And before you jump to another conclusion, he's gay."

"Oh, I like him already."

"I think we better go back. My friends will be worried about me. I'm glad we danced, Dominic. Thank you."

"Caro mia, if I had to bid a million dollars to hold you in my arms tonight, I would have." Dominic took Laura into his arms meeting his lips with hers. She hesitated only a second before opening to let him invade her mouth as she joined him in the touching dance that made their bodies lean into each other. The waves lapped on shore and the band's music drifted out across the lawn to the sea, but the two people entwined in each others arms, heard nothing but the beating of their hearts with electricity zipping through them.

Dominic pulled back from their kiss, but he continued to hold Laura. A smile showed his white teeth. "You still kiss like an innocent."

"Is that so?" Laura felt cocky, "I'll have you know that I'm considered one of the best kissers in Stowe."

Dominic laughed. "Is that so? Tell me...tell me about your experienced kisses." Dominic knew in his heart she was still an innocent. Being overjoyed he held her closer.

"Don't you know a woman never tells?"

Still holding her close but not as tightly as he would like—he brushed his lips across hers and then touched his tongue on her neck under the emerald erring. Laura could feel his warm breath against her air cooled skin and then his mouth came to devour her and she responded in kind. With sparks flying his kiss traveled to the pit of her stomach and churning it into an unexpected wild storm. When Dominic, using common sense, pulled away yet continuing to hold her neither said a word; their feelings were entwined while Laura was trying to cope with Dominic's magic.

Dominic's spoke, his tone husky, "We can't stay here as much as I'd like to."

"I know." Laura's pulse pounding in her ears looked at the man, shadowed in moonlight, who easily took her from despondency to ecstasy, answered, "Thank you, Dominic, for giving me this night to remember."

"Caro mia," his deep tone simmering with checked passion, "Surely you cannot believe that this is only an apology? Or that I don't want you with me? This is the beginning of our lives together."

Dominic, do you really mean what I think you're saying? Laura's voice was shaky but with determination, said, "Really?" And then with courage she never realized she had she reached up and kissed the corner of Dominic's mouth and let her tongue slowly trace his lips and then with her mouth moist caressed only his bottom lip and then nipped it. "Now, Mr. Deluca," her voice low and a bit raspy said, "do you believe I'm experienced or not?"

"Why you little tease," grinning, "knowing we can't stay out here any longer. Tell me," he was walking them back to the ball, "do you always kiss everyone like that?"

Blood still pounding in her brain and her knees trembling, she stopped and looked into the shadow of his face and admitted, "You are the only man I've ever kissed like that in my life."

Dominic suddenly kissed her soundly and laughingly crowed, "I knew it!"

Laura's tone turned serious. "Dom, my daughter goes where I go. She's very special."

"Not a problem as if she's yours then she's mine." He was about to plant another kiss on Laura's rosy mouth when he heard, "Oh there you are, Dom. I was worried. Did she accept your apology?"

Laura saw the woman approach. The music was louder now as they neared the ballroom, but she heard the words loud and clear. Laura gasped and stopped. Dominic turned and reached for her, but Laura could only stare at the very woman that said she was with her boss and soon to be married.

Dominic holding her arm felt her tense through his jacket as her muffled cry carried out to him. "Caro…Laura, what's wrong?"

Laura's lowered voice that only Dominic would hear, "It's all games with you, isn't it?" She pulled off his jacket and dropped it. Tears rolling down her cheeks caught from the patio lights while looking at him, her emotions shot, pleaded, "Please, no more. Please, I can't…" She didn't run but her steps were quick as she passed others not looking left or right. Stunned, he watched her burnished hair having lost some of its pins had fallen in curls. Her sad pleading ate at him. He had to find her. He took two long steps forward.

Margo's voice was sweet but she was livid. She had been humiliated when Dom held the green-eyed bitch in his arms—looking at her as if she was the only woman in the room and then disappearing. Incensed she hid out on the patio waiting for the opportunity to get even. When she saw them return and Dom's jacket covering her, Margo's fury about exploded. She could tell when someone was thoroughly kissed and it was that mousy woman that Dominic paid one hundred thousand dollars to dance with. What kind of hold did she have on him? Margo didn't know but she did know there was no way she was going to lose this man. *Dom Deluca and his money belong to me.* "I'm glad I found you. Jack and Diane are waiting to leave. We're holding them up."

"Damn," Dominic grumbled. "Thanks, Margo." He picked up his jacket and shook it. Putting it on he sniffed Laura's perfume. *I'll find you, caro mia, this time I won't lose you.*

Margo looped her arm through Dominic's looking up at him with her sweetest admiring smile. Her hope was that the bitch that was wrecking her plans would be there to see her with Dom.

Dominic greeted Diane and Jack. "Sorry for the delay."

Margo looked around but didn't see the woman whom she was sure was in love with her man. *Well no matter, Dom said we were going to stop in New York to visit his friends before returning to London. It can't be soon enough!*

* * * * *

Next day, late afternoon

Dominic clutched the telephone. "Are you sure Miss Kincaid is away?" He massaged his brow, frowning, "Will you be sure and tell her Dominic Deluca…" He listened and then said, "Thank you, I appreciate it. And you have my number? Repeat it, please. Thank you."

Dominic played a miserable game of golf. He couldn't concentrate, but the others didn't mind as his high score made them appear as pros in comparison.

He showered, and with a towel wrapped around his wet waist, he tried Laura's number again. He heard Margo call out. "What is it, Margo? I'll be out in a second." He turned toward the bathroom when she opened his bedroom door.

"My"—she smiled—"this is a nice surprise."

A spasm of irritation crossed Dominic's face. "Please, Margo, I need to dress. It will be better if you wait in the other room." He turned to go and said, "Get the file for the Islander's museum. Be sure all the papers are in order." He went into the bathroom and closed the door.

Margo understood the brush-off. She had listened to his telephone conversation when she sneaked into Dominic's suite. At least the bitch didn't want to talk with him, which gave her time to work on Dom. They were leaving for New York this evening. Disgruntled, she left to fulfill her secretarial duties.

19

Four days after the ball

"We've traveled to Fort Lauderdale, Miami Beach, and over to Fort Meyers, on to Sarasota and now we're home." Eve unlatched her seatbelt. "Have we put enough space between you and the Hunk?"

Laura smothered a yawn. "Thanks, Eve." Laura ignored Eve's taunt. "Look at our babies sound asleep."

"Well, I still think you should have talked with him. I'm telling you, Laura, he is one gorgeous man." Giving Laura the eye, went on, "And from what Gabe said, very, very well to do."

Getting out of the car and stretching, Laura grimaced, "Money has no value if there is no honor."

"You're too much. Come, let's get our girls to bed. I'm beat. I'm glad Paul was called in for an emergency—it gives me a chance to freshen up. A warm bath is going to be heaven."

They carried their babies into the house preparing to end their day. It was eight-thirty, the sun set long ago, and they were exhausted.

*****

"Good morning, Eve. Coffee smells terrific." Laura poured herself a cup. "I've decided it's time for Cella and me to head back to Stowe."

Eve put down her cup. "Laura, you're running away. Stay and talk with him. Look at the number of messages he's left."

"I know. But I'm a realist, so I won't make a fool of myself again. I really need to go home." She stared out at the pool's aquamarine water with Sage's plastic swan bobbing in one corner. The blue sky and green grass were surreal in the middle of winter. "I don't know how to show my appreciation to you, Paul and Gabe. If ever I can do something for you, you will tell me. Promise?"

"It's been our pleasure, Laura. And you have more than thanked me for being kind to my parents. I'm embarrassed to admit that I don't miss Vermont."

Watching a breeze sweep the swan to the other side of the pool, Laura said, "I can understand why—Florida is another world."

"Even so, when I think of Vermont I'll know that you and Cella are near my Mom and Dad. The store is their life and too, now I know Cella fills the void I've caused: I thank you for that."

"Well, just so you remember my offer still stands."

"I'll remember. Now I'll make your plane reservation. I'll use the same limo service to pick you up in New York and take you to Stowe."

Laura laughed. "Thanks. I'll be honest when I get into the big city, I'm lost."

Eve smiled. "You know you were a smash at the ball," and then turned serious, "Gabe said several men asked for your telephone number, but he shilly-shallied in his own particular manner and said he'd let them know."

"Don't believe it—it's because of Dominic bidding all that money."

"Laura, you've got to have more confidence in yourself. You are a gorgeous lady, a beautiful mother, and my wonderful friend. In fact, if you wish to stay we can drum up some of those men and see what happens."

"Uh-huh. I best go home, but thank you for this fantastic visit. You've swelled my head to last for years to come."

They laughed and toasted each other with their coffee cups.

20

New York

Margo sat quietly in Mancini's plush New York apartment. She didn't care much for the Isabella and Lorenzo but they were Dom's friends and she was careful not to show her displeasure.

Dominic unaware of Margo's infatuation considered her a good PA and introduced her as such.

Isabella knew the moment she met Margo that the woman was after Dom. She kept it to herself. When Dom was near, Margo behaved in a sweet reserved mode seeking his attention. Meanwhile Dom was totally oblivious to her mischief. In fact, when Dom spoke openly about Laura, Isabella observed Margo's expression become strained.

"I'm telling you, Issy, you were right about me. I won't go into it, but"—Dom laughed—"perhaps what you said might be true."

Lorenzo noticing that Margo being left out of the conversation, spoke, "How do you like New York, Margo?"

She looked at Dominic and then at Lorenzo. "It doesn't remind me of London."

"Why compare the two?" Isabella asked.

Margo's demur smile didn't fool Isabella. "What I mean is London's quiet fog compared to New York's robust traffic is quite different—noisier."

"I think Margo prefers Palm Beach. It spoiled you, hasn't it, Margo?"

Margo's eye lit from Dom's notice. "Dom's right, of course. The weather is unbelievable and the people were so welcoming. I hated to leave. But Dom said duty calls." She smiled at him with hopeful eyes, "In fact, we'll be leaving for London tomorrow; unfortunately returning to Palm Beach isn't possible."

Dominic looked stunned. "What do you mean we're flying out tomorrow?"

Margo exchanged a polite, bland half-smile. "You have a meeting the first of the week and I thought you'd want to take some time to go over those contracts."

"Oh well, not to worry. I can do those in time. I'd like to stay in New York a few extra days. You'll have to change the reservations." Dominic took a sip of whiskey, "In fact, Margo, cancel my reservation and you can go on. Handle the office and I'll let you know if I want to postpone any of the meetings coming up." He looked at Isabella, "Issy, I've invited myself to hang around if you and Ren don't mind?"

"You're always welcome."

Margo fumed. Damn, these Americans. I'll make sure Dom's meetings must take place. "I'll do that." She stood, "If you'll excuse me I'll get busy making the changes."

Dom spoke, "Leave my reservation open, I'll call when I'm ready." He didn't see Margo grimace, but said to Isabella and Ren, "She's the very best secretary—she came with the firm."

Margo heard. You better learn to march to my drum, Mr. Deluca or you're going to be out one best PA. I'm not working for you just to make your office hours easier. She wanted to slam the door but quietly closed it.

* * * * *

Dominic entered the apartment, finding Isabella sipping orange juice. "Did you find a cab for Margo to get to the airport?"

"I finally flagged one down. It's a mad house out there." He poured himself some coffee. "You know, Issy, I feel good about sending Margo on ahead. She seems different away from the office. I have a good antenna, and it was a mistake to bring her with me."

"She's got the hots for you."

He raised an eyebrow, "Margo?"

"Yes, your beautiful, intelligent secretary—Margo. You know, Dom, for someone sharp, who can run circles around mathematicians, build phenomenal bridges and buildings, and control scads of properties besides being as rich as Croesus, you are somewhat simple-minded when it comes to women."

"Coming from you, Issy, it's useless to argue. How can you say that about me?"

Isabella almost slammed down her juice glass, frustrated. "Laura Kincaid…I rest my case!"

Dominic leaned his elbow on the table, resting his chin on his knuckles, and stared at Isabella's smug expression.

Lorenzo walked in. "What are you two about?"

Isabella smiled at her husband. "I was just telling Dom I feel fat."

"Don't let her lie to you, Ren. Your darling wife just said I was an idiot."

Lorenzo laughed. "Really, Bella, if you're going to insult our guest, wait until he checks out and pays his bill."

"Never mind you two," as she rose, saying, "Let's finish our coffee in my sun room. It's the right time of day to absorb the sun."

They moved to Bella's private sanctuary.

Dom sank down on a lounge. "This is nice, Issy."

"Consider yourself privileged, Dom, since my wife took over this room, few people are invited to share its feminine comforts."

"It's my domain," Isabella defended, "just as the library is yours."

Dom stood and began studying the books in her bookcase. "Have you read all of these?"

"If you're referring to romance novels, the answer is yes."

"Ahh, you are a true romantic."

"Never mind my books," she lightly scolded, "Tell us, Dom, what happened with Laura? How in the world did she end in Florida?

That lady doesn't travel. I've asked her to visit so many times and she politely refuses. I like her."

"I do too."

"Then let's hear all. I didn't ask before as Margo was there and I think of Laura as our personal friend. Did you really bid one hundred thousand dollars to dance with her?"

"I had to. The guy she was with must have promised to bid for her dance and the fool meant it. He kept bidding higher and so I did too. Finally when it reached seventy five thousand I had enough and bit a hundred." Dom laughed, "That put an end to the bidding."

Lorenzo sat near his wife and Dominic noticed how Lorenzo laid his hand on her shoulder while fingering her hair. Dominic felt a twinge of envy.

"And so?" Now it was Lorenzo who pressed.

"She is everything I always thought she was. I misjudged her and asked...no, I pleaded for her forgiveness."

"I presume you worked your charm," Isabella cocked her head and waited for his response.

"I will tell you that things were going great. I explained I had an extenuating family problem and lost all sense of reason and then later I was angered when I found she had a daughter because I assumed she had married." Dominic moved around the room, forgetting his coffee. "In fact, I thought we had cleared our misunderstanding and things looked favorable. We were returning to the ball when Laura seeing Margo, she stopped and just stared. She didn't say a word. I'd given her my jacket as it was chilly and she actually yanked it off, dropped it, and rushed off. I can't figure her out. Believe it or not, it happened in less than a minute, but seemed longer."

"You mean you haven't talked to her since then?"

"Issy," his brow pulled into an affronted frown, "I've called and called and left message after message. It's the same as before, I hear nothing from her."

"Listen to me, Dom, something had to occur for her to leave in haste. You said it was when Margo came. I'll bet you a dollar that your PA has something to do with it."

"That's silly. They've never met."

"Didn't I just tell you," she teased, "that when it comes to women, you really have no understanding? Seriously, my suave macho friend, to prove my point Laura and Margo must have crossed paths at that ball each not knowing you were connected to them both."

"Go easy on him," Lorenzo chided. "The poor guy is confused."

Isabella laughed. "At least you agree with me."

They looked at Dom, waiting for his sassy response, but he was studying pictures Isabella had on one of her bookcase shelves. Dom said nothing for the longest time. Isabella and Lorenzo looked at one another—Lorenzo shrugged meaning he didn't understand Dom's attraction to the pictures either.

Isabella moved slowly to get up with her round belly. She went to stand next to Dominic. "What's gotten you so interested? Those are Christmas card photos I dislike putting them away."

Dom reached for the photograph of a little girl holding a teddy bear. His fingers gripped the card as he read the name, Cella. Isabella reached for his arm.

She smiled when she saw the Christmas card. "That's Whisper and Cella, Laura's little girl. You remember my telling you that Laura adopted her baby?" Unaware of what Dom was thinking, she continued, "Cella named the teddy Whisper."

Dominic remained silent as his features hardened, his face lost color.

Lorenzo looked at Dominic. "Bella get Dom a whiskey, please."

"Really?"

"Bella," Lorenzo's brow creased with worry. He looked at Dom still staring hard and unmoving at the picture. Dom's jaw tightened as his fingers bent a corner of the Christmas card. "You knew Laura had a daughter." Dominic still said nothing. Lorenzo's voice quieted, "Surely you're not holding that against her?"

Lorenzo poured Dom a double. "Here, drink! It's early but for some reason I think you need this." His voice with quiet emphasis, "And then tell us what's wrong."

Dominic swallowed the whiskey—all of it, astonishing both his friends. That was not like him. Something was radically wrong.

Isabella's voice had an infinitely compassionate tone, "Tell us, Dom. Why has that picture upset you?"

Dominic still clutching the Christmas card continuing to stare at it. Tris said her baby's name is Cella. I know this is her daughter. But how? He kept looking at the photo of a little girl wearing pink pajamas holding a worn teddy bear. Her smile, like Trista's as a happy child. Cella sitting in front of a small Christmas tree. It was a precious picture. Trista's daughter, yet the card says from Cella and Laura Kincaid. Cella Kincaid? Dominic's heart hammered as a sudden spurt of adrenaline whooshed through his veins, anger building—how could Laura keep his niece from him? Why didn't she tell him all this time that she had Trista Deluca's baby…his very own sister…Dominic's knuckles turned white staring at the Christmas card. Innocent? Laura Kincaid? She'll pay for this and I'll have my niece with me where she belongs…with me.

Isabella and Lorenzo remained silent, waiting for Dom to explain.

Finally, Dom looked at Isabella. He didn't want to break his promise with Tris, yet he might have to. "Who…who does that little girl remind you of, Issy?"

Isabella reached for the card but Dominic wouldn't release it. He held it up to her.

Innocently, Isabella studying Laura's Christmas card, said, "Its little Cella and her teddy bear. Laura and I exchange cards and sometimes a letter. We keep in touch. Why? What is so special about the picture?"

Dom pulled his wallet from his pocket. He took out a picture of his sister and handed it to Isabella. He didn't have to look at it as he had studied Trista's image a thousand times.

"That's Trista." Isabella's mouth gaped as her eyes shifted from Dominic to the Christmas photo and back to Dom's picture of Trista. "Dom, surely you don't think there is a connection? Trista never married," Isabella let out an audible breath. Now Isabella's hands were shaking, she compared the two pictures and could see a resemblance but wasn't completely sure. "Dom, forgive me for thinking so, but did Trista have a baby? She must have told you." She reached for

Dominic's wrist and squeezed it gently, "But how did Laura become involved? Your sister lived in Italy and Laura in America. How? It's incredible. If so, why didn't either one tell you?"

Lorenzo poured Dominic another drink and took one himself. "I think we better sit down and take this a step at a time. We must not rush to conclusions." He handed Dom the whiskey, "Fortify yourself—you're going to need it if what you think proves true."

Fury resonated in Dominic's pacing as his hand fisted and slapped into his other palm. "I will get to the bottom of this. No more will I be played the fool." He glared at Isabella, "You thought me an idiot," his tone tolerated no comeback, "you are one hundred per cent right." He slammed his fist into his hand again, "To be taken in once again by that green-eyed sneak, as that is exactly what Laura Kincaid is. But let me tell you," his tone low and lethal, "never again."

Lorenzo's voice cut through Dominic's thoughts. "Dom, don't make any rash decisions until you've formulated each step. Until you have all the facts, attacking Laura for having Cella can be detrimental to your building a case. Now you only have suspicions."

Dominic stopped, anguish rolling through him. "Ren, you make sense and I know that you're thinking in my behalf. I truly believed Laura was different." His laugh was not warm, "I allowed myself to be conned. All this time she had my niece and didn't have the decency to tell me. She played me a fool for the last time."

"Do you know how Trista arranged to have an American adopt her baby? How did she put her baby into Laura Kincaid's possession? First and more important is how did your sister know Laura? Dom, you have the advantage to find answers without raising suspicion now that you know where Cella is. Storming into their lives with accusations can delay finding answers. There must be a paper trail allowing the little girl to be legally adopted by Laura, if she was. Where is the birth certificate? Also, there has to be adoption papers. Waiting a few more days or weeks is to your advantage."

Dom fell into a chair near Lorenzo. He rested his head in his shaking hands. "I've been searching for my sister's child for years. The only information I had was that her name is Cella. That is an uncommon name. I'm sure she is Tris's daughter. Tris died as she was telling me what happened. She made me promise not to tell anyone." He looked up, sadness shadowing in his eyes and voice, "She didn't want to bring shame for her behavior on our parents and so disappeared until she returned and ill. I kept my word. I hired the best investigators and nothing was discovered." Dominic said with a bit of pride, "Tris mastered her secret and we couldn't find a clue."

Isabella didn't move, but stayed quiet on the lounge.

Dominic looked over at her. "So, Issy, you have nothing to say?"

"I'm not saying a word as you'll climb all over my opinion. But since you've given me an opening," Isabella leaned forward to make her point, "I'll bet another dollar that Laura doesn't know you're related to Cella."

"Oh come on, Izzy!" Dominic's disgust obvious, "How can she not know? If she knew Trista, then she knows that I'm Tris's brother. Can you explain that?"

"No, I can't explain any of this, but then neither can you."

"Stop it, you two." Lorenzo butted in. "We need to plan what steps are needed to establish your right to legally take your niece with you."

"I have every right. Do not doubt it."

"Then let's start from there. What do you know? Do you know when the child was born? Where? Who is the father?"

Isabella spoke. "Cella's birthday is March second. In fact, she will be three in a few weeks." She looked at both of the men watching her, "Laura adopted Cella when she was a tiny baby." Isabella's eyes seemed to burst big and bright when she said, "Oh my god, I remember Laura saying that Cella was hers and she'd be hers forever. I thought it strange. Maybe she thought there could be problems and she was reassuring herself. Laura loves Cella and is a good mother, unless you can come up with some information to prove otherwise, it isn't going to be easy for you."

"Why would she have said that if there wasn't a question about the adoption?"

"You have a good point, Dom." Lorenzo was upset with his friend. "Let me help find out what we can; we'll work with deliberate speed but carefully so we make no mistakes. If Laura has adoption papers then it becomes another matter that has to be investigated. How did she get them? Who handled the adoption?"

"As you say, Ren, Cella is not in harm's way. For now, my primary concern is to keep her safe without hinting to Laura that I'm on to her."

"Why don't you go to Stowe, Dom, and make nice with Laura? You can meet your niece and judge the situation firsthand, and you can personally verify that Cella is Trista's baby."

Dominic growled, "Make nice with Laura, that's easy for you to say, Ren. It means I have to come in contact with that liar and pretend I'm there to see her. Dio, will I never get away from her?"

Isabella eyed her husband. Their thoughts coincided as they believed Dominic still had clandestine feelings for Laura but would never admit it. Finding Cella with Laura complicated his life even more.

"I'm going to do it. Some way I'll arrange a meeting with her and I'll see my niece. I'm going to Stowe pretending to smooth things over with Laura. If I'm positive that Cella is my niece, well then I'll let things stand as they are temporarily."

"Smart!" offered Lorenzo.

"I've got responsibilities to my firm that I can't just ignore but anything I can sideline I will. Then I'll go full force in taking Cella home with me."

"Dom," Isabella's voice gentled, "you're not going to tell your parents, are you?"

"No. I promised Tris not to tell our parents so only when I'm able to take Cella to them and explain. It will make them happy and sad."

"How about the father? Do you know who he is? Did Trista ever tell him, do you know? Can he cause you any grief? You have questions that only your sister can answer and she must have had very good reasons to hide the birth of her baby if she did and if not can he make a claim for his child?"

"Once I have more facts, no one and I mean no one will take that child from me. Cella is my sister's child and I am her uncle.

Whatever it takes, I don't care the cost, I will have Cella as she belongs with me…her real genetic family."

Isabella shuddered. Hearing Dom's declaration was unsettling. Poor Laura, she doesn't stand a chance. "Dom, promise me that you will be careful. Remember Cella knows Laura as her mother. Both of them have bonded and to think of crushing that bond is something you must consider."

"Don't tell me, Issy, that you're thinking Laura has a right to my niece?"

"I don't know. If Cella is your niece, well what I'm saying is to keep in mind that those two have been one—so to speak, going on three years. You can't just walk in and think that your claim will not have an affect on the child."

Dominic grimaced, "Naturally the child comes first. I don't give a damn about the so-called mother."

"You will, Dom, when you see them together. You're going to be in for a shock."

"I get it…you want me to go easy on Laura. What I do from now on will be in the interest of Trista's daughter; my niece." He stood, "Now if you'll excuse me I'm going to Stowe."

* * * * *

While shoveling snow, Laura tossed small snowballs to Cella. The little girl was laughing while trying to catch them.

Dominic parked his rental on the road watching. Sliding down a window he heard Trista's little girl giggle and then say, "Snowball, Mama."

Laura dropped the shovel and picked up Cella and twirled with her—they both were laughing.

Dominic's heart seemed about to burst with rage at having lost years of having his niece with him and missing her young life. It irritated him that he was observing as a stranger because of the cunning of a sneak.

Laura turned and saw a van parked near the front of her drive. She took a second look and froze. Her lips move. "Dominic?"

Dominic made his way over to the two people he'd been watching. He noticed Laura tense and pressed Cella closer to her.

"Down, Mama."

"No, darling. Not yet." Holding Cella gave Laura a sort of shield from Dominic getting too close. She squeezed Cella tighter.

Smoldering, Dominic put on his best face. He agreed with Lorenzo to take it slow to get answers. He stopped three feet from Laura. Laura's green eyes were bright in the cold air, but it was Cella's eyes that captured him. In the sunlight, they appeared almost black, not like Trista's burnt almond color. Cella's rosy cheeks and smile brought Trista to mind. Dominic swallowed to keep from shouting, *This little girl belongs with me. She is mine.* "Hello, caro, I had to come. I owe you an apology."

"You don't owe me anything, Dominic."

"Don't own, Dom-ick," Cella copied and then giggled.

Her words brought a big smile to Dominic, showing his even white teeth against his olive skin. "You must be Cella."

Laura raised an eyebrow. "How do you know? Oh, Bella." The cold turned Laura's cheeks rosy red, matching her lips that still haven't curved into a smile. "Cella, this is Mr. Deluca. Remember what to say?"

"Hello."

Dominic's heart swelled. "Hello." He reached to touch her cheek with his gloved finger before turning to Laura. He forces a matter-of-fact voice. "Yes, Isabella sends her best to you both."

"Down, Mama." Cella was trying to pull out of Laura's hold.

Laura has no choice or Cella will fuss and how can she explain that she is using her daughter as a barrier from the man that constantly exists in her dreams and is now here in the flesh.

Laura sets Cella down. "Be careful, sweetheart."

Cella tries to pick up the snow shovel that Laura was using.

Keeping one eye on her daughter, Laura says, "I can't imagine why you're here. You owe me no apology."

Dominic bit the inside of his jaw to keep from blowing his top. "When I couldn't get to talk with you after the ball, I wondered why you refused my calls. I thought we corrected our misunderstandings."

Incensed, Laura's lips thinned, lowering her voice, said, "We did or I thought so. It just happens, Mr. Deluca, I don't like being made a fool. You seem to have the knack to do just that with me. Do you get your jollies by stirring my emotions?" Her look hard, went on, "Why me? What have I ever done to you to warrant your derision?"

Dominic glared, his teeth gritted, uttered, "What the bloody hell are you talking about? And your act of disappearing is childish."

Laura wanted to stamp her foot and wipe the arrogance that belonged strictly to him—off his face. "You took me out of the ballroom. We gave our explanations and we kissed. It was not just a kiss, Mr. Deluca, it was as though you meant it." She looked away from his staring eyes, checked on Cella and then turned back to him. "What kind of game do you play? You're going to be married and yet you engage in kissing someone other than your fiancée?"

Dominic automatically took a step forward to stand in front of Laura. "Now hold on. Where did you get that idiotic idea?"

"From your fiancée's mouth."

"You mean Margo?" He laughed to cover relief as well as his annoyance.

"It may be funny to you, but I assure you I find it sordid as well as humiliating. What kind of man are you? Certainly not the man I believed you to be." Laura turned to walk away, but Dominic grabbed her arm to stop her.

"Let go of me," her tone suddenly loud.

"Mama," cried Cella. "Go way."

Dominic had been so wrapped in his conversation with Laura he forgot about Cella hearing. He kneeled and softly cajoled, "Please, tesoro, I only want to talk with your mama."

Cella's chubby face broke out in a big smile. "My mama calls soro." Cella walked closer to Dominic but she didn't take his outstretched hand. "You make snowballs? I catch'em."

"Cella." Laura's tone was steady. "Mr. Deluca has to leave. It's time for lunch. Auntie Gretel will be calling soon."

Cella looked at Dominic. She turned her head one way and the other—her little red knitted hat with its tassel bobbing, "Want lunch? Make snowballs."

Before Laura could object, Dominic said, "Yes, I'd like that. Do you think you could catch my snowballs?"

Cella earnestly answered by shaking her head yes, laughing while trying to clap her mitten-covered hands.

Laura didn't want to make a scene. Her heart beating so fast she was sure Dominic could see through her jacket. She wouldn't admit it to him but she wanted him to stay.

Taking Cella's hand, Laura said, "I suppose, Dominic, you've been invited to lunch. Soup and sandwich. Nothing fancy."

He forced a smile. "That sounds great." It will give me an opportunity to check on my niece's living conditions and your devious methods. This little girl is mine and I intend to claim her as soon as possible.

"Auntie Gretel," Cella bounced into the kitchen pulling at the buttons on her snowsuit. "Mr. Luca makes snowballs."

Gretel eyed Dominic. "That's great, honey. How about we first wash your hands?" Turning to Dominic she offered her hand. "I'm Gretel, but to Cella I'm Auntie. I hope you like peanut butter and jelly."

Dominic smiled warmly. He liked the woman. "Thank you, in fact, peanut butter and jelly is my favorite sandwich."

Gretel laughed. "I bet!"

Dominic shoved his gloves in his jacket pocket and then hung them on the tree next to Laura's. His maroon sweater hugged his broad shoulders. Gretel held her smile thinking he was a big one.

Laura returned and lifted Cella into her booster chair, pushing it to the table.

Gretel set a small bowl of vegetable soup in front of the little girl.

Dominic bent his head to see the soup. "It's not too hot, is it?" Then he seemed embarrassed and looked away. He was still standing as neither Gretel nor Laura had sat. "I'm sorry. I remember being small and anxious to eat so I could go out to play and the first spoonful blistered my lip."

"Not to worry," Gretel answered, "we always make sure her food is just right."

"Please sit down, Dominic," Laura pressed. "Gretel and I work together in getting lunch, but we usually get Cella started first." Laura eyed her daughter moving to bring the bowl closer to her.

Cella spooning vegetables into her little mouth stopped to eye Dominic, "You like soup?"

Dominic's heart swells with pure joy for this little angel. "Yes, I do."

Cella, no longer interested is busy finding the peas in her soup.

Dominic watches his niece conceding that she is healthy and happy. He is going to have to leave her with Laura for a while longer until he finds proof that Cella belongs to him.

Having finished a bowl of soup and buttered bread, Dominic refuses Gretel's offer of coffee. "No thanks. This is fine." He takes a drink of water. "Isabella said Cella is going to be three soon. She's very bright."

Gretel lifted sleepy Cella for her nap. Dominic noticed how both women took care of her.

Dominic saw Laura's eyes brighten. "Yes, she is. She repeats words she hears so we have to be careful how we say things."

"You mean talk carelessly?"

"Of course not. That's a ridiculous thing to suggest. My daughter is very precocious and quick to learn."

Dominic bristled at Laura calling Trista's daughter hers. Then out of the blue, Dominic said, "Have dinner with me tonight?"

Laura looked straight into his eyes. "And be jilted again? No, thank you."

"Please, I promise to be here on time. Seven o'clock. Say you will." Dominic's voice mellowed knowing how to turn on his charm and use it to his advantage. He hid his resentment at having to act as a gentleman to the manipulating lying witch.

Laura wanted to be with Dominic in the worst way but something wasn't jelling. Is her mind telling her that he's pretending? But why? She didn't want to say no. "Dinner it is then, and seven will work."

"I'll be here. You can bank on it."

He rose, taking in Laura's rosy lips that he remembered kissing and chastising himself at the same time for even thinking about it. "Thank you, Signora Gretel, for your delicious lunch. It's been a pleasure meeting you."

His eyes went to Laura. "Until tonight, Signorina. Tell the little angel that perhaps another time I will make snowballs for her." And then he was gone.

* * * * *

When Dominic made reservations at Angelo's, he requested a table in a quiet corner. The wall sconces kept the lighting soft music adding to its ambience.

Dominic pulled out a chair for Laura and purposely sat on her left so he could touch her hand. His intention is to manipulate and gather as much information as possible.

Laura, wearing black slacks, a long-sleeved emerald blouse with a black cashmere sweater draped around her shoulders, feels good about her clothes. Shopping in Florida, Eve told her she looked classy. She added a little blush and sparing eye shadow; she felt pretty. She wanted to look her best for Dominic; she couldn't keep her heart from quivering. She kept telling herself his dinner invitation had no special meaning.

Angelo came over to their table to say hello. Dominic ordered wine. Laura smiled. "Mr. Angelo, you make the best eggplant parmesan—better than I had in Rome."

Dominic's ears perked. "Rome? You were in Rome?"

Laura felt the nape of her neck twitch. Dominic's tone was more than curiosity. "Si"—she laughed—"I vacationed in Italy, and Rome was one of the cities we toured. It's a magic place. You don't remember but I mentioned it that day we drove to Montpelier."

Angelo grins. "When one visits Roma, they will always return."

Dominic, anxious to learn more, didn't realize his facial expression was troubled. "I'm sorry I don't recall. When were you in Rome?"

"It was years ago. I had taken a vacation tour of Italy." You must promise never to tell anyone that you have met me, Trista had warned. Laura never forgot. She picked up the glass of water, sipping. "It was glorious." Returning Dominic's stare, said, "Was Rome your home? And now it's London. You must have to travel a lot."

Dominic was onto Laura changing the subject and for now he would let her. "My family has a villa not far from Rome. I work out of Rome but have enlarged my interests. Consequently, I must be in London. It is a busy life, very time-consuming."

"I can't imagine the scope of what you must do." She had no idea that Dominic was biting the inside of his jaw to keep from shouting at her one minute and then next wanting to take her in his arms and kiss her. "It's no wonder then that when you stayed at the Cloud and demanded to be undisturbed."

"Si. I think we will order and then take our time to visit."

Dominic here with me in Angelo's as if that other time with Matt never happened. Laura felt turmoil wending through her. Unable to catch her breath Laura could only nod.

Dominic was angry with himself for the jolt of heat he was experiencing from just the mild touch of her skin. He had to remind his brain that Cella was the reason for this dinner. "You suggested the eggplant. What else do you favor?" Dominic ordered another bottle of red wine and then kept his eyes on the menu.

"Angelo's cannot be topped for delicious foods." She eyed Dominic, her heart soaring, she reached for his hand that rested on the table entwined on the stem of his wine glass. The light touch, the spark, brought a flush to her glowing cheeks. "Thank you, Dominic. This is really a treat and your company makes it special."

"Ah, but, signorina, it is still early. Let us not rush off. We can enjoy an espresso or if I remember correctly—you prefer cappuccino."

Laura's smile turned Dominic's insides to mush. "That you remember is surprising."

"So we have discussed the weather, skiing, ice skating, and our preference for food. Now"—he reached for her full hand and caressed her palm with his thumb—"tell me what a beautiful young woman does with her time."

Goose bumps multiplied by the dozens from Dominic's caress and mellow voice. "I...I live a quiet life as you can tell. It's a good life, and with Cella, it is never boring."

"You have a very sweet"—he couldn't make himself say daughter—"little girl."

"She is the joy of my being. I know I'm bragging but Cella is smart and it's natural. She picks up on everything. You know when she turned two she could recite part of the alphabet and count to ten." Laura laughed, "Don't ask her to count for you now as she will go on and on." Laura's laugh tingled, "She will mix up the numbers but it matters not as she becomes so intent in a sing-song way."

Dominic was smoldering. Because of you, I have lost those moments of her life—they are gone forever. But fair is fair when you'll never see my niece again. "I wish I had asked her."

"You're welcome to visit again."

"I'm sorry, but I will be leaving in the morning. I must get back to work. But," he offered her a wide smile, "I should like to return soon. I hope you won't mind." His voice became husky, "I don't have to ski to make me want to return to Stowe."

A warning voice whispered in her head, but she ignored it. "Cella and I would like that. You like children, do you not, Dominic?" Laura wanted her dreams to come true. The power of this man overwhelmed her. She wanted to trust him and perhaps with his next visit she'd do just that. After all, he didn't jilt her this time.

Dominic held her wrist, finding her pulse and feeling his beat in unison. Don't be a fool, he told himself—she's a manipulative sneak. "Yes, I like children. You're a wonderful mother, Laura. I'd never imagine a young woman willingly adopting a baby and taking on years of responsibility."

"Cella isn't a responsibility, she's a treasure." Her voice held depth, "I wouldn't give up one minute of my time with her for," she laughed, "as the saying goes—for all the tea in China, but I think I should change that to India." Laura wanted Dominic to know right off that Cella would always be with her.

"That's commendable." He kept moving his thumb on Laura's wrist. Electricity seemed to zoom into each of them, but he acted as though he didn't know it. "Tell me, how does a single woman get to adopt a child? You must know someone with authority to arrange this. In Italy, I think it would be impossible."

Laura hesitated. Never would she reveal Cella's birth mother. "I was just fortunate to be in the right place at the right time."

Dominic nodded, careful with his next words. "Then she's always lived in Vermont?"

"Oh yes," Laura answered enthusiastically, "born here."

Pleased with the information yet befuddled as to how Tris came to America, Dominic wanted to be rid of this sneak as he surmised he would get nothing from her as she displayed she was good at hiding her discretions. But he had enough to search the state's birth records. "I believe, Signorina, we must be on our way."

"Of course." Surprised at the abrupt ending of their conversation, Laura went to rise as Dominic held the back of her chair.

Dominic walked Laura to her door. "I would like to come in and see your little angel, but it is late. I'll say good night."

He was about to turn when Laura whispered, "Dominic, won't you kiss me goodbye?"

Kissing her was what he thought of half the night. It was dangerous to go in that direction so he steeled himself. So you want to play games with me, do you? Dominic said not a word as he gathered Laura in his arms, crushing her to him. His tongue traced the fullness of her lips. He covered her mouth hungrily and she responded in kind. He took cruel ravishment of her mouth over and over again. His kiss was punishing and angry.

Standing on tiptoe she pressed herself against him. She felt heady sensations zoom through and wanted it to go on and on when suddenly Dominic pulled away.

"Dio," he exclaimed, his voice deep and husky. "You are a witch."

Her breathless voice reached him wrapping him in her silken cocoon. "I love you kissing me, I can't help it."

"Really, caro?" His furor, especially with himself for getting carried away with this firecracker that continues to light his fuse every time she is near.

Laura didn't understand. "Dominic, remember I told you about my kissing experience when we were in Florida?" She chuckled. "Surely you aren't holding that against me?"

All Dominic knew was that he had to get away. He left her standing on the porch looking up from the bottom step, he said, "Good night, Laura." If it weren't so dark, she would see anger in his facial expression. "Until we meet again." He left and didn't look back, not once.

Laura, her lips burning with fire that he started, stood gaping as tears fell. *Once again I'm a fool. Why, Dominic, what have I ever done to have you pretend to like me one minute, and then I feel your animosity the next?* Laura watched the red taillights disappear before entering her sanctuary.

21

New York

Hire the best investigator there is, Ren. I care not the cost. He is to go over every birth certificate in the state. Have him cover the 1st to the 10th of March first. Leave nothing to chance."

"But, Dom," Isabella injects, "Cella's birthday is the 2nd. Why go through all those extra days?"

"Because she is manipulative. I don't trust her."

"You're wrong, Dom." Isabella held up her hand to ward off his retort. "Laura is exactly as she appears. I trust her. For some reason that none are privy to she became involved with your sister." Isabella sipped some juice, "Admit it," she looked at her husband and then Dom, "you said Trista was very secretive about her whereabouts. How did their meeting come about? If Cella was born in Vermont it was because Trista chose Laura; the one person she felt she could rely on and not be traced."

"Please, Issy, right now I've got more to contend with and that's claiming my niece."

"I've given my word I'll say nothing to Laura about your quest, but I don't like it. If she loses Cella, you'll crush her. She loves that little girl."

Frustrated, Dominic groaned, "I haven't the answers but I will get them. Somehow Laura enticed Tris to leave Cella to her."

"How? Did Trista sound worried when she told you she had a daughter? She must have known Laura and then somehow managed that Cella be born in Vermont."

"I don't know. I have Trista's passport and it doesn't show her traveling to America."

"Then how is it Cella was born in Vermont? How did Trista get from Italy to America? And now the big question…is Cella your niece? Maybe the name is a coincidence and nothing more."

"I don't know…yet." Dominic, weary of debating with his friend, said, "This may prove that Laura is lying about Cella being born in America." He looked at Lorenzo, "I still want all birth records searched and also any in information pertaining to Laura Kincaid delved into, too. I want my sister's daughter and one way or the other I will succeed."

"We'll do all that we can. You can't be in two places at once so go to London and I promise I will keep at this for you."

"Thanks, Ren. I know I can count on you." Dominic looked at Isabella, "And Issy, I feel the same about you. Mostly take care of yourself and Ren's baby. I don't want anything to happen to upset you. Understand?"

"Of course I do. You also take care." Then she winked, "And when you get back to London I don't want to hear wedding bells between you and Margo. She's not for you!"

Lorenzo laughed. "Bella always thinks she knows what's best for you."

"I'm glad she's in my corner." Dominic stood. "I'll get ready; my flight takes off in a few hours."

22

Stowe

Today being Cella's third birthday she sat in her high chair with birthday cake frosting smudged over her lips and cheeks as her little fingers pushed more cake into her mouth. Laura and Greta sat with smiles singing "Happy Birthday" to her.

Unexpectedly the front doorbell rang. Laura peeked through the glass. A delivery man called out that he had packages for Cella Kincaid.

"Let's take them into the living room, sweetheart, and see who they're from."

Cella was tearing into the first box after Laura broke the seal. It was a doll with long blond hair and a fancy satin dress trimmed in lace. When Cella squeezed it, the doll said, "I love you." Cella laughed.

"I love you," she said to the doll.

Laura unsealed the other package. It was heavier.

Cella's anxious little hands were pulling at the paper. It was a book. The cover's colorful characters were lifelike of Mother Goose stories.

Cella opened it and all the characters for Old Mother Hubbard's Cupboard popped up. Cella forgot about her doll; this one enchanted her.

Gretel smiling, whispered to Laura, "That is some book. It must have cost a pretty penny."

SECRET PROMISE

Laura nodded watching her little girl enthralled turning each page and seeing the pop-ups while the other open pages would fold back in place.

"Cella, we must see if there is a card. You must say thank you."

"Okay, Mama." But she went right on turning the pages.

"Your pretty doll is from Mrs. Mancini." Laura looked for a card for the book but found nothing. She helped Cella lift the big book and when she opened the cover and wrote in a long hand with heavy strokes caused her stomach to tighten.

To Tesoro,

I haven't forgotten you. Happy Birthday.

Signed,
D. Deluca

Gretel, eyeing Laura, asked what was wrong.

"Nothing. Remember when Dominic Deluca visited weeks ago? It's from him."

"How can I forget that handsome devil? How about him remembering Cella's birthday?"

"He and Mrs. Mancini are friends. I guess she mentioned it."

The next morning Gretel packed her belongings. She was going to her home in Pennsylvania. Pete would be picking her up. She parted from Laura with tears, though they were happy ones.

Laura decided to telephone Isabella and thank her for Cella's gift. She mentioned having Cella attend a half-day school so she could mix with the children. Isabella laughed when Laura said Cella would probably be telling the teacher how to run her class.

"She's three going on twelve," Laura told of Dominic's gift and asked for his telephone number. She didn't admit that she wanted to hear his voice. Dominic hadn't contacted her since he took her to Angelo's. Laura figured it was because she was aggressive in asking Dominic to kiss her. Still, she never regretted it for a second. She could feel his kisses as they still tingled and gave her a rush. She'd go for seconds if she could.

Laura's telephone call went directly to Dominic's PA. When Laura asked to speak with Mr. Deluca and gave her name, Margo didn't hesitate to say that he was out of the office and wouldn't return for the rest of the day. Dominic was at his desk at the moment and Margo knew he'd take the call. She said she'd pass on Laura's message.

The next day Laura tried again and was told Mr. Deluca received her message. There was no reason for her to call again.

Laura asked that she tell Mr. Deluca that Cella was very happy with her birthday gift.

"Of course," Margo replied. *Bloody hell will I give him your message?*

Disappointed in not hearing from Dominic, trying to convince herself that he was very busy, Laura muted her heartache and put her effort into helping Cella make new friends.

* * * * *

It was the first week in April after Cella's birthday when Jason visited with Laura. Sitting in her sunny kitchen, said, "I got kind of suspicious, Laur, so I had to come and tell you."

"Jace, you're not making this up to tease me, are you?"

"No, I'm telling you the guy came up to me pretending to be your school friend from Maine. He asked if you were married. I told him you weren't."

"Did he give you a name? What did he look like?"

Jason shook his head. "No last name, just Jack. He's tall, has gray hair, and no face wrinkles. He had nice clothes."

Laura shrugged.

"When he began to ask about Cella I wondered why he'd ask if you're married and then ask about your little girl. I told him he should talk to you. Did he?"

"No."

"See," Jason gloated, "I knew I was right. What do you think he wanted?"

Laura's stomach knotted. She did her best to cover her nervousness. "I haven't a clue. He's probably looking to sell me insurance and wanting to know if I'd be a good risk."

Jason got up to leave. "We sure miss you at the Cloud. Mr. I's got me acting as a tour guide. He said if I'm going to hang around this summer I might as well work."

Laura had to laugh. "For someone who likes girls, maybe you'll find your special one."

"Nah!" He winked, "You were always my favorite girl. These will be groups of families with small kids or old people. But it's a living."

As soon as Jason backed out of the driveway Laura went to her secret hiding place and took out the silver key. She studied the key. Trista, what am I going to do? Her hand shaking, glad Cella was in half-day school, she grabbed her jacket and headed for the bank.

Laura sat in the little room with the metal box, its lid up. She was white as the paper she was holding. She was going to vomit. The perspiration didn't stop at her brow but covered her entire body. Cella's birth certificate for anyone to see printed plainly that Laura Kincaid was the mother of Cella Rose Kincaid and the father was listed as Dominic Deluca.

Tremors racing through her, her hands shaking she looked at more of the papers. A sealed envelope for Dominic Deluca and Laura remembered Trista saying she left a letter for her brother if he was needed. Dominic...Trista's brother...my god! Looking further a note was left to Laura telling that she used her mother's maiden name—Serrano and that she was sorry for having lied. The money remained in a separate envelope. There were other legal papers that concerned Cella when she came of age. Laura didn't bother with those. Discovering Dominic to be Trista's brother devastated Laura. She knew she was in trouble. Dominic wasn't interested in her; his interest was only for Cella.

Why didn't I look at these papers when Trista was putting them in this box? What am I going to do? Dominic has somehow found out about Cella and he must be planning on taking Cella away from me. He's not interested in me at all. Why so sneaky, Dominic? Why not discuss Cella with me? She's mine. Your sister gave her to me. Laura gripped the edge of the table until her knuckles whitened. No wonder you showed up suddenly and pretended you cared. Laura's terror veered over to rage, *Oh no, Mr. Deluca; Cella is mine: you cannot have her.* Yet Dominic's name on Cella's birth certificate would give him some rights. She knew with his money and power he could do just about anything to have his way. She wasn't going to let him do it. Cella is mine; not yours. Laura was shaking so badly that the papers scattered. She choked back her sobs as she slowly and methodically folded all the papers returning them to the box except Cella's birth certificate. Determined now, she opened the envelope with the money and removed a few thousand dollars. With my savings, it'll be enough to take Cella and me far away.

Trista's sealed letter to Dominic was left in the box.

Dear Dom,

Please forgive me for what I am going to tell you. You were right when you said Antonio was no good. I found that he pretended to love me only to steal information from you through me. But it is too late now. I am pregnant, and the shame I will bring to our family is something I cannot let happen, so I am going to take advantage of a new friendship I made with an American. I'm going to have my baby use her name. I have arranged for papers to identify me as Laura Kincaid. She knows nothing of this, and hopefully she will accept my baby as her own. I have to do this, Dom, as I cannot leave an innocent child tied to the likes of Antonio. I have no choice as I am dying. The remission is over. How can I burden our parents with my illegitimate baby along with my death? So I am going to America, give my tesoro to my trusted friend. She will have the papers to confirm the child is hers. I have not told her my real name. I used Mama's maiden name.

This letter will be included with my baby's birth certificate as Laura-mother, and I have named you as father. I do not want Antonio to have any inkling he is the father. It would lead to blackmail and scandal.

I'm sorry and ashamed. I beg your forgiveness. If you have received this letter, it is because Laura needs your help. I told her she could count on you. I did give Laura money for my baby. Also, I have made provisions that my inheritance will go to my baby when she becomes of age. Laura has the envelope. She can show you.

I love you, Dom, with all my heart. I'll leave it up to you if you want to tell Mama and Papa about my baby. I made Laura promise to never mention my name or let anyone know that we ever met. I covered my tracks well, Dom. I had to protect my baby, your niece, and Laura's daughter. So this is the burden I have put upon you. I am truly sorry that I didn't listen, but my little baby is innocent.

Be good to yourself, Dom. Stop working so hard. Find a good lady, fall in love, and marry.

Tris

* * * * *

Laura left the bank and picked up Cella at school. Not wanting to raise questions she would do as Trista did and leave no trail. She had to hurry. Dom showed up, and then a stranger worried her.

First, she went to Mr. Carlsson telling him that she was going to Maine for a while. Then home to pack. She didn't take her credit card; she'd travel with cash only. She remembered the many advertised cruises when she visited Florida and somehow she was going to get Cella and her on one of those ships.

Pete picked her up to catch the bus. "Now don't worry about a thing. I'll keep checking on your house. Take as long as you want."

Laura, with Cella and Whisper, began her clandestine journey.

It was the long way around but getting off the bus midway and not returning to it and then buying a ticket on an express bus full of parents and children going south to Disney in Orlando, she fit right in. Arriving in Orlando she boarded another bus to Miami.

Nervous, Laura held Cella's hand while staring in awe at the ship. Cella clutched Whisper to her. "Here we are, sweetheart. We're going to have an adventure and lots of fun."

"Whisper says okay, Mama."

Holding Cella's hand Laura looked for their line to board. Even knowing she left no clues she wouldn't feel completely at ease until they were sailing on the Atlantic and far from Vermont.

23

April, New York

When the investigator showed Lorenzo what he discovered in Burlington's court records, Lorenzo stared at the report. "The authenticity of this is indisputable?"

"There is no mistake. It is a true copy."

"I'm going to put your service on hold. Send me your bill. I'll be in touch." Lorenzo had to get hold of Dom. "Your investigative service remains confidential, correct?"

"As I stated at the very beginning, unless we discover a felony we report what we learn to no one other than our client." He left.

Lorenzo sat at his desk, rubbing the back of his neck. His face spread into a wide grin. He picked up the copy of Cella's birth certificate. "Laura Kincaid and Dominic Deluca are the parents of little Cella Rose Kincaid," Lorenzo spoke to the empty room and then began laughing. He was about to reach for the telephone to call his friend, but stopped with his hand in mid air realizing this isn't funny. Certain Dom didn't have a clue so that left Laura. Dom must be right about Laura being devious.

Lorenzo changed his appointments and headed home. He had to talk with Bella.

The paper rattled as Isabella stared at it. "My God, Ren, do you know what this means?"

"Sweetheart, all hell is going to break loose. How in the world did Laura get named Cella's legal mother and yet Trista is the child's biological mother? Can we be sure that Cella is Trista's?"

"Don't be ridiculous. It says Dom's her father."

"We know that isn't true, Bella. How and why is Dom's name on the birth certificate with Laura Kincaid, but yet the baby is Kincaid and not Deluca?"

"Who knows? Trista must not have wanted the real father to have any claim yet didn't tell her brother. What are you going to do?"

"I don't know. This will be a double blow to Dom. It appears Laura Kincaid is in the midst of this skullduggery. If not, why didn't she tell him? She had many opportunities and said not a word. Lord knows what he'll do when his Italian temper gets riled. He's going to rush over here and I wouldn't be surprised if he just takes Cella away with him."

"But, Laura…oh my god, Ren. Poor Laura."

"I don't know, Bella. You always believed in Laura. But this is beyond trusting." Lorenzo paced. "I'm going to call Dom. It's his decision."

"Hello, Margo. This is Lorenzo Mancini. Is Dom there?"

Margo bit her tongue as she'd really like to tell him what she thought. Instead, she did what was expected, "Hello, Mr. Mancini. Dom isn't here. He's on one of his jobs checking specifications."

Damn, thought Lorenzo. "Please have him get in touch with me as soon as possible."

"Is there anything I can help you with?"

"No, Margo, thanks. Tell Dom I'll wait for his call. How are you?"

"Busy as usual. I'll give Dom your message."

Lorenzo put the phone down.

"Dom's not in his office?" Isabella leaned back in the chair with her feet up and pulled her blouse over her round belly. "You're not going to send it to him?"

"No." Lorenzo sat across from his wife. "I don't want to send Cella's birth certificate. This is personal and for Dom's eyes, only."

Isabella's eyes sought her husband's. "Call Dom's home and leave a message on his machine."

"Why? I just told Margo to have him call me."

Isabella eyed him with an amusing look.

With a touch of sarcasm, he uttered, "What?"

"You are so naïve, my darling. I told you Margo has the hots for Dom, and it wouldn't surprise me if she didn't see him again for the day, and the message would be given to him tomorrow. I don't trust her."

Lorenzo snickered. "She is Dom's right hand. He trusts her. Get over it, my sweet."

Isabella scooted off the chair as best she could and went to the telephone. She flipped through her address book and dialed direct to Dom's London apartment. Meanwhile she smiled at her husband while he shook his head. "Dom, this is Issy. Call Ren or me as soon as you can. Bye."

It was late when Dom dialed Mancini's number. He yawned.

"Hi Ren. I got Issy's message. Good news, I hope." Lorenzo swallowed. Bella was right. "I just got home and figured I'd call before I jumped in the shower."

"I have news, Dom. I think you should sit down."

Dominic laughed. "Right. I'm sitting."

"The investigator located Cella's birth certificate and..."

Dominic leapt forward, "Fantastic!"

"Cella is an American. She was born in Burlington, Vermont on March second. She is three years old."

"The certificate—what does it say? Is Trista Cella's mother? Did it name the father?" Dominic couldn't restrain his anticipation, "Finally!"

Isabella was on another phone and broke in. "Dom, please, you're going to blow your top. I just know it."

"Issy, I will not. I'm prepared for the worst. Ren, tell me, is Cella my niece?"

"Yes and it shows that Laura Kincaid is the mother of Cella Rose Kincaid and ..."

"Bloody hell," Dominic shouted. "That can't be. How the hell did she pull that one off? Who's the father?"

"The only way to tell you is straight out. You are, Dom. Your name is recorded as the baby's father." Lorenzo waited for the explosion but all he got was silence.

"Dom, are you still there? You're worrying me."

There was another long pause before Dominic answered. "I'm here, Ren. You're right, I need to sit."

"It's inconceivable if I wasn't looking at the birth certificate."

"How? I didn't know Tris knew Laura. How did they pull this stunt and think to get away with it, especially Laura and she has never breathed a word." Ren could hear vehemence rising in Dom's tone, "I'm not only upset I'm gnashing my teeth to keep from blowing up. I'd wring that sneak's neck if she were here."

Isabella's voice raised an octave, "Dom, until you get answers as to why Laura has remained silent; please take it easy. This birth certificate states that Laura is Cella's mother. Laura must believe that possession is 9/10ths, you know?"

"Well, it says I'm Cella's father. That gives me clout as well as control for my niece…daughter." His tone bitter, "I don't know how Trista and Laura connived to make this mess; of course my sister had to be involved. I wonder how Laura coerced Tris into doing this so secretly. Trista must have wanted me to have a say in her baby's well being. Why else did she name me?" He chuckled nastily, "Now it's my call and I am going to take responsibility for my daughter."

"You can try, Dom, but this is America and legally Laura is Cella's mother and she has raised her from infancy."

"I'm not going to get into that now, Issy. I have to delegate orders for my crew tomorrow so I can get out here as soon as possible."

Lorenzo spoke. "Come to New York, Dom. Let's map out the best way for you to go. Laura hasn't a clue that we know."

Dominic's tone was loaded with heavy sarcasm. "All these years that lying sneak could have contacted me. We could have worked through this like sensible adults. I don't trust her. I'm not giving her an opportunity to lie and try to make up a story that paints her as the innocent."

"I believe Laura must have her reasons."

"Issy, Issy, your faith wears thin. Be careful you don't get your toes stepped on."

"No, my dear friend, I suggest you take careful steps. Laura is a good mother. You have to admit it even though you don't want to.

Because if she wasn't you'd never have walked away and left Cella with her."

"You've made your point."

"Exactly." Her voice gentled, "Dom, please consider Laura's as well as Cella's situation in this."

Dominic took a long breath. "Okay, Issy, for you I will not do anything irrational. In the meantime, you take care of your baby and Ren." His tone mellowed, "You're going to make a beautiful mother."

"Thanks, Dom. That means a lot."

Lorenzo broke in, "And I'm going to make one hellava' papa."

"No question—I'd bet my money on you." Dominic yawned. "I'm going to sign off. I can't thank you enough for getting me this information to me. I'll fly in as soon as I can. And Ren, get the investigator back. We better keep tabs on Laura. If she should get wind of our knowing, who knows what she'll do. I want my sister's baby. Cella belongs to me and the proof is on the certificate. Dio…what was Tris thinking?"

They disconnected. All three knowing there were going to be big changes ahead.

April

Dominic walked in as Lorenzo was hanging up the telephone. "The coffee smells great, just what I need."

Lorenzo folded his newspaper as Dominic filled a cup.

"Sorry I slept late, but I couldn't relax coming over, a bit of turbulence while trying to figure out what possessed Tris to pull a stunt like this."

"Could be she worried about the impact it would have on her family."

"But if she came to me I would have helped her. Now I've got to contend with Laura Kincaid." Heaviness settled in Dom's gut. "She knew about Cella and never said a word. What kind of bloody game is she playing?" Dominic reached for a slice of toast, "I've been thinking, Ren, to offer Laura a million dollars to sign custody of Cella to me."

"And guaranteed she won't take it," Isabella said, walking into the room.

Dominic couldn't help but smile at his tubby friend. "You sound like a broken record, Issy."

She returned his smile. "Want to make a side bet?"

"Bella!"

"Never mind, my sweet, I'm going to show this know-it-all that long ago when he first decided Laura's innocence, he was right."

"How much do you want to lose, Issy?"

Lorenzo set a glass of orange juice in front of his wife. "Listen you two, before you start this nonsense I have more news." Grimacing, he said, "You're not going to like it."

"As long as Cella is okay, I can handle anything now."

Lorenzo didn't hesitate, "No one knows where Laura and Cella are. She's gone."

"What?" Dominic and Isabella both spoke in unison.

"That was the investigator on the phone. He went to Stowe yesterday and learned that Laura and her daughter left for Maine a few days ago. That's all anyone knows. Laura lived in Maine and she was taking a few days to visit up there. That was April thirteenth. It's been four days. She traveled by bus, but with his checking, she didn't go all the way to Portland, and he couldn't find a trace of what she decided to do. He's going to keep on it."

Dominic slammed his fist on the table rattling his coffee cup and saucer. "Sorry," furious, he growled at Isabella, "guarantee, Issy? The sneaky witch found out. But she won't get away. I'll find her and when I do she will have no choice but to agree with me or else."

"I'm sorry, Dom," Isabella held her juice but didn't drink. Isabella felt heartsick.

"I'm going to Stowe!"

"Don't do it, Dom." Lorenzo argued, "Give the investigator another day or two. If you barge up there and raise questions about Laura you're going to start a firestorm. Those people are tight-knit and suspicious of outsiders."

"I know you're right, but just sitting here isn't solving my dilemma." Dom's mind reeled, "I've got it. I'll go to Laura's house and see if there is anything that will lead to Laura's motive in keeping

Cella's identification from me. If we only knew, I'd be in a better position to get Cella."

"Dom, you can't break and enter. You haven't the right, especially with Laura away."

"I'll think of something."

Isabella grinned. "Like what? That you're madly in love and you want to surprise her with a homecoming party?"

"Issy, I love you but you're pushing my buttons." He looked at Lorenzo, "I don't know how you put up with her."

Lorenzo laughed. "And she's all mine."

"Seriously, Dom," Isabella said softly, her eyes narrowing. "Is the idea as far out that in some strange way you have a deep attraction for Laura?" She raised her hand to stop him from disagreeing. "I remember when you thought her spirit exceptional. It's very possible that what you believed of her is true."

Dominic shook his head. "If that were true, why didn't she tell me about Cella? She told me she once thought of me as noble"—he grinned—"can you imagine…me noble? If she really believed that she would have trusted me about my niece. She must have the original birth certificate. Dio, my name is on it with hers." Dominic slapped his fist into his palm. "No, she is not innocent. She is being sneaky and lying and up to no good. When I finish with her, if she doesn't take the million she'll wish she had."

"Oh, Dom," Isabella cried, "this is so unlike you."

"Like hell!"

"You know what I think?" She looked him square in the eye. "I think you are angry with yourself for having feelings for Laura and rather than face them you're concocting all kinds of measures to assure yourself that you don't like her. Cella is important to you, I don't doubt for a second, but somehow Laura has gotten to you."

Dominic turned to stare out the window; seeing nothing. "She played me a fool. She's gotten to me all right. She has had three important years of Trista's baby and has not shared them with me. She is not only a lying sneak but selfish."

Isabella refused to continue the discussion. She didn't want to alienate their affection for each other. "However it all goes, Dom, you know Ren and I are with you."

He moved toward the door. "I'm going to Stowe. She has to return, and I'll be there waiting. You can reach me at Cloud Nine."

*****

Mr. Irwin explained that Cloud Nine was only half-staffed. Dominic said he didn't mind and wouldn't require any extra services. Any room would suffice.

Mr. Irwin, surprised, offered, "If there is anything my staff can tender for your comfort, let us know."

"Thank you. One other thing, on one of my visits Laura Kincaid drove me to Montpelier. Would it be possible to hire her to do some work for me?"

"Miss Kincaid is no longer employed with us. I'm sorry."

Not wanting to raise suspicions, Dominic asked, "Do you have anyone of her caliber that could do some work for me?"

"I doubt it. As I said, we're only half-staffed, but you might try the library. Sometimes the ladies there are willing to do side work."

"I'll do that. Thank you."

Dressed in faded jeans, a white tee that fitted his muscled chest, and an unbuttoned navy cashmere cardigan, Dominic hopped out of the rental car on Laura's driveway. Pete was mowing. He stopped watching Dominic approach.

Dominic remembered Laura's house guest, Gretel, mentioning Pete being her brother-in-law. This must be the same man from the inn.

Pete studied Dominic's long stride. He remembered him from the Cloud and Laura driving the Lincoln. Pete sort of scowled, "Can I help you with something?"

Dominic held out his hand. Pete had no choice but to take it. "I thought I'd drop in and say hello to Laura and Gretel."

"Gretel? You know my sister-in-law?" Pete's mouth fell open.

Dominic choked back his grin. "Yeah," he purposely used slang, "we had lunch and a nice visit. I know Gretel said she was going back to Pennsylvania, but I don't remember when."

Pete's demeanor warmed. "She left a few weeks ago." She comes every year and stays till March with Laura. My wife's her sister."

"Oh yeah, she mentioned that. You're Pete, her brother-in-law. I think I remember seeing you at Cloud Nine."

Pete laughed. "You got that right."

"Sorry, I missed her. I've got some free time and thought I'd come up to Stowe for some peace and quiet."

Pete's face split into a wide grin. "You'll get plenty of that, especially this time of the year. We all take a breather until the leaves color, and then we're bamboozled with folks again."

"I've never been here in autumn. I understand it's God's paint shop—no other place like it in the world."

"You can say that again."

Dominic leaned his shoulder against a maple, "So is Miss Kincaid around? She's got a beautiful little girl." Dominic eyed a swing hanging from a tree limb. "Bet you put that up for her."

"Ayah. Sure did. That is the smartest little girl I've ever seen. Why she'll talk a leg off you if you've got the time."

Dominic's laugh was pure. "She wanted me to make snowballs for her." He thought by throwing that in Pete would think Laura welcomed his presence.

"Isn't she something? I love that little one." Now Pete was turning into the gossip he naturally is. "You know to this day no one knows how Laura got to adopt that sweetheart, and now no one cares. Everybody thinks the world of Laura. We miss her at the Cloud, but understand why she quit."

"She quit?"

"So she could stay home with her daughter."

"I suppose having a daughter keeps her too busy to date."

"Laura date?" Pete stopped to take his pipe out of his shirt pocket. He tapped it on the mower's handle and then replaced it back in his pocket. "Gret says she doesn't go out, but I think she was going with a college professor."

For some reason, the thought of another man taking Laura out didn't sit well with Dominic. He had to bite his tongue. "Well, she's a fine-looking woman. I'm surprised she hasn't married."

"Now that always surprised me, but I suppose after she adopted Cella she didn't have much time." Pete scratched his head, "Or maybe no one wanted a ready-made family. Don't know."

Dominic didn't want to overstay his welcome or have Pete think he might be too interested in Laura, he said, "I guess I better be going. As long as no one is home I'll take a drive and see more of your country."

"Take the back roads, they're the nicest. Not traveled much."

"Thanks." Dominic smiled. "Sorry to keep you from mowing."

"It doesn't really need it, just chopping up stray leaves. I want it to look nice when Laura gets home. She's good to Gret, and I like to think it's a nice way to thank her."

"Yeah, it is, Pete. You're doing a great job."

The compliment caused Pete to puff up his chest as he pulled the cord starting the motor.

Dominic drove away. Gripping the wheel he tried to figure out Laura's motive in never telling him about Cella. He'd just have to wait to confront her.

Dominic turned into the diner parking. He'd have a bite and check with Margo. He had no choice but to stay in Stowe until Laura returned. He was going to get his niece through scheming means if necessary and the devil with Miss Laura Kincaid. He cut the motor and got out of the car remembering green eyes ablaze when she walked away from him in this very diner.

24

Last day in April, End of Cruise

Laura held Cella's hand while gripping their souvenir packages.

Cella yawned. "Whisper told me he wants to go home."

"I think Whisper has the right idea. We're going home the fastest way. Okay?"

"Okay."

The fastest way was to fly to Boston and rent a car to drive to Stowe.

Laura yawned; it was one in the morning. Cella, wrapped in a blanket, was asleep with Whisper beside her. Laura smiled. *If only your mother could see how you love her gift.*

The quiet early morning hours along with the hum of the motor taking them closer to Stowe allowed Laura more time to think of her situation. The dashboard lighted the dark interior of the car—Laura peeked at her sleeping daughter.

She turned on the radio but the static was fierce. Laura clicked on the headlights to high as the beam spread across and down the road—far into the darkness. She blinked every so often and looked away so the white line wouldn't mesmerize her. The curves and roll to the road with its double yellow lines easily kept her in her own lane. No other cars passed.

She was tired, but not so tired that she could dismiss the upheaval coming. Dominic somehow found out about Cella.

Her mind was spinning as fast as the car's wheels. *How could Tris not tell me that Dominic Deluca was her brother? And that* she named him Cella's father. I should have looked at Cella's birth certificate right then with Tris. Why Tris did you use a different name? Where did that come from? How can I rectify this with your brother—he doesn't believe anything I say. He'll call me a liar again. But I'll keep my promise. Your secret is safe with me. Laura's fingers tightened on the steering wheel. *Cella comes first so maybe Dominic will only want to visit.* Laura released a breath she didn't realize she was holding. *Maybe I'm making too much of Dominic's visits. Well, Tris, I won't run again. I'll consent to visitations. After all, he is her uncle. There is no way your brother can be allowed to take my little girl from me.*

With that settled, the miles passed, and in no time, she welcomed the sight of Stowe, deserted in the early morning. She relaxed.

Laura turned into her driveway. The moon lighted her neat surroundings. She sighed, and the knot in her stomach eased. She and Cella were home safe.

"Come on, sweetheart, we're home." Cella didn't move as Laura struggled to lift her.

"Let me help you," the deep voice came out of nowhere, its serious undertone brooked no refusal.

Laura still bent toward Cella's sleeping form looked over her shoulder and knew who was waiting. Her mixed emotions at the moment had her stymied. Shadowed in the moonlight Dominic's powerful body blocked her escape, her heart pounding. Her emotions whirled and skidded. Her agitated whisper sounded like a shout to her, though she knew it was not. "What are you doing here? Go away!"

Dominic's white teeth came into view, but it wasn't a warm greeting. "I've been waiting for you. I have no intention of going anywhere until you and I talk." He stepped nearer. "Now let me help you with my niece…yes, I know, Miss Falseheart…I have every right to be here. I am after all Cella's father."

Laura quickly looked at her baby to make sure she was sleeping. Her voice was a hard whisper. "You are not and you know it." She was doing her best to keep her knees from buckling.

Dominic moved in. He touched Laura's shoulder to move her away and was struck by a sensation that rippled through him. He pulled his hand away steeling himself from the sharp vibration. "Dio, she's a magic witch," he mumbled under his breath. He didn't miss Laura's shiver before she slipped lower to the ground.

His husky voice cut through the night. "This will not do. Come, let us do this together." He reached for Laura's elbow to lift her and felt the zing again. Dominic bit his jaw and went on to help her up. His grasp was light so that when he lifted her Laura lost her balance and fell against his solid chest. "Dio." He didn't want to let her go. The night air was cool but the heat he felt from her warmed him like a blast from a hot furnace.

As Laura struggled to get her balance in the small space the more her body leaned into Dominic's. She trembled and clutched at his sweater. She could smell the soap he used. He was so warm, and she was so tired, that she momentarily forgot that he was her enemy. Nothing mattered; all she wanted to do was stay in his arms. For that moment all the blinding rage she carried within her melted, this was where she wanted to be. Laura looked up and wanted Dominic to kiss her. She needed his mouth on hers. "Please," she moved her lips but no sound came.

Dominic came to his senses first. His harsh, raw voice penetrated, "You are a witch."

Laura jumped back and hit the car. "I must be out of my mind. Get out!" she shouted.

"Mama, are we home now?"

Tears hiding under her lids, she turned to her daughter, "Yes, sweetheart. Take hold of Whisper, and Mama will carry you."

"Hello, tesoro," Dominic's voice mellowed, carrying into the car. "Let me help you and Whisper." He literally elbowed Laura out of the way.

Sleepy, Cella made no fuss.

Dominic scooped Cella in his arms. He held her close and stared at her sleepy image in the moonlight. His voice faded, losing its steely edge. "You are beautiful—just like your mama."

Laura knew Dominic didn't mean her. Pain consumed her as she hid her upset. She wanted nothing more than to get herself and Cella to bed and be away from this man, though he enraged her and insulted her she couldn't get him out of her dreams. Shaken, she had to end this nightmare. Fighting tears, she opened her purse to retrieve her house key. She walked toward the back porch knowing Dominic would follow.

Leading the way to Cella's bedroom, Dominic gently laid Cella on her bed. Laura reached to unbutton Cella's jacket as Dominic bent down to remove Cella's shoes.

"Leave those," Laura said through gritted teeth, "I'll take care of my baby."

Dominic stood, the light from the hall casting shadows in the room. His voice dropped a volume, "You forget that your baby is also my baby." He left to go to her kitchen.

Angry and agitated, Laura finished caring for Cella, laying her teddy next to her before entering the kitchen.

She stopped and leaned on the door frame. "I'm tired, Dominic. Can't this wait until later?"

"I think not," his sarcasm palpable, "I don't trust you."

Laura smothered a yawn. She had dark circles around her eyes; she needed sleep. "At this moment, Dominic Deluca, I could care less whether you trust me or not. You've attacked me with absurd assertions, and because your mind is made up, you can't see the truth if it were painted on your eyelids." She tried haughtily to lift her chin and persevered. "I didn't know you very well, but what I do know now, I don't like." Laura turned to leave. "I'm going to get some sleep. Please close the door when you leave." She didn't look back. She peeked in on Cella and then went to her bedroom, and for the first time since living in this house, she locked the door. She brushed her teeth, splashed water on her face, dropped her clothes, climbed in between cool sheets, and fell asleep.

Dominic sat at her table. His mind tripped from sympathy to fury. Sympathy for her tired features and yet she looked more beautiful without a bit of makeup, her hair tussled as her wrinkled clothing covered her luscious body. Fury...mostly at himself because as much as he tried to forget that one heated airport kiss, Dio, still wanted to take her in his arms and kiss the bloody hell out of her.

* * * * *

Dominic sat in Laura's kitchen, his leg spread out under her table, holding a fresh cup of coffee. After Laura went to bed he slipped back to his room at the inn to shower, shave, and change clothes. His mind was made up to fulfill his goal. *Laura isn't the only one that can connive.*

Yet for some reason, he didn't find glory in having to be devious. He'd always been upfront and integrity was the law within him that he abided. Now he had no choice—he argued with himself. Step One will be to earn Laura Kincaid's trust. It is wise to secure her trust knowing it won't be easy after all the things he'd said, but the challenge energized him. Knowing the deals he closed, Laura will be a deal he'll close no matter what it takes.

Quietly, Dominic entered Cella's bedroom. He smiled at her while putting his finger to his lips. "Shh…your mama is sleeping. Do you remember me, tesoro?"

Holding her teddy, Cella answered seriously, "You call me that name like Mama, and you're going to make snowballs, but there's no snow."

"I will when it snows again. Will you come into the kitchen so as not to wake your mama? She's very tired."

Cella got off her bed and took teddy with her. When she reached for Dominic's hand; elation swept through him. Her precious soft little fingers wrapped in his. His heart thumped.

"Are you going to take me to school? I miss it."

"I would like to do that, but we'll have to get your clothes and then we'll have breakfast."

"Okay. I can tie my shoes."

Dominic thought he died and went to heaven. Trista's little girl was right here with him. "That's great. How did you learn to tie your shoes?"

"My mama showed me."

Dominic wanted to pick his niece up and hug her to him, but knowing it wasn't the right time, held off. "Let's get your school clothes."

"I better ask Mama."

Dominic's pulse roared in his ears. "I think we better let Mama sleep. She drove a long time and needs to sleep."

Cella stared at Dominic as though sizing up his words. "Okay."

He was amazed that this little girl went to the right drawer and pulled out a pair of panties and an undershirt and in another drawer she lifted out a pair of blue pants and a white tee shirt. She handed them to Dominic as though it was the most natural thing to do and went into another drawer for her blue sweater. "I'm ready." Then she went to put Whisper in her small rocker in the living room. Dominic followed.

"Let's put your school clothes on in here, shall we?"

"I have to tinkle and I have to brush my teeth. Do you brush your teeth?"

Dominic smothered his chuckle. "Yes, I do. It's important to do that every day."

"Mama says I have to do it every day two times," she held up two fingers. Cella studied Dominic and then blurted, "I didn't brush my teeth."

"Not to worry, tesoro mia, your mama wanted you to sleep. Go do it now." He watched her run into the bathroom closing the door. He hoped she wouldn't lock it like Laura did last night—he distinctly heard her key turn as if he'd be interested. As he ruminated Cella came out with her face washed and her hair wet around the edges. He went back to her room for her shoes and socks—holding them as if they were priceless.

"Let me help you." Enjoying every minute with Trista's little girl yet wanting to hurry before Laura woke.

"We went on a big boat. There was a slide. It went down into the big pool. It was fun." She laughed, "Mama says we're brown like Whisper."

"You are and you're beautiful. Come, let's go have breakfast, and then I'll take you to school."

SECRET PROMISE

Dominic located the school by asking the grocer for directions. When he took Cella inside he made it a point to introduce himself. He said Laura would be picking up her daughter at noon. His smile and charm alleviated any suspicions, especially when he bent to say goodbye to Cella. She gave him a hug and told him to take care of Whisper.

Smug, Dominic said, though no one heard, "This completes Step Two."

Laura woke to the smell of coffee and bacon frying. She eyed the clock and jumped up. Ten o'clock! My baby. She grabbed her old blue chenille bathrobe ready to run into the kitchen. But her door wouldn't open. She panicked for a second before remembering that she locked it. Hurrying, she peeked inside Cella's room and saw the empty bed. Her hair hanging every which way she shoved her hand to push it back and heard, "Good morning, Ms Kincaid. Did you sleep well?"

Laura stopped short, her mouth opened, and she stared. "What are you doing here?" She looked around. "Where's Cella? Where's my baby?"

"Easy...go easy," his smile lit her already sun-filled kitchen. "Cella is in school."

"What?"

"Well she told me she missed her school and would I take her and as her uncle, how could I refuse? But not to worry," he rushed on, "I told them at the school that you would pick her up at noon. Is that satisfactory?"

"You had no right. How dare you?" Laura gripped the top of her baggy robe closer to her neck. "You can't come in here and think you can do as you wish."

Dominic tilted his head. He took in her sleep dishevelment and never had he seen a woman look so ready to be seduced. His heart thudded as heat fired up his body. Angry with himself for letting her get to him he lashed out at her. "You forget, Laura Kincaid, that I am Cella's uncle and if you wish to dispute that further, I suggest you read her birth certificate, as her father I have some rights."

"But...but, Dominic, you don't understand."

His voice softened, "Then tell me, caro."

She stood without moving or blinking, silent. Then suddenly turned, "I have to dress, excuse me."

Laura was taken aback, mostly from seeing Dominic in her kitchen. Dressed in chinos, a navy shirt unbuttoned at the neck showing the tip of his chest hairs was a total turn-on. She wanted to wrap her arms around his neck and kiss him under his chin and follow kisses down to the hair showing. His chinos fit low on his narrow hips. Laura hungered for his kisses. And again she realized she was in dreamland again. Dominic didn't care for her, it was Cella he wanted. "Well you aren't going to take her from me," she groused as she pulled on a pair of jeans and a red cotton blouse. Pulling on her leather half boots she marched back into the kitchen. She'd brushed her hair but didn't bother with makeup as there was no reason to pretend. She was determined to get Dominic Deluca to leave.

Walking into her kitchen she felt like a guest. Dominic had coffee, juice and toast ready for her. "How do you like your eggs?" His mellowed voice stirred her stomach.

"You don't have to do this."

"I'm doing it because I want to. Now about the eggs?"

"Scrambled."

Dominic's smile melted her hostility. "Good, I like mine the same. Sit and we'll have breakfast and then talk."

The dishes were in the sink and Dominic sat across from Laura, his easy going manner put her on edge. Laura thought Dominic was being too nice.

Laura pushed her cup and saucer to one side and leaned forward to look into Dominic's beautiful dark eyes. Determined not to let him mesmerize her, she said, "Okay, Mr. Deluca. Let's cut to the chase. We have a small dilemma, but nothing that we can't overcome."

Dominic's mind sifted through her words—Small dilemma? You kept my niece from me for three years and you think it's a small dilemma? He bit the inside of his jaw to keep from shouting at her. Careful not to clench his fists or allow his eyes to reveal his feelings, he said, "What you say is true. So let us be upfront with how we'll each share Cella," he lied.

Laura's tightly squeezed fingers caused her knuckles to whiten. Dominic did not miss her reaction. He hadn't become a successful businessman without being able to read reactions.

He went on, his tone gentled. "Would visitation be in the offering?" He saw Laura relax and kept his smile hidden. "I would come as often as possible but I can't give you any certain days or months, you know a timeline? My business requires I be there and there. I've expanded to London; presently it's a heavy workload and takes much concentration." He half smiled. "I hope to lessen that in the near future which would permit me to see Cella more."

Laura's radiant smile fired up his gut. His arousal should never be taking place, but the magic of this woman continued to live within him. The rush he felt when she was near had to stop but certain parts of his body refused to get the message.

"Dominic, I apologize. I was wrong in thinking you were here to take Cella from me. Of course, you can visit with Cella anytime. I would never think of putting restrictions on you. Cella would love you to visit. Why it might be nice if you could ski and spend the holiday with us." Laura blushed. "I mean with Cella."

Dominic choked back his rage. If he didn't know better he'd think her sweetness was sincere. He was wise to her and her acting. He didn't trust her, but she'd never know. "That is a possibility," playing it cool, he added, "if I can get away."

"Of course, and I won't make plans by telling Cella you'll come or not, it'll be a surprise anytime you can make it." Laura was beside herself with joy to think that they'd be together. When did she fall so madly in love with this man? She couldn't say, but she yearned for his kisses and his embrace taking her against him raising her temperature, and causing warmth to fuse in every part of her when the heat from Dominic's body mixed with hers in the most intimate way. Unfortunately, she knew he didn't have those same feelings and she did her best to keep hers concealed. He'd laugh for sure. She studied Dominic from her hooded eyelashes. Her heart was double-beating and heat again soared through her. She wanted to touch him, to feel their spark. *Oh Trista, the spark we talked about*, she grinned, *is with your brother.*

"Care to share?"

Laura blushed, "It's nothing."

Dominic couldn't imagine why Laura appeared flustered. Eyeing her rosy lips all morning he wanted to crush her to him and ravish her mouth and body. "So will you tell me about Cella? Will you tell me how you met Tris? How did you come to be Cella's mother on the birth certificate? I have so many questions, please; will you honor me with answers?"

Unconsciously, Laura reached over and touched Dominic's hand resting on the table. The hairs on the tops of his fingers tingled with her fingertips. She couldn't move her hand if her life depended on it, the magic zinging from him became overwhelming.

"Dio," Dominic came to his senses. He moved his hand and picked up his cup of cold coffee.

"Dominic," Laura's throaty voice sighed, "Will you consider giving me time to come to grips with all that has happened? It's not that I don't want to tell you, it's that right now I can't." Laura rose and gripped the back of the chair. "I'll do what's right, I promise. Please trust me." Laura felt odd comfort being able to speak openly with Trista's brother; still, she remembered the secret promise. She never broke a promise; would it be right to tell Trista's brother? She just didn't know what to do. Tris, would you forgive me if I shared your secret?

Showing no signs of relenting Dominic wanted to shake her. He should tell her that her acting is superb, yet careful not to give her a hint of his fury, he said, "All right, I'll do as you ask." Step Number Three…done!

"Thank you." She wanted to go to him but didn't as Dominic made no move or gave any indication, Laura smiled. "I have to pick up Cella, but I have a favor to ask."

"Ask. If it's in my power, you've got it." His husky voice penetrated giving Laura goose bumps.

She chuckled. "It's nothing serious. I'm not going to ask to borrow a million dollars." She saw Dominic frown; his eyes turned black as his eyelids lowered. Quickly, she injected, "I'm only teasing. Lord in heaven what would I do with a million dollars?" She laughed. "My favor is that I have to return the rental and I'll need a ride home." She looked at the clock. "Although I don't think there's enough time, I'll have to pick up Cella first."

Dominic concealed his rage A million for Cella? No, I think it is for her. Five million for Cella and she just might consider the deal. "Whatever, let's go get our little girl."

Dominic made a point to keep his distance from the only woman who has the ability to totally upset his equilibrium.

* * * * *

Dominic and Laura were sitting in the coffee shop down the street from Everything. Dominic continued to play the understanding uncle.

Laura's happiness tugged at Dominic's nerves. She wore only a touch of makeup with her hair brushed back with a few of its curls escaping its pins. Her inexpensive clothing looked like a million bucks to Dominic, and it galled him that he'd even think that way. A natural beauty embraced her, and as usual, she seemed not to be aware. This last week he wanted to seduce her and keep her for his own yet common sense prevailed. Laura's talent at sincerity was formidable to his agenda; he stuck to his counsel.

"If you don't mind," Laura's voice intruded in his thoughts, "I have to pick up the receipts and invoices from Mr. Carlsson. I've neglected my work and Matt is having a hissy fit." Looking into Dominic's eyes caused Laura to become lightheaded. Stop, she cautioned herself. "They trust me to bookkeep the store's records; I can't let them down."

"Of course, I would expect nothing less than your loyalty to those you care about." Step Number Four.

"Dominic," she touched his hand and felt the hot spark. She wanted to raise his hand to her lips, so silly; she thought when he should be doing that yet knowing he doesn't have those same feelings. Laura's voice barely audible, repeated his name…"Dominic, I have a letter for you. It's in a safety deposit box."

He stared hard at her wondering what mischief she was concocting.

"Please don't look at me like that. It was among her papers Tris put in the box. I didn't look at them until I needed Cella's birth certificate for our trip." Her voice carried an edge of desperation, "Really, Tris put them in the box and gave me the key and that was that. She did say that she wrote her brother a letter and it was up to me to decide about giving it to you. She said, 'My brother would help' if I asked him. I didn't realize…" Laura's voice failed and then she softly said, "Trista's letter is in the box. I'll get it for you. It is sealed."

Trusting Dominic, Laura added, "I hope I'm doing right." Laura didn't mention her secret promise to his sister.

Anger flared within him. Liar. Dominic looked at his expensive watch, keeping his ire subdued. Step Number Five coming up. "Do you have time to get it now?"

"I can do that." Her eyes filled with waves of passion she felt reach across to him. Laura had been blatant with her emotions for him, but Dominic refused to be made a fool again.

"I'll tell you what we can do," his voice mild, his smile charming. "You go to the bank, then we'll get your work from the store and we can pick up Cella at school."

"That'll work," she said as her decision about Trista eased a weight she carried in her heart.

Laura came from the bank and went to Dominic waiting in the car. She didn't notice his small bag packed and pushed behind the driver's seat.

She didn't get in the car but handed the letter to him. "I'll walk to Mr. Carlsson's and you can turn around and pick me up, is that all right? I need to stretch my legs." She thought he might want to read Trista's letter in private.

Dominic nodded, charming her. "And beautiful legs they are." He looked at the envelope—stunned to see his sister's handwriting. Clearly, his name was written across the sealed envelope. *Why didn't you give this to me at once? I'm right, Laura, you are a sneak and not to be trusted.* "Take your time." *Now it's my turn to lie, see how you like being made the fool.* Yet there was no glee in Dominic's hidden demeanor, only misery. But he knew he had no choice. He had a copy of Cella's birth certificate proving he was her father. He checked and his plane's ready for take-off, all he needed to do was get rid of Laura to pick up Cella and race to the airport. And here she was making it simple for him to put his last Step Number Five in force.

When Laura was out of sight, Dominic didn't bother to read Trista's letter, he shoved it in his pocket. He had to get to Cella. He knew he'd not have any problem as he'd made sure they recognized him at the school and releasing her to him would be acceptable.

Laura cut her visit short with Mr. Carlsson, but Matt went on and on about what he wanted her to do with the invoices. Finally, stepping outside, her arms filled with folders packed in the store's logo bags, she waited for Dominic. She had to smile wondering if he got lost. She looked at her watch. It was noon; she had to pick up Cella. I should have driven my car but Dominic insisted he drive. She knew the school would allow her a half hour to get her daughter, so she waited, looking this way and that for Dominic. Finally, with only five minutes to spare, she went into Everything to call the school.

Laura held the phone, her complexion turned ashen, and she began to shake. "Are you sure? Yes, of course." She mumbled, "He probably had tire trouble." She hung up, but the cold that penetrated her body told her differently—Dominic kidnapped her baby. He'd planned it all along. Laura had to get out there and find them. She rushed from the store and out onto the road, not thinking, her tears blinding her she ran in front of an oncoming car.

Meanwhile Dominic carrying Cella boarded his plane with the engines starting to rev up. One part of him was raring to go but the other part pulled at his heartstrings and the lump he carried in his stomach was as heavy as concrete. There was no burst of joy.

Back on the road in Stowe the driver jumped from his car and kneeled over Laura. His voice panicky, "She ran into me, I couldn't stop."

His wife was beside him in seconds. "My God, it's Laura. Has someone called for an ambulance?"

"It's on the way," someone called out.

Mr. Carlsson was in their midst wringing his hands as he looked at Laura's inert body. "She isn't going to die, is she?" he asked out to anyone.

Laura moaned. She had a goose egg on the outside of her head. "My baby, where is my baby?" She was agitated and wanted to move but the driver pressed her in place—relieved when he heard the siren.

Laura was put in the ambulance and the medic said to Mr. Carlsson as the old man followed them had tears, "We'll look after her. We'll be going to Montpelier General. If her family comes you can tell them where she'll be." The ambulance took off, sirens blasting.

At the hospital heavily sedated Laura was wheeled for an X-ray.

"Dr. Fallon," the orderly said, "I'm told there is no identification on this patient."

"I don't care," he replied. She needs quiet, not in a ward. See that she's in a single or double." He walked away expecting his order to be followed.

* * * * *

Dominic's jet was airborne. The seat belts were no longer necessary; Cella walked around touching this and looking at that. Elation filled Dominic—finally Trista's little girl was his, but he couldn't dampen his guilt thinking at the cost of his deceit. He tried to convince himself that Laura had it coming; to justify his actions for the dirty trick he played on the green-eyed beauty. This wasn't sitting well with him at all.

Cella stopped beside him, looking at him, and asked, "Where's Mama?"

Dominic's heart dropped, roaring in his ears from his pounding pulse. He tried his charming smile, "She couldn't be with us but we'll call her later."

"Okay." So trusting she climbed onto a leather chair that held Dominic's jacket. She was rubbing its' soft leather. Trista's letter fell from its pocket. She handed it to Dominic. "Here."

Dominic reached for the letter staring at his sister's handwriting. His brows drew together in an agonized expression.

Perceptive, Cella asked, "Why are you sad?"

Dominic reached over and pinched the tops of her shoes, wiggling them. "You're a smart one, just like your mama."

That brought a big smile from Cella.

"Do you think Mama has Whisper?"

Dominic's gut kicked in and his muscles tightened. "I think she will," he lied. Holding Trista's letter, using his finger to break the seal—her writing clear, nothing shaky, and written in her strong hand, Dominic began to read. "Dio!" His hand began to shake and a cold sweat traveled over his torso. Right before his eyes, his sister wrote that Laura only knew Trista as Serrano, not as Deluca. The big powerful man who ran huge financial investments around the world wanted to cry like a baby. Never in his life did Dominic feel lower than a snake. He reread some of Trista's writing telling without a doubt she wanted Laura to have Cella.

Cella yawned. "Are we going to get my mama, now?"

Dominic didn't think twice. "Yes. Stay put, sweetheart. I'll be right back." He headed forward to the cockpit. His orders loud and clear, "Turn around, we go back! Rapido-quick!"

The pilot didn't blink, hearing the harsh tone, said, "Si. To the same airport?"

"Si! Si!" Dominic went back to his niece. He could feel the plane begin to bank and hurried to strap Cella into the seat.

The plane landed; a car was waiting.

Carrying Cella he took hurried steps toward the car.

"Are we going to see Mama?"

"Yes, tesoro, you can count on it."

"I hope Mama has Whisper."

"If not, we'll find your teddy."

Dominic was beside himself. Never in his life had he misjudged a person or been cruel. Panic traveled through him faster than the speed he pressed on the accelerator. "I've been a damn fool," he uttered under his breath.

He looked over and saw Cella had fallen asleep. Anguish filled him as well as heartache for his sister, her daughter, and especially for Laura and for the misery he caused by exacerbating this situation. Laura had not lied; she kept his sister's secret. Dominic recognized loyalty and in all his business dealings where millions of dollars passed around like cards had he never been so wrong. Never had he been off the mark as with Laura. Had he any inkling about his sister's working mind he was certain none of this tragedy would have transpired. Dio, Tris, why didn't you trust me?

Perspiration settled on his collar. The speedometer hit eighty, and not wanting to take time explaining and getting ticketed, he backed off to seventy-five and held steady, sweet caro Laura I am so very sorry. Gripping the wheel remorse swept through him. He knew he would confess and declare his stupidity. He'd plead for her forgiveness, once again. My caro, I am truly sorry. Bereft, Dominic reached to swipe at a huge teardrop.

He moved his head a little from one side to the other, thinking Issy had been right all along. I've been jealous over wanting Laura and refusing to face it.

Nearing his destination, he had to convince Laura he was the nobleman she once believed him to be. Dominic has been credited for being the master of success, and now he couldn't remember when an outcome meant so much to him. This undertaking will be the biggest deal in his lifetime and he'd not accept failure. Arrogance joined humility as he had every intention of having his way.

He slowed his speed and turned on the road to Laura's. When he pulled in the drive he saw her car and relaxed a bit. She was home. He immediately wondered why she wasn't flying out the door.

"Come on, sweetheart, we're home. Wake up." Holding her, he walked to the back porch expecting to see Laura. But all was quiet. Not a sound when he opened the door and stepped into the kitchen.

Cella now fully awake, wiggled to be put down. "Mama... Whisper...Tinkle." The house was silent, she looked at Dominic.

"We'll find your mama but first let's get you to the bathroom. He then took this minute to check the quiet house discovering Laura's absence.

Cella came back into the kitchen clutching her teddy. "Where's Mama?"

"Let's put on your sweater and skedaddle."

SECRET PROMISE

Cella laughed, "What's ski daddle?"

Smothering his worry Dominic picked Cella up and gave her a hug, "It means let's get out of here."

Entering Everything Cella saw Mr. Carlsson and smiled. "I got Whisper."

Dominic asked, "Is Laura here?"

Stricken, Mr. Carlsson lowered his voice. "You don't know?"

Dominic's gut knotted. He barely choked out the words, "Know what?"

Mr. Carlsson looked to see Cella studying the candy case, he leaned toward Dominic and whispered, "Miss Kincaid had an accident."

Dominic clamped his eyes shut for a second, apprehension racing through him, his innards tightening.

Mr. Carlsson continued, "She got hit by a car and they took her to the hospital in an ambulance."

"When?" but Dominic knew when.

"Around noon. The strangest thing, she just ran out and didn't look. She was going to get her little girl."

If Dominic could have dug a hole, he would have jumped into it right then. *Dio, what have I done?* "What hospital? I've got to go to her."

Kindly, Mr. Carlsson noted the distress in the big man that he'd seen with Laura. "I see you are worried, Mister…?"

"Deluca, but call me Dominic…Dom. What do you know?"

"Miss Kincaid is at Montpelier General. Matt called, he works with her, and all they'd say is that she is stable."

Dominic leaned on the counter to remain upright. Dio, what have I done? His veins standing out in ridges along his temple, he said, "I'm going to the hospital."

"I 'pect so. Would you like to leave Cella with us? We'll take good care of her."

"That's very kind of you. I'm sure Laura would like that. Thank you, Mr. Carlsson." He turned, "Cella, will you come here a moment, please."

195

Before Dominic could say anything, Cella blurted, "Can you be my daddy? Sage has a daddy. I want one too."

Dominic picked up Cella and hugged her. "I'd like that very much. I'll be your daddy and you can be my daughter now and forever." Giving her another squeeze, he whispered in her ear, "I love you, Tesoro mia." He didn't know how Laura would accept his pledge but he'd deal with that later. "I'm going to go see your mama and Mr. Carlsson would like you to keep him company." Dominic pecked each of her cheeks, "Will you wait here for me and your mama?"

"I keep Whisper with me?"

"Of course." He kissed her on the forehead. "I'll be back as soon as I can."

Cella looked at him; shyness seemed to take place over her usual exuberance. She said, "Bye Daddy." Then Cella eyes Mr. Carlsson, "See, I have a daddy just like Sage."

He had to hurry away to hide tears collecting that he could no longer confine under his lids. He heard Mr. Carlsson say that there were cookies and milk waiting for her.

Dominic, disheveled, his whiskers adding to his messy appearance in wrinkled clothes—all that meant nothing as he stopped to fill the gas tank anxious to get to the hospital, to Laura. Thinking of her in pain and the cause terrified him. I did this to her. One minute, he was elated when Cella asked to call him daddy and then his failure to trust Laura crushed his hope. Why didn't I read Tris's letter right then?

Speeding toward Laura, Dominic's mind went to London knowing he must contact his office. He knew his responsibilities to his firm, but presently Laura was his number one priority. Losing a million dollars meant nothing if it meant Laura was well and would forgive him and let him show her the love he had buried deep inside with only her name. "Please, caro mia, please say you will marry me…be my wife. Not for Cella but for me."

The Mancini came to mind. Ren loved Issy and never shied from showing it. He understood it fully now as the corners of Dominic's mouth turned up. I want that green-eyed beauty to be my wife. I love her.

SECRET PROMISE

Content with his thoughts, he didn't think for a moment Laura's response would be negative. Self assured of Laura's love for him as he saw it plainly this last week and now he would tell her about his true feelings. *Caro, my love, trust me, please.* Dominic knew as never before did his plea for this woman's love become the biggest contract in his life. There was nothing he wouldn't do to regain Laura's trust and belief in him. Then the realization slammed into the forefront of his thinking as his knuckle whitened from gripping the wheel, *I'm going to a hospital because it is my fault that my caro is there. Dio... help her be well. I'll take care of her for the rest of my life. I swear.* He despised the actions of the person he portrayed. *I'm sorry, caro mia, I'm sorry.*

* * * * *

It was nearing eleven o'clock when Dominic drove into the hospital parking space. Having calmed he wished he had his bodyguard with him. He knew he couldn't walk in and expect to be given Laura's room number let alone be allowed to see Laura at this late hour. His bodyguard could have been a distraction.

A florist van pulled up to the emergency entrance. Dominic moved with speed when a woman opened the back of the delivery van.

"Excuse me." He smiled. "I hope you can help me."

The gray-haired woman, not a bit wary, eyed him from head to foot. She didn't smile but her tone was nice, "Why should I?"

Now Dominic's smile turned into a broad grin. "Because I am a man in love and have driven like a madman to get here and I don't know the room number of the woman I must see."

"That's what all you Romeo's say." She went about her business getting flowers in order while checking her list.

Dominic wasn't giving up. "I know I look a mess," his Italian accent seemed more pronounced, "Laura was in an accident today. They say she's all right, but I've got to be sure. I must see for myself that is true."

"What did you say her name is?"

This time, Dominic didn't smile. His face, haggard with worry, said, "Laura…Laura Kincaid. If you have extra flowers I'll buy them for her."

The flower lady lifted a vase filled with mixed flowers, Dominic was about to help her—she waved him off. "I've been doing this for years and years, I don't need help." He quickly stepped back. "Stay here and I'll see what I can find out. But if you're giving me a line and you're an abusive husband, I swear your life will be over the next time I see you."

"You are a Signorina after my own heart. I would expect nothing more…for me or anyone."

She nodded and left pressing the code pad to gain entry after hours.

Dominic leaned against the truck, anxious yet knowing at this time of night the florist being his only hope. A half-hour passed and Dominic was sure he was forgotten but also knew that giving up wasn't the way to go.

His patience paid—the florist returned. "You are right. Laura Kincaid is in this hospital and she did have an accident, bit of discomfort she'll be having. Her foot is in a cast and she's under sedation."

He released a pent-up breath. "Gratzi, thank you."

"Well come on, then. I'll help you get into the hospital. Her room number is 242. When you get off the elevator the nurse's station is to your left. Get off and go right. The 242 is on the right side in the middle. They have two nurses on duty so if you're lucky you'll make it." She shook her head, "Oh hell, you might as well let me help you," she pushed a big bouquet of flowers into Dominic's arms. "But I'm warning you if you're so much as telling me a trumped-up story, you're a dead man."

Overcome with gratitude, Dominic's smile against his white teeth and whiskers charmed the old lady. "I promise you she is everything to me."

Dominic followed the florist into the hospital holding the flowers up high in front of him. He felt exhilarated, also like a schoolboy trying to sneak back into school.

"I finally got myself a helper," the florist said.

"Good for you, Alice. You're no spring chicken, you know?" And Dominic heard laughter. They entered the elevator.

Dominic entered Laura's room. The fluorescent night light created a mean atmosphere. The green walls and tiled floors did nothing to surround Laura with warmth. He cringed seeing Laura's inert form. The beeping machine sound filled the silent room. As Dominic stepped toward her he felt as though he was battling a gale to reach her. His chest expanded, and he could hardly take in air. His gut twisted into a rock while his legs weakened—barely able to hold up his large frame. *Dio, I did this.*

Laura was asleep—her head bandaged; her color ashen. Her right foot was wrapped in a cast and an IV dripping steadily into her arm.

My beautiful Laura, what have I done? He went around the bed and took her lifeless cold hand wrapping his warm one around it. Bringing it to his lips, he kissed her palm and then held it against his cheek. "Forgive me, caro mia, I was so wrong." He used the corner of Laura's sheet to dry his eyes though tears remained under his lashes as he tried to clear his clogged throat, "I will never hurt you again." Torment assailed him along with sinking despair. He kissed her fingers. "Will you open your eyes for me, caro? I'm here," his voice in a broken whisper, pleaded, "Laura…it's Dominic. Cella is waiting for you to come home. If you can hear me, know I love you." Misery was so acute he could feel his pulse throb, "Please, I need you so." Sudden warmth filled him with a proprietary feeling. "Laura, you are the only person I want in my life. I fought loving you but never again. You can trust me for the rest of my life. I promise."

The door swung open with a quiet swish. The nurse stopped short, her voice cautious, yet with clout. "What are you doing in this room? Who are you? I shall call Security if you do not leave immediately."

Not wanting to raise a ruckus, seeing his Laura safe, he nodded. "Of course, I understand." His deep voice with his accent, he said, "Please, can you tell me how she is?"

His gentle voice and the same way she saw him holding her patient's hand to his cheek, she did something she rarely did. "No,

I can't." The nurse laid Laura's chart on the foot of the bed. "I'll be back right back."

Dominic lunged for the chart—reading: Hema toma (large goose egg) on the outside of the skull. Watch for concussion. Many bruises. No fractures or torn ligaments. Some patients suffered severe pain when pressure applied cupping her heel and shin. Patient was sedated to enable rest. Will sustain horrific headaches when awake. Patient was to stay off their feet until the swelling goes—possibly one week.

Dominic placed Laura's chart on the bed as the nurse returned. "Thank you. She will sleep through the night?"

Taking pity on the handsome frazzled man, she replied. "Yes."

"Gratzi." His soft kind voice reflected his feelings as he opened the door just wide enough to pass through sideways.

* * * * *

Dominic decided to remain parked on the tarmac and not travel back to Stowe this late. Running his hand over his whiskers, he bounded up the steps. "I'll have a light supper after I've showered," he said to his steward.

He added, "We will remain here. Notify the airport."

Kicking off his shoes—yawning, he began to undress.

Toweling the water from his silky black hair he reached for his terry robe. Flexing his muscles, he felt the pull from not using them. A sandwich, fruit, wine, and a carafe of coffee filled a tray next to the bed. He savored the club sandwich not realizing he was hungry.

Swallowing, Dominic picked up his phone dialing Mr. Carlsson having promised that he would call even if the hour was late, and he wanted to check on Cella. Affection spread through him—"I'm to be her daddy," he said before taking a drink of coffee. Hearing Cella was sleeping, he said he would pick her up first thing in the morning. He hung up and stretched out on the bed, pushing his damp hair back off his forehead. He couldn't stop yawning.

Not one to let necessary business wait, he scrambled for his numbers book. Dialing Lorenzo's number while taking a bite of a quartered apple.

"Dom, where the hell are you?"

Dominic laughed and swallowed some apple. "And hello to you, too."

"I'm serious. How the hell am I to brag that I'm a father of the most handsome son in this world if I can't find you?"

"Ren...a son. That's great. How's Issy? When did this happy event take place?"

"May 2. I'm telling you I wanted to walk up walls until Bella was all right. She's doing fine. I'm going to bring her home tomorrow or the next day." Lorenzo crowed, "I can't tell you, Dom, what it feels like to know that I created such a tiny little human being. It's incredible."

Dominic couldn't help but feel that twinge of envy. "I'm happy for you, amico."

"I gave Bella a sapphire ring and told her for every child we have I'll add another sapphire."

"Then you couldn't splurge for a finer cause...by the way," Dominic said, laughing, "you know you can't start working on that second sapphire for a couple of months, don't you?"

Lorenzo chuckled. "Don't be a smart-ass." He cleared his throat, "So are you still in Stowe? What's going on?"

"Ren, Issy was right. I've been wrong. Laura is innocent and has always been. I've made a mess and hopefully in the process of correcting it. So tell your sweetheart-wife I owe her an apology." He growled, "It seems I better practice up on apologizing."

"Your message will make her day. She asked if I heard from you."

"I'm glad for you, Ren, having a son. Give Issy my best and I'll get back to you as soon as I can. I'm going to catch some shut-eye—it's been a long day."

"Good night then and," he remonstrated, "keep in touch."

"Will do, Daddy." Before both men disconnected Dominic heard his friend's hearty laughter.

Dominic poured another cup of coffee and proceeded to telephone Margo. "Yes, I know I've been out of touch." He went straight to work. "I've delegated Tom to act fully on my behalf as I told you. Check with him and follow his instructions." He heard Margo's acerbic tone but ignored it. "Also, get me a realtor that is familiar with rental estates. Preferably near London if possible. Give her my number, no, no, I'll speak with her. I don't know when I'll be returning but it shouldn't be much longer. Yes, I talked with Lorenzo. Thanks." He was about to end the call when Margo asked what his exact plans were. "Margo, I appreciate your keeping my office going without mishap. I know it's not easy, but everything is in a bit of turmoil and as soon as I straighten this fiasco I've created, I'll be back." He disconnected and flopped back on the bed. Rubbing his eyes knowing tomorrow would be the beginning of a new start for him and Laura and for their little girl, he fell asleep.

25

Dominic hurried into Everything. Not disheveled as the previous day; whiskers gone and hair neatly in place and wearing a gray pinned suit, tailored especially for his broad shoulders, with a crisp white shirt and a dark patterned silver silk tie, he exuded power. "Good morning, Mr. Carlsson. I hope I'm not too early, but I've come to take Cella for a change of clothes. Her mother is doing well. She suffers a headache that is easing by the hour and her ankle should be better within a week. It's good news. She will be home soon."

"I'm so glad. It was such a shock. You know? I know you're in a hurry, let me get little Cella; she's helping my wife make cookies."

While Dominic waited he weighed on his decision to take Cella to the hospital. Cella needs Laura and Laura must see that Cella is here. Dominic believed both would have a calming affect for both of them, especially for Laura.

Carrying Whisper, Cella ran toward Dominic. "Hi Daddy. Where's Mama?"

"Good morning, little caro. We're going to your mama right now." Thrilled to be called daddy, he beamed. "Say goodbye to Mr. Carlsson. Did you thank Mrs. Carlsson for letting you help her?"

"Yes," Cella answered seriously, "we made cookies."

Dominic shook Mr. Carlsson's hand and thanked him saying he'd be sure to tell Laura he asked about her.

* * * * *

Dominic carrying Cella stepped out of the elevator; stopping first at the Nurse's Station and placing two huge boxes of Godiva's chocolates on their counter—, for you and the night nurses, he said with his warm Italian accent. Gratzi. He nodded and then walked directly toward Laura's room. No one stopped him as he awed the staff. His melodious voice along with his handsome features and tall lean muscular torso in an Armani suit appeared as though he walked off a magazine's cover. Besides the doctor said to expect him with his daughter.

Putting Cella down near Laura's room, he said, "Remember, Tesoro mia," he said with gentle emphasis, "Your mama bumped her head and has a big bandage." Cella gripping Whisper nodded, her lips pressed together. "So we must be very quiet. Her head hurts but it will go away soon. She will be so happy to see you."

Entering the room the blinds were still closed and the machine still beeping. Dominic felt Cella tighten her hand on one of his fingers, fear taking over as she took in the surroundings and then pressed her little body against Dominic's leg. His eyes were on the high bed. Cella pulled on his hand bringing his attention back to her. She raised her arms, alarm in her eyes. He didn't hesitate to pick her up, "Shh, it's all right. Your mama is resting…see," he walked toward the bed and Cella hugged him closer. Seeing the IV board taped to Laura's arm and the beeping machine was frightening.

"Mama." Cella's little worried voice reached Laura. She opened her eyes and blinked. "Mama, here is Whisper." She held out her teddy. Laura uttered a soft groan. "Does your head hurt, Mama?" Cella reached to pat Laura's arm while still holding onto Dominic.

Dominic wondered if he made a mistake bringing Cella to see Laura, but when Laura opened her eyes again and saw her little girl, her lips moved whispering, "My baby." A tear escaped.

"Si," his voice, soft and tender, said, "Caro, we are here."

Cella's tension eased, "Whisper says come home, Mama."

Dominic reached for Laura's hand and gently rubbed his thumb over her knuckles and quite naturally raising it and holding it against his cheek.

Confused, Laura couldn't grasp what happened but relief brought a sigh. Still holding Cella, he heard Laura murmur "My baby."

The nurse came in and said they would have to go and let her patient rest.

Dominic bent over Laura and lightly brushed her lips with his, his voice husky whispered for her ears only, "Cella and I will be here with you until we can all go home together."

The nurse ready to give Laura pain meds forced both of them to leave. Holding Cella, the little girl waved and said, "Whisper will come back, Mama," Dominic saw Laura smile and wave with her good hand. "Bye for now, my baby." Pleased that he insisted to the doctor to allow Cella to see her mother—he still lamented over Laura being in pain.

Later in the afternoon Dominic and Cella entered Laura's room. She was awake and sitting up. When she saw Cella her face reacted with a warm smile. Though her head still ached, it wasn't as bad as it had been.

Holding Cella he couldn't stop his heart from hammering and his sudden need for Laura overwhelmed him. Thankfully his jacket prevented him from being embarrassed. Though it didn't take a second more for him to realize the smile wasn't for him, but he didn't care. Just seeing Laura happy was all important to him. Still what he wouldn't give to take Laura in his arms and do what his heart and body demanded, instead he offered his own warm smile.

Holding her teddy, Cella giggled. "Mama, you've got a big hat."

Laura touched her bandaged head. "I know, isn't it funny?"

Dominic set Cella gently on the bed. Laura's left hand grasped her daughter's. "So what have you been doing, sweetheart? I've missed you."

"I made cookies with Mrs. Carlsson."

Laura glanced at Dominic standing at Cella's side so she wouldn't tumble off the high bed. She wanted to be angry with him for frightening her, but she must have jumped to conclusions as he didn't kidnap her baby. They were here.

For a moment Laura's eyes probed Dominic intently as confusion apparently darkened the color in her eyes.

Please, not now, do not ask questions. I promise to tell you later. Hopefully, he wanted it to be much later. He took hold of her and Cella's hand in his big one, giving them a gentle squeeze. "Are you feeling better, caro mia?"

Laura's features eased as her green eyes brightened. "I think so, but with this foot, I'm in a pickle."

"Not to worry. Cella and I will take care of you."

Cella giggled. "What's pickle, Daddy?"

Laura's mouth fell open, staring at Dominic. She mouthed Daddy?

Dominic quickly explained, his eyes capturing Laura's, "Our little girl asked me if I would be her Daddy and…"

Cella interrupted, forgetting about the pickle, stating, "Sage has a daddy and I want one."

"Do you mind?" He held his breath.

Laura knew she had no choice, especially in her current situation; she winked at Cella, "I think that's a good idea."

Cella beaming, eyed Dominic. "Can I get down, Daddy?"

"You may, but you must stay in this room." He lifted her and before putting her down kissed both her cheeks.

Cella seriously explained to Laura, "Daddy always does that, two kisses." She held up two little fingers and then repeated the same two kisses on her teddy before wandering around.

Dominic's heart flipped; his throat constricted making it hard to swallow. Cella's innocence turned him into a marshmallow. "She is so precocious, thank you."

"Dom," her voice turned into a suffocating undertone, "we have Tris to thank."

His voice low, Dominic asserted, "True, but it is your doing that our little girl is carefree, happy, and healthy." Then taking Laura's hand in his rubbing the top of it with his thumb, feeling their current transferring into each other, especially again to Dominic as he changed his stance for comfort, said, "I can't wait to take you out of here. Will you and Cella come with me? I want it so very much."

His touch seemed magnified sending shock waves up her arm. "Where?" was all she could manage.

Not immune to the rush he felt—he guarded against his groin taking precedence over their conversation, so he gently lay her hand down and couldn't stop himself from brushing his knuckles over Laura's. "I want to take you and Cella to London with me."

"What?" She grimaced and closed her eyes from the sudden head movement.

Quickly, he softly said, "Please don't excite yourself." He leaned closer lowering his voice, "This is not the time or the place, but my intentions are honorable. Will you marry me, Laura?" His voice a soft caress; "I'm asking you to please be my wife."

All these years, dream upon dream and now Laura could see he was feeling sorry for her. How could she live with this man who offers marriage out of pity and also to gain Cella's custody? Knowing she is the obstacle in getting Trista's little girl without a lot of hullabaloo, she had to be careful in how she responded. For now, she was in no condition to disagree, he had her baby. Playing for time, she said, "You don't mean it?"

"Of course, I mean it. I want you both with me. I'll take care of you and see that you have all the comfort you desire."

It was as she surmised, he wanted Cella. She tried to shrug but it didn't work that well and the pain lodged in her neck as well as her heart. Dominic was right there touching her and sending lightning shivers through her. "It's all right, Dom, just a short kick. It's gone. Now about your proposal," she bit the inside of her lip, "let me consider it." His scowl wasn't a good sign. "I mean that right now I feel like I've been hit by a train and…"

Cella ran to the bed on tippy-toes, her little head not reaching the top of the mattress. "A train, Mama?"

"You never miss a thing," Laura chuckled. "No, sweetheart, it just feels like it."

Dominic having picked up Cella, said, "We better go and let Mama rest. We'll come back tomorrow. It will all work out, you'll see."

Cella leaned over and kissed Laura's cheek, and then the other copied Dominic's way.

The pleasure in Laura's reaction made his heart double-beat. He leaned over planting a light kiss on each of her cheeks and then on her lips letting his tongue trace her bottom lip. His groin was reacting as he smothered his groan. Clearing his throat, said, "Rest, caro, until tomorrow."

"Goodbye, Mama." Anxious to leave now that she saw her mother, said, "Let's go, Daddy."

"Dominic," Laura called, "thank you for the beautiful flowers."

"I'll buy you all the flowers you want anytime." He wanted to say I love you but with Cella right there, he didn't. "Ciao, caro mia." And he was gone.

Laura didn't see his love-blossomed eyes. If she had her present attitude might have been different toward the man she coveted in her dreams.

* * * * *

Dominic left fixed instructions for his pilot—the plane to be ready for departure upon his arrival.

Dominic left Cella with Laura while he settled Laura's hospital charges.

The nurse appeared with the wheelchair for Laura and Cella asked, "Can I push Mama?"

Dominic smiled. "That's not a good idea. How about I carry you? I would like that."

Cella raised her arms upward. "Okay, Daddy."

Laura eyed her daughter so willingly going into Dominic's arms—Daddy? Everything seemed to be happening too fast. Not feeling all that well, Laura felt overwhelmed, or could it be a streak of jealousy that Cella giving Dominic her undivided attention?

Dominic's van was at the entrance. Laura could bend her knee so putting her in the van wasn't difficult. With Cella situated, Dominic touched Laura's arm, "All set?"

SECRET PROMISE

When Dominic pulled up to the plane, Laura's glare could have hung icicles in the van's interior. Gritting her teeth, she mumbled, "What are we doing here? I want to go home."

But Cella rushed to explain. "We're going to fly, Mama. It's fun."

Dominic didn't want Laura to know that he had kidnapped her baby. He planned on confessing but only after they were securely wed. Before Cella said more, he enlightened Laura, "We've been using the plane as our hotel. We spent the night here rather than drive all the way to Stowe."

"So what are we doing here…now?"

"Daddy has a soft bed for you."

"Cella!" Laura's sharp tone caused Dominic's eyes to gape while Cella's face crunched ready for tears.

"I'm sorry, baby. Mama can't move, please come here and let me hold you. I'm upset but not with you, sweetie."

Dominic lifted Cella onto Laura's lap. "Easy, tesoro, you're heavy on your mama's sore leg."

"Please, Dominic, I don't need your help."

His tone was brisk but softly spoken. "You're going to get my help because I want to give it. Now I have Cella's passport ready. I've collected yours and now we three are going to get on this plane and fly to London. You will rest while we travel, and once we are settled, you and I will have a serious talk. After, when your foot is healed, we will make another decision together. In the meantime, you will be with your daughter. Know this, Laura, I have no intention of taking Cella from you."

"Daddy keeps us," Cella joined in.

Neither Laura nor Dominic commented but neither could withhold the corners of their mouth from turning up. In fact, Dominic's turned into a wide smile.

Dominic nodded his head and the plane's door opened. Two men came down and one female nurse. Energized, Dominic said, "I'll carry the lady, please help our little girl and see that all our belongings are on board." A car pulled up. Dominic reached into his pocket and slipped some bills into the driver's hand. Thanked them for their help. They waited to take the van away.

Laura's throat closed as she tried to breathe. Here is Dominic's private plane, and he's taking her with him. She didn't know if she should laugh, cry, or be angry over his high-handedness. Yet there was Cella talking to the stewards as though they were old friends. Laura wanted not only to be home in Stowe, but she also wanted to be with the man who continuously causes her heart to double beat and whose touch is magic. She'll go along especially since he said he'd never take Cella from her. She believed him.

When Dominic carried Laura in his arms up the steps heat between them ignited their bodies. He whispered into her ear, "You are my tesoro." He pulled her closer, his hot breathing transferring onto Laura causing perspiration to warm her straight through her clothes. Dominic said, his breath tickling her ear before he nipped it, "You're mine."

Why can't you say you love me? Because you don't. She felt his romantic spark but his words didn't speak of love and that she needed to hear more than anything.

Lying comfortably buckled in on a feathered lounge she smiled at her daughter as Dominic buckled Cella. He kissed them both and sat down. The plane's engines roared and began to roll. Once airborne it wasn't ten minutes and both his girls were asleep.

Dominic's heart banged against his chest with longing. Lately he's been in a perpetual state of arousal and hiding it was a problem at times. I need you, Laura. I need your caring, your goodness, of course your love and I want YOU. He stared at his new family with reverence knowing they were his to love. Though tired, he needed to call his office and reached for the telephone. His brow creased when he was informed that Margo was away for the rest of the day. He decided to check back after he got his family settled. Too, he was thinking of phoning Lorenzo and telling his good news but decided he'd do that tomorrow.

The steady hum from the jets engines enticed relaxed vibes in him. Smiling, sure of his decisions, Dominic leaned back and closed his eyes.

26

London, Dominic's Penthouse

Dominic keyed his floor in the lift whisking Cella and Laura directly to his floor. The doors swished open into his foyer. He pushed the button returning the lift.

Awestruck by Dominic's lifestyle, Laura couldn't say a word. Though Cella didn't lack voicing her thoughts, "Is this my new home, Daddy?" She looked up at him her voice excited. "Whisper likes it."

Laura couldn't help laughing. "I think you better put me down, Dom. I'll manage."

"I like holding you. Not yet, I…"

It was at that moment Margo walked into the room wearing a gown revealing her figure in its fullest. She gaped at them, anger ripping through her, said, "I heard you were returning—I didn't know you were bringing company."

Laura gasped, struggling to be put down, but Dominic held her closer to him. His face hardening as his lips curled with distaste. "What is the meaning of this, Margo? Explain yourself."

She took in Dominic holding Laura and a little girl clinging to his leg—her palms grew clammy, but suddenly she smiled maliciously, "Why darling, you always like me to be here for you when you've been away."

Dominic ground out his words between clenched teeth. "Liar. Get out! You are no longer employed with my firm."

Margo's face became a glowering mask of rage before she darted back into a bedroom. She wanted to scream.

Dominic carefully set Laura on the sofa. Cella went to sit beside her.

Dominic picked up the phone calling Reception at his office. "This is an authorized memo. Margo Selan is no longer employed with our firm and is not to be allowed into the building from this moment—mark the time and date. If she gets past security at any time, you will all be terminated, there will be no exceptions. Now connect me to Tom in Finance." He relayed the same message to Tom. "I want this order typed, sign it and pass it to all offices. Also contact James Pierce and have all passwords changed. Lock my office and also Margo's. No one is to enter. Put a guard on it if necessary. Thanks, Tom. I'll see you in the morning. Call if there's any question. Yes, I'm in London."

Margo stormed out of the bedroom properly dressed in a suit while carrying a small leather bag. Dominic walked toward her. "Leave the bag, Margo. I'll see you out."

"These are my things," she shrilled.

His tone forbidding while he stared at her, "I'll see them returned by carrier tomorrow."

"You...you can't do that."

"Come, Margo, you know better than that. Now move. I want you gone." He took her elbow and rushed her toward his lift. He turned to Laura, "I'm escorting Margo down. I won't be long."

When Dominic returned he found Laura and Cella in his kitchen. Laura hopped on one foot while holding on to the counter. Cella drinking orange juice.

He combed his fingers through his hair, his tone deeply apologetic, "I'm sorry about that. I had no idea she planned a homecoming for us."

Laura teased. "I think it was for you."

Dominic winked, "The only one I want to welcome me is a certain lady with a sore foot—she has my heart." He bent and brushed her lips with his.

"Daddy, you didn't kiss Mama's face."

"You are so right, my little girl, I shall do that right now." Laura warmed at his teasing and waited for his lips to touch her again.

When he kissed bother her cheeks he let the tip of his tongue touch her. Sparks and more sparks made her insides feel like doing summersaults as she grasped at Dominic's lapels for balance.

Dominic's groin was in motion as he clasped Laura to him knowing he had to explain his action to Cella—watching. "I better hold on to your mama so she doesn't fall." He held Laura carrying her back into the living room.

"I'll show you around later, but first I'll take you to your bedroom so you can tidy up if you like. Then we'll order some food and enjoy a quiet dinner. Will that be all right?"

"Thank you for asking and yes, that sounds wonderful."

"There are four bedrooms, but I think for the first few days, it will be wise to let Cella sleep in the room with you. After we'll set up a room for our little girl and let her be part of choosing things she likes."

Laura couldn't hold back her tears.

Dom wrapped his arm around Laura, his voice whispery soft, "What is it, Love? What's wrong?"

"Nothing's wrong, Dom. It's how nice you're treating us."

He kissed the tip of her nose, "How is it you Americano's say— you ain't seen nothing yet!"

Laura couldn't hold back her laughter. She was riding on soft fluffy clouds and didn't want to get off while hoping her clouds wouldn't collapse.

Their dinner having been favorably devoured, Laura and Dominic sat on the sofa together holding hands.

"Are you sure Cella won't roll and fall off the bed?"

"Very sure. I have boxed her in with pillows and put Whisper on guard. Relax, my sweet—we must talk."

"Dom, I'm curious…why didn't you let Margo take her bag?"

Dominic let go of Laura's hand. "Wait a second." He came back with the bag and opened it. Margo's belongings were squashed in it but also inside were a couple of folders. Dominic held them for Laura to see. "These are calculations that I've been working on for a client. She was stealing them. That's why it was necessary that I have her barred from entering the building. I believe Margo wouldn't have done this if I returned alone, but seeing as she was not about to be involved with me she must have wanted some kind of revenge."

"You're not going to bring charges, are you? That would be horrible."

"No, I haven't any intention of doing anything more than I already have put in motion." He dropped the bag on the floor and went to sit with Laura. "Let's forget Margo."

Laura looked starry-eyed at the man of her dreams. "Will you kiss me please?"

Dominic's gut expanded. "Believe me, caro mia, it will be my pleasure. I always want to kiss you." He gathered her in his arms. First, he kissed each corner of her eyes before moving to kiss her eyelids. She sighed and leaned into him. He kissed each of her cheeks using the tip of his tongue to taste her luscious skin before taking her bottom lip between his teeth and light-nipping it while she opened for him and he delved into the warmth wanting to really taste her. His touch was delicious and demanding which set her afire. She couldn't disguise her body's reaction. Laura responded in kind, and the kiss they were sharing was like no other. The spark burst into—not one flame but a progressive blaze igniting a burning desire and an aching need Laura couldn't readily define. They were both pressing—snuggling to get closer.

Dominic pulled away; he had to—his breathing trying to take in as much air as possible. Never had he felt this turbulent tide of passion, his whole being flooding with need. Laura set his body ablaze as his beloved nuzzled her face into his neck just under his chin—her warm breath and her tongue teasing his skin increasing his desire.

Laura moved, her voice quaking, "Will you please remove this wretched shirt so I can feel more of you? I very much want to bite you." She smoothed his hair with her hand letting her fingers trail down his cheek. "I've never had these feelings before...I don't know how to control them. And it's all your doing." She smiled at him, adding, "I'm glad. I don't want them to stop."

His heart swelled knowing of her innocence. I was right about Laura from that very first day long ago. He was in awe that he would be the only person to hold her and show her what loving is about.

"All you have to do, my sweet, is follow your heart and go with what you feel. There are no rules." He shifted his position as his trousers were pulling across his groin making it impossible for him to relax.

Dominic's eyes darkened his voice mellow as he looked at her. "I want you to know, Laura Kincaid, that I love you. I have for years but have been too stubborn to admit it. I want you to be my wife if you will. Marry me…not for Cella's sake but for mine. I need you to be part of the rest of my life."

Inhaling Dominic's heated scent—sending goose bumps through her, she needed his heart and his soul as he already had hers. Instead of answering, she pressed herself against him and ran her tongue over his whiskered chin while kissing him and nipping wherever she could. The unusual ripple radiating below her waist made her want to climb on him. She ran her tongue over his bottom lip copying his way, finding she liked its touch—especially when he moaned.

"You're driving me crazy, caro, crazy for you, and if you don't stop, we're going to do tonight what we should be doing on our wedding night." He nipped her bottom lip back. "However, that won't make me angry."

Laura wanted to lie beside Dominic in his bed. She wanted to feel the length of him naked beside her, but something held her back. Her body afire with hot embers that only he could extinguish. Being with this man had always been her dream and now she could make it real. Biting the inside of her jaw she was about to tell him she didn't want to wait for marriage when the telephone rang. His voice warm and husky, he groaned, "Sorry, love, but I have to answer." When he moved, the separation cooled her ardor enough to make her rethink her impulse. She best go to bed alone. But she didn't have to tell Dominic as he began to apologize, "I have to go to the office, caro, they're having a problem, and I think the name is Margo."

"Don't apologize. Will you help me to my room?"

Dominic picked Laura up as though she was feathers light. "You know," he whispered into her ear as his tongue traced its inner curve, "we have unfinished business."

Laura turned and kissed him lingering, savoring every moment.

"No fair, my adorable witch." He bit her earlobe until she yelped.

Keeping her laughter down, she said, "Now that's not fair."

Putting her on the bed, he said, "Do you want me to help you get into bed?"

"Okay," she teased.

Walking toward the door, he whispered back at her, "You know I'm going to get you for that." He stopped and looked at her shiny face and rosy lips, "I love you both…very much." Then he was gone.

Laura's heart beat like a tom-tom as a broad smile beamed, "And I love you too," she said to the closed door, "if you only knew how much."

The next morning, Dominic rose early and was gone before Laura and Cella woke. He left her a note saying he'd call.

Meeting Mrs. Haskins, Dominic's housekeeper, Cella was chattering with the new lady while enjoying her breakfast. Laura and Mrs. Haskins spoke pleasantries.

Laura later moved slowly to investigate their temporary home. Beautifully decorated rooms held no warmth. A mixture of glass and brass, thick cream carpeting—adequate to nap on brought a smile as she remembered Gran's worn rugs gracing their small living room that Gran called her parlor. Eying framed paintings that intentionally added splotches of color to cream walls along with colorful pillows didn't invite a welcoming atmosphere as far as Laura was concerned.

Laura, with Cella, made her way into Dominic's bedroom. The smell of his aftershave made her tingle. His room was stark, except for the long windows catching the morning sun. She bit her tongue to keep from voicing what she was thinking upon seeing identical décor—cream walls and more splotches of colorful paintings. Everything blended with no inviting warmth—only cold magnificence.

Cella ran ahead into Dom's dressing room. "Look, Mama," she called. When Laura hobbled in Cella was standing before a walled mirror giggling. Laura laughed and then spied her image and wanted to cry. There was nothing about her that inspired a tad of loveliness. Her hair pinned back certainly didn't shine; her complexion had a pinch of pink with green eyes staring back at her told dull. Her wraparound dress hung lopsided off her shoulders with her bandaged foot being the main attraction. "I'm a mess."

"No, you're not, Mama." Cella, watching Laura's reflection, said, "You're my mama." She held up her teddy, "Look at Whisper."

Laura opened another door. This room took her breath away, this was Dom's sanctuary. She could picture him in this appealing space. Wood paneling, dark hardwood flooring—a rug with an array of mixed dark colors and an extra long leather sofa stretched before a fireplace. Huge end-tables that could easily hold a complete place setting were piled with magazines and books. A crystal fish bowl half filled with mixed candies told Laura a lot about her dream man. One wall held books she trudged to read their titles. Architecture, engineering, landscaping, and flower gardening—were the first of many title subjects. Further down a collection of Charles Dickens' and another of Fitzgerald's. She laughed when she spied Huckleberry Finn.

Dominic's massive desk took one corner of the room. Laura ran her fingers over the polished wood. There were papers, folders, and his handwritten notes. She felt a streak of heat pass through her knowing that this was his workplace and where he sat. She spied a silver framed picture and studied it. She recognized Trista—and swallowed Trista smiling and holding hands with an older couple. Laura knew at once they were Dominic's mother and father. Cella's grandparents with her real mama. Laura began to shake. She put the picture back in place. She had to leave the room.

"Let's go to our room and freshen up. Then we will investigate your daddy's roof garden.

Cella nodded and ran ahead with Laura's thoughts in turmoil.

Dominic telephoned three times during the day to be sure Laura and Cella had everything they needed. He also said he'd be working late, apologizing once again.

"Not to worry," Laura assured him.

* * * * *

Laura woke to Cella's talking to Whisper telling her teddy that they live in the sky.

Dominic tapped on the door and peeked in.

"Daddy, Daddy…can Whisper and I come out?"

"Dominic held out his arms and Cella ran into them. "Si. You may do anything you like as long as your mama says it's okay." He looked over at Laura and saw her eyes closed but a smile crossed her beautiful face. "Let's not wake Mama"—he put his finger to his lips—"we'll go and see what Mrs. Haskins has for breakfast."

"Will you stay with me?"

"If you want me to." Listening to Cella telling Mrs. Haskins about Whisper's airplane ride, Dominic slipped away with a cup of coffee for Laura.

Wearing a navy suit, stark white shirt, silver cuff links, and a silver silk tie scattered with red thread through it filled Laura's dream fantasy about Dominic. His whiskers were gone, his hair combed, and there wasn't another man on earth as handsome as the man handing her a cup of coffee.

"Good morning, my love. I've left our little girl jabbering away with Mrs. Haskins. I hope she doesn't tell all our secrets."

She grinned. "You think not?" Her face glowed. She sat with Dominic's silk robe wrapped around her. Her voice was low as she looked into his eyes. "Good morning." She fingered the belt. "I hope you don't mind. It was on the bed."

"I know I put it there wishing we could both wear it at the same time."

Laura blushed.

His eyes swept over Laura wanting to take her in his arms, smother kisses over her body, and thoroughly make her his. An erection was occurring. He was glad his suit jacket covered him. "Sorry, but I have to go. Mrs. Haskins will be here to help you. Forgive me, caro mia."

Disappointed but not wanting Dominic to know, she braved a smile. "Please do what you must. Your roof garden is a beautiful place to spend the day."

He took her hand and kissed her fingers…each one at a time. Clearing his throat, said, "I'm sorry I can't stay."

"Dom, if you don't mind I'd like to make a few telephone calls. I owe Mr. Carlsson and Matt an explanation and an apology. Too, I'd like to talk with Eve. They have all been so kind."

"Sweetheart, call anyone you like and talk as long as you wish. Whatever you want to do, go right ahead…anything at all. What is mine is also yours. Know that and use it."

Laura got a dreamy look and said, "You know if you keep fooling with my fingers I'll forget about the coffee and you're going to be late for your meetings."

"Tease, that's what you are when I know we can't do a thing about it." Cella ran in at that moment. They both laughed.

Dominic leaned over and kissed Laura, not like he wanted to but enough to get a taste of her. Then he kissed Cella. "Sorry about leaving my two favorite girls." He winked, "Just remember that I love you both."

* * * * *

For the next few days, Dominic and Laura communicated mostly by telephone. Returning late each night saying backlogged work required his personal attention. He'd sneak into Laura's room wanting to kiss her every night, yet didn't—he'd take in his fill looking at her. In the mornings he was gone before she woke.

On the fifth night when Dominic came in after midnight, Laura was waiting. Drawn circles around his eyes reflected surprise and then a big smile appeared.

"This is a wonderful surprise." He brushed his lips with hers. "I must shower as I've been out on one of the jobs. I'll be right back. Please," intensity in his pleading tone, "stay right where you are."

"I'll be right here." She called as he headed toward his bedroom, "Wait, Dom, are you hungry?"

"Only for you," he called back; his voice resonant.

Laura knew Dominic wasn't going to like her idea but she had to tell him and that was why she waited for him. If he didn't agree, she smiled knowing she'd blackmail him into agreeing.

He returned smelling of soap, his whiskers gone. "I'm sorry, caro, about having to be away from you."

"Dominic, I didn't wait up for an apology."

"Good." He swept her into his arms and kissed her as if it were the last kiss to a drowning man. Holding Laura soundly against him, his voice raspy, said, "I miss you. I miss holding you. I miss touching you." Using one hand he gently touched her face and captured her mouth; savoring, thrusting, devouring sending heady sensations and currents electrifying them both. Laura responded pushing Dominic's resistance to his lowest ebb. Looking into her dewy green eyes he pulled on her lower lip with his teeth. His breathing seared a path as he nipped her ear lobe, "Caro," Dominic let out a long audible breath, "I want to make you mine in every way. I love you, tesoro mia, surely you can feel what you do to me."

Laura reached to touch Dominic's face and then her fingers moved his hair to one side. As she did this he turned his face and kissed her palm. Laura felt hot and clammy not only from her own body heat but from Dominic's too. "I love you, Dominic Deluca. I have for a very long time. I miss touching you, I miss you holding me, and I miss your kisses"—her eyes glistened as her voice gave way—"especially when you kiss me from your heart. You do funny things to me every time you're near me. I want you too."

He nipped her bottom lip. "Then we will…"

She moved back just enough to interrupt him and said, "First, listen to me, please."

He nodded, though his eyes narrowed.

She laid her hand against his cheek. "I'd like to take Cella and go to Stowe."

"What! You can say that after what you just declared. You love me? How?"

"Please listen." Laura tightened her hold on his hand. "We left in such a rush and right now we're in your way."

"Absolutely not! Impossible for you to be in my way." Dominic swallowed, not wanting Laura to be away from him. Anger was roiling inside of him. His tone was firm, "How can you even think of parting when we care so much for each other?"

"Again, I'm asking you to listen, please. Stowe is my home. I left without taking care of things."

"Hire someone to do that for you. Pete is looking after the place for you right now. All you have to do is call him."

"No. I want to take care of my things my way."

"Tell me," his voice purposely composed, "you love me, do you not?"

A slight tremor in her voice touched Dominic when it turned soft like velvet. "More than I can say. That's why when I come back I don't want to have to be apart from you ever. This is a good time for me to go, Dom. You're busy and here I feel confined, doing nothing when I could accomplish more in Stowe. Please let me do this my way. Too, Cella should be around other children. Not just Mrs. Haskins and me."

Dominic rubbed his smooth chin. His perchance of bedding Laura, he knew no longer existed. He loved her too much not to take her feelings seriously. He didn't like Laura making sense and he didn't like the thought of her being so far away. He trusted her and her love for him. *Am I being selfish?* He knew if his acquaintances could see him now they'd have a good belly laugh. Wealthy, powerful and not tolerating noncooperation to his demands—he was now agreeing to cower to some degree to her demands. However, Laura watched a sudden gleam brighten in Dom's eyes as his smile broadened showing his teeth against his gorgeous olive skin.

"I think we should negotiate, Miss Kincaid. Are you willing?"

Tilting her head, she said, "That depends."

"Oh, you don't trust me or it is you don't trust yourself?"

"Never mind," she teased, "what are you engineering in that superior mind of yours?"

"I'll agree for you to temporarily go back, note I said temporarily, to Stowe. In fact, I'll have my plane fly you. I'll have a chauffeured car waiting to take you anywhere you wish to go. I'd like for you to hire Gretel, she can help you. Cella is comfortable with Gretel, and anything you want is yours without question."

"So what's the catch? There's no doubt in my mind you've got something working to your advantage. And before you explain, until I'm your wife, I don't want you paying my expenses. I can manage."

Dominic reached for her—holding each side of her head and using his thumbs to caress her cheeks while looking into her eyes, whispered, "Will you do me the honor of letting me take you to bed this night and make love to you? I mean totally...completely?" He feathered kisses across her inviting mouth. "If you do, I'll do as you ask and let you temporarily part from me." Dom's body was already responding to Laura's nearness.

Laura's emotions whirled and skidded as her body succumbed to his touch—his caress a command to tighten the bond between them. Her body felt heavy and warm as her heart beat wildly as though out of control. The spark igniting over and over caused Laura to succumb; she couldn't say a word as his force enveloped her and then they both heard Cella's cries.

"Dio." Dominic's heart pounded against his ribs. He read Laura's eyes and body movements, telling him she would agree, and he wasn't going to give her a chance to change her mind. Sweeping her up in his arms he headed for his bedroom. He looked at her and his heart lurched madly knowing that she would be totally his before the night ended.

"Dom, stop. That was Cella crying. We've got to see what's wrong."

This was the very first time when Dominic would have liked to strangle his sister. "Si."

They found Cella hugging her teddy and sound asleep. "She must be dreaming."

"Come caro, love of my life." His warm breath caused a chill to race across her nape. "We have unfinished business." Dom touched Laura's shoulder and felt her tremble. His aching body needed release that only she could cure.

Shy, Laura looked at the man she dreamed of for years. Without him kissing her she began to think, "I don't..."

Dominic's arm shot out and he pulled her to him. She was backed into his chest and could feel his hardness wedged against her bottom. "No, Laura," he ordered, "you cannot change your mind, not now." The heat from him penetrated her. She felt the change in her own body melt into his. Yet she was frightened. Not of Dominic but whether she could measure up to fulfill his desire. She tried to move but he held her in place stepping backward to leave Cella's room. Once having backed them away he lifted her—carrying her to his bedroom. Placing his lips in her ear he proceeded to tickle it with his tongue. She trembled.

Slowly he lowered her body down sliding it against his torso. Neither missed the electrified jolt passing from one to the other. Cupping her face he kissed her long, longer and longest. Ending the kiss gently he kept her gathered in his arms. His heavy breathing beat against her breast.

Laura entwined her fingers in the back of Dominic's silky black hair at the nape of his neck sharing their intense physical awareness. "Dom, what I feel is not lust but a smoldering passion energized by my love from deep inside of me only for you."

Stepping away but continuing to hold her, he said, "We are agreed I will make you mine tonight." He had no intention of letting this night pass without them sharing their love.

Laura's answer was to cover his mouth hungrily as her hands moved over his torso. "You have on too many clothes." She was about to take off her robe and then stopped. "Dom, her voice broke, "I don't know what to do."

Dominic's smile could have lighted all of London. "Ah, my love, let me show you. You don't have to do a thing if you don't want to. But," he moved his tongue over her bottom lip, "feel free to follow your feelings." He loosened her robe and let it slide to the floor in a silent heap. He hid a chuckle upon seeing Laura in a granny nightie. With a flick of his finger he loosened the ties one at a time at her neck and on down the front of her breasts letting his fingers linger touching the softness of her breasts before sending her nightie to join the robe. Laura looked for something to hide herself. "No, caro, please… you must not. You are beautiful."

Laura had no idea her breast buds would come alive from Dominic's intense stare adding to the unidentifiable throbbing below her waist. "Dom," her blush blossoming, "I've never been naked in front of anyone. I've got to have my robe."

Dominic clasped her to him—adoring her blush—trailing his hands over and down her back, her soft skin an aphrodisiac. "You honor me and only for me will you show your beautiful body." He leaned his head and kissed first one breast and then the other—his hot mouth causing Laura's nipples to swell. "Oh my," he heard her sigh and it brought a possessiveness into his soul that he never felt before for anyone. "You're mine and you will always be mine." He laid her on his smooth sheets kissing her breast and then her cleavage going to her neck, biting her ear lobes and once again capturing her lips.

Laura was lost. Excitement wrapped around her body like a hot blanket. His kiss sent the pit of her stomach into a wild swirling storm. Delicious aches augured into her body as she found herself drunk with his nearness as waves of the unknown rippled from the tips of her fingers to the tips of her toes. Squirming, reaching for him—trying to keep him with her when he moved to undress. Flustered, she opened her glittering green eyes, "Don't leave me," her throaty tone implored.

Dominic's raspy chuckle shook his head. "Not a chance, my innocent, six elephants couldn't pull me out of this room away from you."

Laura beamed—her body yearning for his. "Only six?"

"That's only for starters. They'd soon have to trumpet for help." He lay beside her warm body making his manhood jump more than ever to attention. "Dio, what you do to me." His gaze was a dark yearning as he pulled Laura to him. She went willingly into his arms nuzzling him—the feel of his rough skin against hers exalted in spreading more fire. Dominic embraced her keeping her close. Kissing her face, ears, and neck—in fact, there wasn't any place his tongue didn't touch before invading her mouth. Dominic's loving spiraled desires into the pit of Laura's stomach and struck an unfamiliar vibrant chord while flooding her senses with delight.

"All mine…I'm on fire for you."

She could feel his heart thudding against her own. "I…I don't know what to do," her voice breaking.

"My dearest love, let me catch my breath for a minute. When you move against me like that I feel like exploding—a good explosion mind you." He didn't want to admit he was on the brink and almost losing control. After all, it has been a long time. In fact, since he first met this heavenly angel he has not thought much about sex with anyone.

Laura peeked down at Dominic's magic and froze. Her cheeks colored but she continued to look. Dominic made no attempt to hide the fact that he was watching her. Her fingers ached to reach over and touch him and then boldly she did. Her touch made his erection leap—she yanked her hand back.

He wanted to let her investigate as much as she desired, but nature wasn't going to allow that. He had stayed away all week, keeping long hours at work simply because the temptation of wanting her was too great. She'd been driving him crazy with his need to make love to her. So he pretended to need long working hours.

"Enough, a man can only take so much." He rolled Laura on her back and lay beside her. His hands never left her body as they found their way to the core of her sex while he kissed her thoroughly. Dominic knew Laura was his—he lifted his mouth from hers, his voice hoarse, "I love you with my soul and know that that will never change. I do not want to hurt you, but I crave you and your body. Trust me, please, it is said there is some discomfort at first." His body searing, his tone croaky, added, "But after there are sensations, I promise you and contentment our having reached the stars together."

Laura's passion vibrated throughout her body as she felt his hand and then finger feather her personal place where no one had ever touched. The strange aching in her limbs added to the wonderment he continued to create—another and another until she was ready to beg him for help. "Dom please," her voice was pleading, "do what you must, I trust you, please. I don't understand all these amazing currents shocking me into wanting you so much, please do not stop but finish however you can."

Thrilled at Laura's declaration his kiss was a slow drugging kiss—then became urgent as her mouth became more persuasive. "Please," she cried, "tell me what to do." His dark eyes shining, his breath hot, he gasped, "My caro, you are doing everything perfectly. Now I'll do the rest. You are perfect."

They made love three times and snuggled together dozing but not sleeping.

"Dom," her voice whisper soft, "don't let me forget to tell you that you're magic. I won't ever share you. Just so you know." And Laura fell asleep.

Dawn cut through the morning mist with Dominic, lying sideways next to Laura, resting his head in his palm watching her sleep. Being deeply in love with her and knowing that no other man had ever touched her so puffed him up he could have become a cloud. His free hand rested on her stomach; he couldn't keep his finger from circling her navel. He knew he should get up and shave and shower, but he didn't want to be separated—not for a minute. He wanted her again, to make love to her over and over, but also knew it would be kind to let her rest. They'd showered once and he smiled remembering her cheeks pinking when he insisted on bathing her most personal place. She surprised him when she said they should negotiate—she would permit him to bathe her but only if she could do the same to him. Thinking about it he smothered his chuckle. "I love you my wife to be."

Laura turned. "I heard that." She beamed a smile that lighted the dawn. "What time is it?"

"Early."

"I hate to think of you having to work today." She put her hand over her yawn.

He kissed her nose. "I can see you need to rest."

"True, but I'd rest better if you were beside me."

He laughed. "Well my darling temptress, if you insist I may be convinced to stay home."

"Really?"

"Si...really. I have a confession to tell you. The reason I stayed working all those long hours and left early every morning was to eliminate the temptation you paraded around me."

Flattered, Laura grinned. "I paraded? Really?"

"Si, believe it." He snuggled her next to him becoming more content than he'd ever remember being so in his life.

They lay silent for a while, naked-unencumbered with only a sheet covering them. Their bodies generated warmth.

"Dom," Laura's tremulous whisper alerted him.

"What is it, my sweet?"

"I've given this a lot of thought. I know you're an important man, and I worry that I won't measure up as your hostess. I'm not all that gregarious, and I don't want to embarrass you. I don't have the know-how that Bella and Eve have."

Dominic gathered her in his arms pulling her on top of him. Looking into her sexy dewy eyes, said, "My dearest, all you have to do regardless of who, where, or when...is just be yourself. Be who you are...the woman I love...my wife. Don't try to change; don't think you have to. You're perfect! Also, you'll have all the help you need to keep things running as you choose. We can afford to do what we please, when we please, and how we please. Understood?" He frowned, "If anyone makes you uncomfortable—tell me. Promise?"

Feeling better, she nodded. "You make everything sound so easy."

"Not to worry. I'll look after you and Cella for the rest of our lives. Speaking of our little girl, when we marry I'd like to change her name to Deluca." He felt Laura stiffen. "We will be family, Laura. We will all be Deluca's."

"Dom"—her tone forceful—"I will never break my promise to Trista. Cella's birth is not open for discussion, ever." She reached for his hand and squeezed it. "But I agree, Cella is a Deluca. I'm sure Trista would like that too."

"I knew I could count on you."

"Also," she hesitated for a second, "what about your parents? I will not tell them about Cella. Trista worried that they would find she was pregnant, especially without marriage. That's why she concocted all this secrecy. I will honor my promise to her, Dom. Tris and I discussed telling Cella, agreeing perhaps when she is eighteen. It is my judgment to make. Right now Cella is too young to have any upheaval in her life. I won't have it!"

Dominic kissed her chin and then running his tongue over her lower lip, he smiled. "It will be your call, caro, I trust you. Trista's letter offered that I decide if our parents were to know about Cella. Right now I think it's best to leave everything as it is." He ran his fingers down her arm, "Cella said she wants a grandma and grandpa like her friend, Sage. That's no problem. My parents will be elated to have part of Trista still with them. I'll think about when to tell them."

Laura stretched out on Dom's naked torso slowly moving her body back and forth. "I think that's right for you to do. However, I'd feel it would be more right if you'd put that magic of yours where it belongs and let me float in the clouds while thunder roars and lightning strikes."

"Are you sure? I want to make love to you as you can plainly tell, but not if you are hurting."

He gasped as she brought her bare chest to meet his. Skin to skin they were one—feeling his erection, she said, "Teasing me like this will only get you what you want."

Dominic flipped Laura over as she giggled and it was then they both heard Cella calling. She was about to come into the bedroom. He leaped off the bed—the bathroom door closing and the shower raining to cool his heated body. Laura laughed at his quick departure yet wished they'd have had time to fulfill her desire for him.

"Hi, Mama. Why are you laughing? How come you're in Daddy's bed? Are you sick?"

Having pulled the sheet around her, Laura choked back her giggles. "Daddy didn't feel good so I thought I'd stay with him. He's feeling much better now and is taking a shower. Did you sleep well? How about Whisper?" Laura knew she could always change Cella's thinking when she mentioned the teddy.

"Whisper is sleeping all the night. I had to wake him up this morning. Mama, can I have an apple?"

"Of course, sweetie, and it's may I have an apple? Why don't you go to the kitchen and I'll be right there. I want to make sure Daddy is all right."

"Okay." Cella bounced out of the room and Laura had to bite her lip to keep from laughing. "Methinks Dominic and I better wed and soon."

Cella was sitting at the table with a bowl of cereal and a glass of milk, Coffee was perking, and its aroma traveled through the kitchen. Laura grinned when Dominic walked into the kitchen and kissed Cella on both cheeks and then went to Laura and did the same only wetting her cheeks with kisses.

"Are you feeling better, Daddy?"

"Just peachy. Couldn't be better. The best I've felt in ages and ages."

"Are you going to work again?"

"No, today I'm going to spend with you and Mama. How about that? We'll go shopping and then we'll go to the park and walk around the serpentine."

Cella giggled. "What's a certain-teen?"

"Serpentine…it's a big lake made by people. It's something to see—special just like you and Mama. It winds all around the park. We'll have fun today."

Surprised, Laura asked, "Really?"

He grinned. "Well seeing as I don't have to hide from temptation anymore, I can take all the time off I want. I am the boss," he cockily explained.

"What's tempation, Daddy? Do I have to hide from it too?"

Laura looked at Dominic and smothered a giggle.

"No, sweetheart, temptation is when you want something and can't have it."

"Oh."

Laura wanted to laugh, but Cella was so serious, she said, "Well, I have some interesting news." She sat beside him laying her hand on Dom's upper thigh where Cella couldn't see. "I've decided that Cella and I won't have to go to Stowe. I mean not right away." She squeezed his muscled thigh, winked, and said, "There are too many important matters that I must take care of right here in London." Her hand slowly moved up his thigh.

Dominic moved her hand away from his magic wand bulging against his chinos, and murmured, "I'll get you for this."

Overflowing with happiness, glowing—she lifted her coffee cup to her mouth all the while letting her green eyes take in the man of her dreams.

Dominic couldn't remember a time in his life when he was this content.

Laura looked at him—her eyes teary as she softly said, "Tris and I were talking about love and she told me if it's true love there has to be a spark from both parties. That if it was one-sided, it wasn't real and I should wait for the real thing." Laying her hand on top of Dom's, she felt it and asked, "Is Tris right? Do you believe in that spark?"

Dominic leaned over, brushed her lips with his, and grinned. "Oh yeah, we do spark together. In fact, I think our sparks could light all of England."

Laughing and so very happy, Laura said, "I love you, Mr. Deluca."

"Mama, do you love me too?"

Both adults burst laughing and Laura whispered to Dom, "Told you she doesn't miss a word."

Dom said to Cella, "Your mama loves you, and she loves me. I love you, and I love your mama. Okay?"

"Okay, but do you love Whisper?"

"Without a doubt, sweetheart…we love Whisper too."

EPILOGUE

On a bright sunny England afternoon in their estate garden, Laura Kincaid and Dominic Deluca were married in a private ceremony. Centered between them was a little girl, Cella Rose Deluca, accompanied by Whisper.

Cella looked up at the married couple. "Does this mean that I'm married too?"

Dominic bent down and collected Cella and her teddy up in his arms, balancing them he gathered Laura closer. She felt his warmth as he gently clasped her shoulder. "Yes, sweetheart, we are all married together." He kissed each of her cheeks, and she giggled.

Their wedding guests beamed smiles. Waiters appeared carrying flutes of champagne. Dominic's parents, knowing Cella was Trista's daughter radiated joy. Isabella and Lorenzo with their son, and Eve and Paul with Sage joined in wishing the couple happy.

Dominic brushed Laura's lips, exposing a wide smile. He lifted his glass and genuinely said, "Thank you all for sharing this splendid day with us. This magnificent woman…my wife, my caro lights up my world, I adore her. The gentlemen here know exactly what I'm feeling. May these blessings of love in our lives always be with us."

* * * * *

Two months later, lying in each other's arms, savoring their love, Laura bit Dominic's ear. "Guess what?"

Sated, he yawned. "Guess what, sweetheart?"

Laura moved to lay on top of his naked body with her own. Glowing, her rosy face and dewy eyes, she feathered his lips with a kiss and then murmured, "Do I have your attention?"

He ran his fingers over her back following her spinal column causing shivers, "I'll say!"

Her scorching look matched his smoldering one—her voice soft—filled with wonder, whispered into his ear, "We're pregnant."

Dominic's smile erupted as he showered her with kisses until he captured her mouth devouring his wife. Clasping her to him he ran his fingers over her and then to her stomach. "*We're pregnant!*" Again kissing the hollow of her neck, he nipped her skin, saying, "We really are pregnant?"

Laughing in pure joy, she responded, "No doubt about it. I told you…you are my magic."

"I love you, Mrs. Deluca, I love you so much. How wonderful you are and you've enriched my life in so many ways. I often try to think of what I've done to deserve someone like you. You are perfect. I love you." His next kiss was a long sweet caress.

They lay together silent—taking in each other's feelings and both knowing that having each other and a new baby as well as Cella, and of course, Whisper—their lives were complete.

Laura thought back to Italy, her long-ago dream vacation, when she met Trista by chance and then when leaving Trista—I doubted we'd ever see each other again. And here I am, Tris, that spark we talked about—how true and you were so right—both have to feel its power. Oh yes, I hope it will please you that Dominic and I are married and Cella is our daughter now. I'm very much in love with your brother and thank you for trusting me to care for Cella. I'll tell Cella about her Mother when the time is right. You will always be in our hearts. Laura turned and pressed a kiss on her husband's naked shoulder and then nipped his ear emitting a soft blissful sigh.

Dominic lay silent, his head resting on his bent arm—content; feeling his wife's body snuggled next to him. Never believed a person could feel and love and be loved as I am. This is a new world for me and I'm glad I'm in it and have the most trusting and loving lady to share it with me. He felt Laura's kiss on his shoulder and quickly moved to his ear. She loves me. He turned and pulled her closer to him, "I love you, too, Mrs. Deluca—I'll not let you forget."

After making love, Laura's head resting on her husband's heated chest, asked what he had been so seriously thinking about.

Grinning, Dominic answered, "Before? You mean before you bit my ear?" He teased, "Oh, nothing too important…just glad that I liked skiing in Vermont."

They were both smiling at each other and were about to rendezvous' again when a little girl knocked on the door and called, "Can Whisper and I come in?"

Both smothered their giggles and Dominic whispered in Laura's ear, "There are moments when…"

More laugher and then Laura called out to their daughter, "Cella, it's may I come in? And yes, darling, come in and yes, you may bring Whisper."

Naked, Dominic zoomed into the bathroom hearing his wife's giggles as he closed the door.

End

ABOUT THE AUTHOR

Joan Livieri and her husband, Arthur, moved to Middle Tennessee because of the moderate four seasons and friendly people. Always a reader with a vivid imagination ignited her passion for writing. She prefers auto traveling with no schedule. Golf and baseball are her favorite sports and feeding stray animals that happen by.